GW00684676

MAPLES

MAPLES

Fine Furnishers

A HOUSEHOLD NAME FOR 150 YEARS

Established
1841

Hugh Barty-King

QUILLER PRESS
LONDON

Copyright © 1992 Allied Maples Limited

First published 1992 by
Quiller Press Limited
46 Lillie Road
London SW6 1TN

ISBN 1 870948 67 X

All rights reserved. No part of this book
may be reproduced or transmitted, in any form
or by any means, without permission of the publishers.

Produced by Hugh Tempest-Radford *Book Producers*
Printed in Great Britain by St Edmundsbury Press

Contents

Foreword

JOHN Maple was a pioneer of modern retailing.

An opportunist, he seized the chance to make his fortune, leaving behind the quiet country life of Horley in Sussex for the largest and wealthiest city in the Victorian world, London. At the age of 26, his zealous entrepreneurial instinct enabled him to take advantage of the City's fabulous riches. John, with his budding imagination and enterprise, created a retail concept which continues to flourish under his influence today, more than 150 years later.

Since its birth in 1841, Maples has witnessed, and undoubtedly influenced, a vast array of changing styles. Throughout its lifetime, the very latest furniture fashions and design trends were always to be found in Maples' inspirational stores. Of course, these rested harmoniously alongside the traditional classic pieces that made Maples a household name. It was this enviable combination of functional and decorative beauty which has been the hallmark of Maples.

Today, we are fortunate to say that little about Maples has changed, particularly the original priorities of customer service, quality and style. We, like our founder, are completely committed in our pursuit of the Victorian standards which propelled the Maples name into international acclaim. We have added to this a touch of contemporary retail technology, which has brought the delights of Maples to a wider audience.

Like no other home furnishings retailer, Maples has 150 years of expertise gained through service to royalty, statesmen and people from all corners of the globe. Today, as in 1841, Maples has universal appeal, attracting customers from throughout the United Kingdom and throughout the world.

If we have been successful in capturing in these pages the unique exciting spirit and inspiration which lives today within our stores and within ourselves, then I suspect that John Maple would have been proud.

Grahame Winter
Managing Director
Birmingham, 1992

MAPLE FAMILY TREE

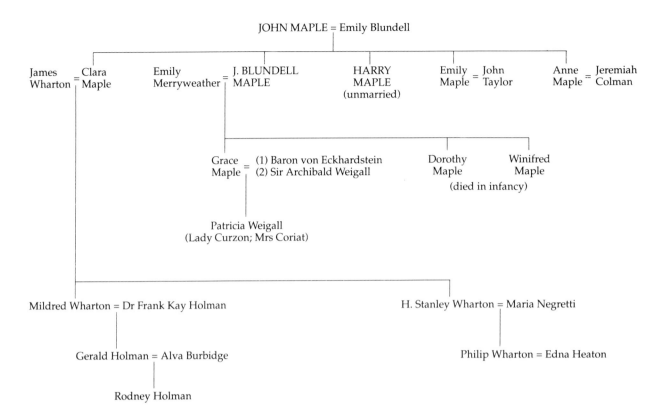

Acknowledgements

M<small>Y</small> thanks are due in the first place to Carol Greene (Mrs Jeffery Hembry) who commissioned me to write a potted history of the firm for the sales brochure she was producing for the Maples Antiques and Fine Art showroom she was opening in New Bond Street in November 1972, when the Tottenham Court Road building was being demolished. When, in somewhat different circumstances, I was asked by Mr Grahame Winter, managing director of Allied Maples Group, to write the full-length history which Carol Greene was unable to persuade the then Board to produce for the opening of the rebuilt store in 1975, such material as I had managed to gather in the intervening 18 years stood me in good stead – and that included much authoritative information from Malcolm Dungworth of Waring & Gillow (Holdings) at Sheffield, to whom I am also grateful. Allied ·Carpets' deal with Gillow plc (now Saxon Hawk Group) did not give them – or me – access to the Maples archives either in London or Sheffield.

I have reason to be very grateful therefore to Mrs Alva Holman for the loan of Press Cutting books, reports and other documents; to Mrs Margaret Pounce for lending me a complete set of *The Maple Leaf* house magazine of which her late husband John Pounce was editor; to Messrs Stanley Darvill, Frank Emes, Norman Andrews and Patrick Rowe, retired Maples staff, for their reminiscences; to Mr Peter Connolly, managing director of Duresta Upholstery Ltd (with Maples 1961–1987) for catalogues and brochures; to Mr Christopher Peddar, General Manager, Maples, Bournemouth, for briefing me on recent events; to Miss Frances Richardson and Miss Kimberley Fernihough of Allied Maples, West Bromwich, and Miss Jane Aspin and Miss Caroline Selby-Green of Countrywide Communications, for their help throughout.

Among those who have helped me with research my thanks are due in particular to Mrs Edna Wharton; Baron Clemens von Schey-Koromla of Buenos Aires; Mr John W Whitaker, grandson of H H Martyn; Mrs Pauline Agius; Miss Pamela Haydon; Mr George White, Consultant Editor, *Cabinet Maker*; Mrs Sarah Medlam, Hon Secretary, The Furniture History Society; Dr R J Holder, Senior Architectural Adviser, The Victorian Society; Mr Stuart Miller, Director, ABE Ventures Corporation UK Limited; Mr Geoffrey Marsh of Event Communication for permission to reproduce as an Appendix his note on The Creation of Frederick Hotels from his history of the Great Central Hotel; Herr Gönke Roscher, Second Secretary Protocol, Embassy of the Federal Republic of Germany; Mr D J Johnson, Deputy Clerk of the Records, House of Lords Record Office; Mr Frank Atkinson, Librarian, St Pauls Cathedral; The Librarian, Windsor Castle; Miss Hannah Lowery, Reader Services, National Art Gallery, Victoria & Albert Museum; The Librarian and staff of The Guildhall Library of London; Miss Wendy Chandley, Assistant Archivist (Library Services), Greater London Council; Elaine Hurt, *Illustrated London News* Picture Library; Miss E Furlong, DMS Watson Library (Manuscript &

Rare Books), University College Hospital; Mr M J Holmes, Local Studies Librarian, Swiss Cottage Library; Miss Judith Yates, Senior Assistant Librarian, All Saints Library, Manchester Polytechnic; Librarian Local Studies, Southwark Public Library; Miss Anne Rehahn, Site Services Librarian, London College of Furniture, City of London Polytechnic; Miss Jan Marsh, Bournemouth Reference Library; Miss Vivienne Prowse, Reference Librarian, St Albans Central Library; Mrs K Haslam, Searchroom Supervisor, Gloucestershire County Record Office; Mr D J Williams, Archivist, Suffolk Record Office, Bury St Edmunds; Mr Alastair Forsyth, Maritime Researcher, City of Southampton; Michael Farrar, County Archivist, Cambridgeshire County Record Office; Miss Nadene Hansen, Archivist, Harrods Limited; Mr Harry Murray, Executive Director, The Imperial Hotel, Torquay; Miss Anne Anderson, Hotel Russell, London.

I would like to thank too those who gave me information regarding the Maples Almhouses in Harpenden – Mr Derek Tynan, Mr John Gillum, Mr Les Casey, Mrs Louisa Watt and Mrs Audrey Edgar; and Miss Jane Colston of Lovell White Durrant for information on Camden Depository.

Ticehurst, May 1991

H B–K

THE FIRST 75 YEARS

❧ 1 ❧

John Maple Sets the Pace 1841–1861

MANY optimists opened drapery shops in London that first decade of the Victorian era. Few lived to the end of the reign basking in the satisfaction of knowing that their name was a household word.

John Maple was one of them.

He was a country lad, born in 1815 of a yeoman farmer William Maple and his wife Hannah in the Sussex village of Thakeham a few miles north of Storrington. The tombstones in the cemetery of the small 12th-century Norman church of All Saints Buncton off the road to Steyning are carved with the names of William Maple's descendants – Elizabeth, widow of Moses Maple who died in 1884; Albert Maple in 1907; Albert Edwin Maple in 1914 and his wife Jane in 1927.

John Maple was still a child when his father died and his mother married again. Hannah's second husband was a Mr Adams, and she left Thakeham to go and live with him at his house in Greenhurst. There is still a Greenhurst Lane between West Chiltington and Thakeham and a house called Greenhurst Manor, though no longer a hamlet of that name. Hannah's second family consisted of at least one son, Henry Adams – John Maple's half brother therefore. But she soon found herself having to raise her sons on her own. Mr Adams died while John Maple was still in his early teens, and Henry was even younger.

It was as 'son of Hannah Adams of Greenhurst in the County of Sussex *widow*' according to the surviving Indenture of 1829, that 14-year-old John Maple put himself Apprentice to James Constable of Horley in Surrey, Shopkeeper, to learn his Art and serve him six years. James Constable appears in the list of 'Shopkeepers, Traders & C' of Storrington in Pigot's Directory of Sussex 1839 as 'grocer & draper'. The directory gives a John

Indenture of May 10, 1829 by which John Maple put himself apprentice to James Constable of Horley, shopkeeper.

Adams among the saddlers and harnessmakers of Fletching – a relation of Hannah's second husband? And Pigot's map of Sussex shows a 'Maplehurst Common'.

As was the custom at the time, by adding his signature on the Indenture to those of his mother (who left the 'a' out of Adams and had to put it in afterwards) and of James Constable, John bound himself to keep his master's secrets, gladly do his commands everywhere; do him no damage nor see it done by others but give him warning of any such attempt. He agreed not to waste his master's goods, nor lend them to anyone unlawfully. He pledged not to play at cards or dice or at (gaming) tables, or any unlawful game whereby his master might have any loss with his own goods or those of others. He would have no hand in buying or selling.

> He shall not haunt Taverns or Playhouses nor absent himself from his said Master's service day or night unlawfully. But in all things as a faithful Apprentice he shall behave himself towards his said Master and all his during the said Term.

It was signed on the 28th day of May in the tenth year of the reign of King George the Fourth.

John's mother agreed to pay James Constable five pounds a year on June 24, until she had paid the agreed total of £25. John was 20 when he completed his six years apprenticeship in 1835, by which time George IV had died and been succeeded by his brother the Duke of Clarence as King William IV. He was happy to accept James Constable's offer to stay on at the Horley general stores as a paid assistant. But as other young men before him, he tired of the quiet country life and, soon after the 19-year-old princess who was King William's niece, had ascended the throne as Queen Victoria in 1837, came to the metropolis to seek his fortune.

London was the largest and wealthiest city in the world. Though its streets were not paved with gold as many believed, it offered the prospect of fabulous riches to anyone of enterprise and imagination. Its growth had been phenomenal. With a population of only 900,000 in 1801, by 1840 it had grown to a city of 2,225,000. In another 70 years it had swollen to 7,250,000. At the heart of this dense concentration of human beings was an ambitious merchant class with money to spend on good quality merchandise, in particular furniture and furnishings for the detached and semi-detached houses or 'villas' which were forming the new suburbs of St Johns Wood, Denmark Hill and Battersea, refuges of the family lifestyle which was now the fashion. And then for each London Season from April to July the nobility and gentry left their country houses, their ceaseless round of picnics, garden parties, croquet and archery, their hunting, shooting and fishing, and flocked to their houses in the West End decorated in the patrician good taste which the social climbing *nouveau riche* took as their ideal.

As a reaction to the heavy drinking, libertine times of the Regency and George IV, which had begun to decelerate under William IV and Queen Adelaide, the home assumed new significance. Comfort took the place of elegance, in tune with the relaxed domesticity of Queen Victoria, who in 1840 settled down to married life with Prince Albert – altogether 'wholesome' except perhaps for the fact that in 1840 Windsor Castle had only one bathroom. Retreating from the 'sinful' over-brightness of the Regency, the mood was for dark and shade, keeping out the sunlight, which faded the wallpaper and the carpets, with blinds and Nottingham lace curtains framed in heavy plush velvet side curtains hung on poles by brass rings.

In spite of the large amount of space taken up by women's dresses – hoop skirts were being replaced by crinolines – everyone filled their living rooms with as much furniture as possible, of the greatest variety of design and material. The parlour, the drawing room, was a cosy clutter of chairs – *papier maché* inlaid with mother-of-pearl and cane-seated, balloon back, bentwood, and the favourite rosewood and mahogany, the prie-dieu chair, the heavily carved and upholstered double tête-à-tête chair, the ottoman buttoned in velvet. There were the looking glasses, china cabinets, crochet boxes, work baskets, the fenders and tongs, the oil lamps, the potted aspidistras, the umbrella stands, door stops and boot scrapers, the wax fruit under the glass dome, the chamber pots and pianos.

Supplying this huge market was obviously a growth industry – and had London as its centre. It needed not only makers but sellers. What better way of making a go of it in the big city, thought John Maple, than applying the Art of the Shopkeeper, which he had spent six years learning at Constables in Horley, to the Furniture Trade?

So, once in London, he looked for a cabinet maker in need of someone to help market his sideboards, wardrobes and desks to furniture retailers, and 'bespoke' pieces direct to customers. Within a short while he had sold himself to one Martin Atkinson, who had extensive workshops and showrooms at 70 to 75 Bridge Road Lambeth (now Westminster Bridge Road). There he met and made friends with a fellow employee called James Cook. After he had gained all the experience and confidence he needed at Atkinsons, he had the urge to try his luck with a shop of his own, and he persuaded James Cook to join him in the new venture as his partner.

John Maple was 26 and the year was 1841.

✳ ✳ ✳

There had been a trade depression in 1837, the year Queen Victoria came to the throne. Unemployment had risen and profits had fallen again in 1840, when there had been a Budget deficit. Unable to cope with the growing problems of a Depression, the Whig Prime Minister Viscount Melbourne resigned in August 1841. In his famous Tamworth Manifesto Sir Robert Peel said he would conserve the interests of the country if elected, and took over from Melbourne as Prime Minister as leader of a Tory Party which from then on was known as the Conservatives.

It would not seem the most favourable time for launching a new commercial enterprise, but Peel soon restored the nation's finances, and there was no change in Britain's position as the world's banker which she remained for another decade. Prosperity was never likely suddenly to desert a nation that fostered innovators like Isambard Brunel whose *Great Western* had crossed the Atlantic with 94 passengers in 15 days in 1838, and Rowland Hill who in 1840 conceived the idea of a Penny Post and introduced the modern postal system. Constitutional stability was ensured in 1841 by the Queen giving birth to the heir to the throne, though she very nearly lost the Prince of Wales's father as she watched Prince Albert fall through the ice on the lake at Buckingham Palace and become immersed up to the chin. Her Majesty was greatly alarmed but, stated the *Annual Register* for 1841, 'with great firmness extricated His Royal Highness from his awkward predicament with the only assistance of one of the ladies of the court'.

John Maple was on firmer ground in Tottenham Court Road, the street in which he acquired from Francis Green, Woollen Draper, the shop he had called 'Tottenham Cloth Hall' at no 145.

Seventy years earlier Tottenham Court Road had been flanked by fields. There had been houses at the Oxford Street end, and in one of these worked Pierre Langlois, Maker of all sorts of Fine Cabinets and Commodes inlaid in the Politest Manner with Brass and Tortoiseshell, many examples of which he had supplied to Horace Walpole for his strange house Strawberry Hill. At the top, the street met the New Road from Paddington which had been built in 1757 and a hundred years later, with the coming of the Metropolitan Railway, became Euston Road. At this junction stood the isolated Toten Hall or Tottenham Court, where in the seventeen twenties they held 'unlawful games and plays, encouraging crowds, riots and misdemeanours, vice and immorality, debauching and ruining servants, apprentices and others'. Fifty years later it had become the slightly more respectable Adam and Eve Tea Rooms and Gardens into which in 1785 the celebrated balloonist Vincent Lunardi made a forced descent, and was the venue of the annual Gooseberry Fair.

In his *Every-Day Book* of 1838 William Hone stated that within his recollection Tottenham Court was

> a house standing alone with spacious gardens in the rear and at the sides, and a forecourt with large timber trees and tables and benches for out-of-doors customers. In the gardens were fruit trees and bowers and arbours for tea drinking parties. In the rear there were not any houses; now there is a town . . .

In the 18th century London's leading furniture makers, including Thomas Chippendale, had had their shops in St Martins Lane but, when their landlords began to raise their rents, the cabinet makers, chair-frame makers and upholsterers moved to Tottenham Court Road. John Harris Heal, feather dresser, had his first workshop in nearby Rathbone Place in 1810 and eight years later moved to 203 Tottenham Court Road. In 1840 Fanny Heal & Son, Mattress and Featherbed Manufacturer, took their business to no 196. James Schoolbred had been trading with his partner Cook (no relation to John Maple's partner) at no 155 since 1817, but not in furniture, which Schoolbreds did not start to sell until 1870.

In 1841 the furniture trade was represented all the way down the street: George Gairdner, upholsterer, at no 80; Daniel Shatford, cabinet maker, at no 83; William Southey, japanner and bedstead maker, at no 87; Benjamin Coote, upholsterer, at no 104; John Rawlings, cabinet maker, at no 170; J William & T Hewetson, upholsterers, at no 204; John Harris, upholsterer, at no 231; Benjamin Lecand, carver and gilder, at no 246; James Purver, upholsterer, at no 258; Bartholomew & Fletcher, cabinet makers, at no 217. A popular rendezvous for all furniture craftsmen in Tottenham Court Road was The Plasterers Arms at no 157.

The shops on either side of no 145 which John Maple had acquired were not in the furniture trade however. At no 144 was Mrs Rebecca Swingler, a flour factor; and at no 146 Leete & Warburton, ironmongers. There was an upholsterer at no 147, Francis Godbold, but a woollen draper, a linen draper and a baker occupied nos 148 to 150. Schoolbred & Co, linen drapers, were at 154 to 156.

In keeping with the trade of these neighbours, and the business of Francis Green whose premises they took over, John Maple and James Cook made the main line at no 145 'ten doors from the New Road and 200 yards from the Adam & Eve Coffee House', Wholesale & Retail Drapery, which is to say linen and cotton sheets, towels, napkins, table cloths. Before houses were numbered (about 1765) traders identified their businesses by signs. Three balls indicated a pawnbroker, a star 'every lewd trade', a hen and chickens a draper. As a stunt, to call attention to the shop being under new management, the two young partners placed a sign reading HEN & CHICKENS on the front wall between the first and second floor windows.

John Maple and Emily Blundell.

Sept/1852

JOHN MAPLE,

145, 146, 147, TOTTENHAM COURT ROAD,

CHIEF ENTRANCE, *Corner of Tottenham Place,*

TEN DOORS *From the New Road.*

WHOLESALE & RETAIL DRAPERY, CARPET, & GENERAL FURNISHING WAREHOUSE.

JOHN MAPLE begs to thank his Friends and the Public for the VERY liberal support he has received during the last ten years, and at the same time assures them he will always strive to merit a continuance of their favors. His Premises are now very extensive, and his Stock IMMENSE, and well-selected. He has only to solicit a visit, being confident all who inspect his Stock will at once perceive the advantages offered to Purchasers. The subjoined List will give some idea of the truth of this assertion.

John Maple, Proprietor, Nos. 145, 146, 147.

DRAPERY AND CARPET DEPARTMENT.

	s	d.		s.	d.
A superior make of Irish Linen, bleached in the yarn, per yard	0	8½	to	1	6
Very fine ditto for Fronts, per yard	1	0	—	2	6
Russia and Irish Sheetings, per yard	0	8	—	1	0
Fine Barnsley ditto, per pair	7	0	—	14	0
Brown Cotton Sheeting, 2 yards wide	0	4	—	0	7
Stout Linen Sheeting	0	6	—	1	0
5-4 Russia ditto	0	10	—	1	6
Full width, without a seam	1	2	—	2	6
Stout Bolton Sheets, per pair	2	0	—	3	0
Russia Towelling, per yard	0	2¼	—	0	5
Nursery Diaper, per piece of 12 squares	1	1½	—	6	0
Damask and other Table Cloths	0	7¾	—	10	9
Handsome Double Damask Cloths				2	8
Double Damask, 3 yards long	6	0	—	12	0
A few slightly Soiled, 2 to 3 yards long, at ...	2	6	—	5	0
Fine undressed Long Cloths, per piece	2	6	—	5	6
Superior Shirting ditto, per yard					3½

A trial of this Article is particularly solicited.

	s	d.		s.	d.
Horrocks's Long Cloth, per yard	0	3½	—	0	9
HOYLE'S yard wide Prints				0	5
MUSLINS of every description.					
WELCH FLANNELS of all Prices, from ...	0	5	—	2	0

White and Blue Serges. Ironing Blankets.

Merinos, Orleans, and Coburgs, from	0	4

CARPETS OF ALL SORTS.

Large Axminster Carpet, 4 yards by 5				1	10	0
Large ditto 3 yards by 4				0	17	0
Turkey Carpets, 4 yards by 4½				3	15	0
Yard wide Carpets, per yard, from					0	6
Stout Stairs ditto	0	4	—		1	6
Good Kidderminster	1	1½	—		1	6
Stout Axminster	1	8	—		2	6
Large size Persia					19	0
Brussels	2	0	—		3	0
Newest designs of ditto	2	9	—		3	6
Best 3-thread ditto					3	8
Handsome Tapestry ditto	3	6	—		3	10
Square Carpets, all sizes, from					4	6
6-4 Printed Druggets, from					0	9½
Stout Druggets for covering Carpets, 1½ yds. wide					1	0
Oil Cloths of every width, the square yard					1	10½
HEARTH RUGS, commencing at					3	6

Oil Baize, and all other kinds of Table Covers.

BEDDING & FURNISHING DEPARTMENT.

Mahogany Chest of Drawers	£1	1	0	to	£2	2	0
Japanned ditto	0	15	0	—	1	5	0
Easy Chairs, in Canvas	0	12	0	—	2	2	0
Ditto in Leather	0	15	0	—	3	10	0
Mahogany and Rosewood Loo Tables ...	1	0	0	—	5	0	0
Set of Mahogany Chairs	3	0	0	—	6	0	0
Mahogany Couches, in Hair Cloth	1	10	0	—	3	10	0
Sofa Bedsteads	1	4	0	—	2	15	0
Ditto (a very prime article)					2	2	0
Stands and Tables, per pair	0	4	6	—	0	8	0
French Bedsteads	0	10	6	—	1	0	0
Tent ditto	0	12	0	—	1	0	0
Mahogany 4-post ditto	1	10	0	—	2	5	0
Handsome cornice top Mahogany 4-post	2	7	0	—	5	5	0
Waterloo Bedsteads	0	12	0	—	1	0	0
Solid top Mahogany Loo Tables	1	1	0	—	2	2	0
Very handsome Rosewood Loo Tables ...	2	10	0	—	5	0	0
Six Drawing Room Chairs	0	16	0	—	1	10	0
Solid Rosewood Chairs, stuffed with Hair and covered in Silk, each	0	15	0	—	1	10	0

Purified Bedding of every description.

Full size Flock Bed	0	6	0	—	0	8	6
Full size Mattress	0	5	6	—	0	8	0
Wool Mattress	0	12	0	—	0	18	6
Hair Mattress, from	1	1	0	—	3	10	0
Full size Feather Beds	1	5	0	—	2	10	0
White Goose ditto	2	2	0	—	5	5	0

Rosewood and Mahogany Cheffioniers, Sideboards, Chimney Glasses, Toilet do., and every article requisite for Dining and Drawing Rooms.

Blankets, Quilts & Counterpanes of every description.

Large White Counterpanes	2	3	to	6	0
Handsome Marseilles ditto	6	0			
Three yards Double Marseilles Quilts	10	0	—	15	0
Witney Blankets, from	2	6	—	5	0
Window Muslins, 12 yards	1	6	—	5	0
Handsome ditto, with border	3	3	—	10	0

Chintz Furnitures, Furniture Dimities, Moreens, &c.

Furniture Dimities	0	2½	—	0	4
Striped Furnitures	0	2	—	0	4
Chintz ditto	0	2½	—	0	6
Stout Watered Moreens	0	6	—	1	0
Rich Washing Damask	0	5½	—	0	10
Floor Cloths of all widths, per yard				1	8

John Maple, Proprietor, Nos. 145, 146, 147.

J. M. begs to state that persons about to furnish will save half the usual trouble and one-third the expense, by selecting from his EXTENSIVE STOCK, as it contains every article requisite for any description of House.

Agent for the Royal Patent Victoria Felt Carpeting, &c.

Fenders, Fire Irons, Brass and Mahogany Cornice Poles, British and French Gilt Cornices, Gilt Frames. Papier Mache Trays, &c. &c.

Henry Mitchener, Printer, 3, Edward Street, Hampstead Road

Maples 1852 advertisement.

Tradition has it that John Maple and James Cook opened their doors for business at 145 Tottenham Court Road on April 16, 1841. However in a notebook with a red cover which survived at least until 1941, but could not be located in 1991, another date is given, 27 days later.

In April 1941 John Maple's grandson told an interviewer from *The Cabinet Maker*:

> I have here a book which is very precious to me, for it is in old Mrs Maple's handwriting, and establishes the business as having been begun by John Maple and James Cook at 145 Tottenham Court Road on May 13, 1841. Expansion was rapid, as no 147 was acquired by the firm in December of that year.

If, after eight months, they bought upholsterer Francis Godbold's shop at no 147, they would have had the ironmongery shop of Leete & Warburton in between. The 1842 directory still gives L & W at 146 but omits any reference to 147. The 1844 directory, reflecting the position at 1843 gave:

145 & 147	Cook & Maple, carpet warehouse
146	Leete & Warburton
148	Hunter & Holt, carpet & furniture warehouse

The sheet on which they wrote their customers bills in 1844 carried an engraving of 145 and 147 as one building, and on a corner. It showed a Hen & Chickens sign between the first and second floor windows of 145 and a ground floor fascia reading COOK & MAPLE; and a Hen & Chickens sign similarly placed on the front of 147 which had a street level fascia reading MAPLE & COOK. On the pavement in front of the tall plate-glass windows were bedsteads, a wardrobe and rolls of carpet. The bill head read:

BOUGHT OF MAPLE & COOK

Wholesale and Retail Drapers

On either side of the picture they listed their subsidiary activities: Carpet Factors, Cabinet Manufacturers, Upholsterers & General Furnishing Warehousemen.

In 1844 John Maple married a friend of his Horley days, Emily Blundell – and James Cook married her sister. Up to then the two bachelors had lived over the shop, but two married men wanted separate establishments. The need to have his own accommodation, and the success of the Tottenham Court Road venture in serving the merchant princes of Marylebone, Tyburnia and Bloomsbury, prompted James Cook to suggest a branch business south of Oxford Street for the aristocratic customers of Belgravia and Mayfair. In 1845 he opened a Cook & Maple carpet warehouse at 22 & 23 Middle Queen's Buildings, Knightsbridge, formerly occupied by upholsterers Slater & Saunders. The premises later became 73 & 75 Brompton Road, just down from Charles Digby Harrod, grocer, at 105.

John and Emily Maple continued to live in the upper part of 145 Tottenham Court Road, and it was there on March 1, 1845 that Emily gave birth to their first child, a boy to whom they gave the Christian names John Blundell.

Living and working apart loosened the bond between the two brothers-in-law, and in 1851 – the year of the Great Exhibition in Hyde Park – John Maple and James Cook dissolved their partnership. From then directory entries read:

Cook, James carpet & furnishing warehouse, 22 & 23 Queens
Buildings
Maple, John carpet & furnishing warehouse, 145 to 147 Totten-
ham Court Road

James Cook carried on at Knightsbridge until 1862 when the premises were acquired by upholsterers Crawcour Lewin & Co. He also had a shop in Leicester Square. In place of James Cook, John Maple took as his partner his half-brother Henry Adams. This time however he decided to trade under his own name. He was now the sole owner (proprietor) of the Totten-ham Court Road store. He had a new bill head printed:

HEN AND CHICKENS
Drapery, Carpet, Cabinet & Upholstery
Warehouses
Nos. 145, 146 & 147 Tottenham Court Road
Bought of John Maple

On a piece of paper with this heading, he jotted down the names of customers and the value of their purchases, which followed on previous orders amounting to £2,471 17s 3d:

Tilley	2 – 3 – 9
Johnson	3 – 3 – 0
Jean	10
McBain	15
James	31 – 2
Wilson & Heath	6 – 14
Waith	29 – 11
Bent	150
Swingler	18 – 18
Parker	50
Read Dufforne	11 – 11
Wagner	13
Hartnell	20
Southgate	4
Roberts & friends	179
Glover	11 – 17 – 6
Clark	22
	3078 – 13 – 0

say £3050 – 0 – 0

The precise significance of this list is by no means clear, but it would seem to indicate a fairly healthy turnover at the start of his trading on his own account.

He produced a trade card reflecting the transition from what began as purely warehousing and retailing to manufacturing.

J. MAPLE
Wholesale & Retail Draper
Carpet Factor, Cabinet Manufacturer, Upholsterer
and General Furnishing Warehouseman
145, 146 & 147 Tottenham Court Road
near the New Road
& 1 to 7 Tottenham Place

Blankets
Counterpanes &
Marseilles Quilts

Irish Linen,
Ready Made Bed Ticks
& Russia Sheeting

In a decade of trading, shrewd management of Maple & Cook and J. Maple, and a flair for knowing what the public wanted and telling them that he had it, enabled John to accumulate sufficient profit by 1851 to afford demolishing the three shops which had once been Francis Greens, Leete & Warburtons and Francis Godbolds, and building on the site a new, single emporium designed to his specification. It had a unified frontage and an impressive row of high shop windows facing the pavement in which to display a selection of his extensive stock of sheets and towels, mattresses and carpets, and furniture of every description. It had its chief entrance at the corner of Tottenham Place where he had the workshops for the craftsmen he employed making tables, china cabinets, escritoires and other products of the cabinet-maker, and the mattress, cushion and sofa stuffers – upholsterers.

For the sake of giving visible evidence of continuity – important in view of the interval between having to close and reopen – the new partners gave the Hen & Chickens sign pride of place in the centre of the new frontage surmounting the wrought iron balustrade, incorporating the name MAPLE picked out in white below an archway. On the fascia above each of the two entrances was written

J. MAPLE

To launch the rebuilt store, the partners had an elaborate poster printed headed with an engraving of the new-look 145, 146 and 147, and setting out what he had to offer. The proprietor introduced his bill of fare with a word of gratitude and an invitation to all and sundry to come and see the place for themselves.

> JOHN MAPLE begs to thank his Friends and the Public for the VERY liberal support he has received during the last ten years, and at the same time assure them he will always strive to merit a continuance of their favors. His Premises are now very extensive, and his Stock IMMENSE, and well-selected. He has only to solicit a visit, being confident all who inspect his Stock will at once perceive the advantages offered to Purchasers. The subjoined list will give some idea of the truth of this assertion.

The Drapery and Carpet Department headed the list and it was topped by 'A superior make of Irish Linen bleached in the yarn' priced at 8½d to 1s 6d a yard – sheeting was by the yard, sheets per pair, Fine Barnsley three times the price of Stout Bolton. The price of a Nursery Diaper of 12 squares ranged from 1s 1½d to 6s; Welch Flannels cost between 5d and 2s; while White and Blue Serges, Merinos, Orleans and Coburgs could be had for fourpence – for ironing blankets.

His most expensive floor covering was a 4 × 4½ yard Turkey carpet at £3 15s (£3.75). A large Axminister of the same size was £1 10s (£1.50). Every width of oil cloth was 1s 10½ (9p) a square yard. A set of Mahogany Chairs could be found in the Bedding and Furnishing Department for £6 – or an inferior version for half the price. A mahogany chest of drawers cost a guinea (£1.5), a japanned chest only 15s (75p). Handsome cornice top mahogany 4-post beds were £5 5s at their most expensive, £2 2s in the cheaper version. But a Waterloo Bed cost only 12s (60p). A Loo Table was originally made for people playing the card game of that name (not unlike whist), but those which John Maple was selling in 1851 for one to five pounds each were merely round tables based on the card table design. The cheaper form of Solid Rosewood Chairs, stuffed with Hair and covered in Silk, could be purchased for 15s.

Under the heading 'Purified Bedding of every description' the wool mattresses were half the price of hair ones; and Full Size Feather Beds, £2 10s at their most expensive, compared with White Goose ditto at £5 5s. Twelve yards of best quality Window Muslin cost five shillings (25p), but double that for Handsome ditto with border. 'Dimity' was a stout cotton cloth woven with raised stripes which was used undyed for beds and hangings. The cheapest article at the Hen & Chickens in 1851 was 'Furniture Dimities' at 2½d (1p). They were listed under 'Chintz Furniture, Furniture Dimities, Moreens & c'. Stout Watered Moreen, a wool and cotton curtain material, cost between sixpence and a shilling.

Squeezed between the dense lines of type, he managed to insert the line:

> Rosewood and Mahogany Cheffoniers, Sideboards, Chimney Glasses, Toilet do., and every article requisite for Dining and Drawing Rooms.

At the front of the poster he made it known that he was Agent for the Royal Patent Victoria Felt Carpeting & c; and, as an afterthought as it were, that he sold Fenders, Fire Irons, Brass and Mahogany Cornice Poles, British and French Gilt Cornices, Gilt Frames, Papier Trays, & c, & c.

> J.M. begs to state that persons about to furnish will save half the usual trouble and one-third the expense by selecting from his EXTENSIVE STOCK, as it contains every article requisite for any description of House.

John Maple was not content to rely on handbills and posters to attract customers to the Hen & Chickens in the eighteen fifties. Someone who knew him in those days described him as a very 'saucy' young gentleman.

> The word is ugly but descriptive. He used to draw attention to the goods that bulged from his shop on the pavement by whacking, perhaps, a china basin with a stout stick, and telling courting couples as they passed that it was time they got married and gave him an order for a bassinette.
>
> I can see him now, a dapper little fellow with a white top hat cocked on one side, very tight trousers and a very loud waistcoat, almost laying hold of the arms of people in his eagerness to make them buy something, if only a door mat, from the Hen & Chickens. He never doubted but what he would make a fortune out of his furnishing line.

John and Emily bought a house for themselves at Hampstead when, in view of the rebuilding, they were no longer able to live above no 145. Their second child Harry was born in the new home in 1851, and a few years later their daughter Clara followed by Emily and Anne. However sales and clerical staff, cabinet makers and upholsterers whom John employed had their living quarters in the new building, as they had had in the old. So they were the sufferers of the tragic event of the spring of 1857.

Hunter & Holt felt they lost out with their old-fashioned carpet and furniture showrooms at nos 148 and 149, and decided to replace them with a modern frontage upsides with the competition next door. They were aware that taking out one section of a terrace risks destabilising the houses on either side, and no 147 was shored up to prevent any such calamity. However, at around seven o'clock on the morning of Saturday May 11 1857, in the words of a local newspaper reporter,

> a cracking noise was heard, and a sound like thunder succeeded, causing the people in the neighbourhood the greatest consternation.

The dividing wall between no 148 and 147 collapsed, and brought with it the whole of nos 147 and 146.

> The building fell with a frightening crash. The shrieks and groans which proceeded from the persons buried beneath the ruins were truly heartrending.

Neighbours were paralysed by so sudden and astounding a shock. It was worse for the 30 or so members of John Maple's staff who were either in bed on the upper floors of the Hen & Chickens, or on the point of getting up and dressing in readiness for their Saturday morning stint in the store below. The housekeeper Mrs Christmas was dusting a piano at the time and fell between it and a beam, luckily only slightly grazing her legs. But Ann Driscoll, the cook, a carving knife in her hands, was one of the six killed. Mr Eaton, John's clerk, had both his leg bones splintered. A young man who had joined the firm as a sales assistant that year had both legs badly bruised, was taken to hospital but was allowed to leave. His name was Horace Regnart.

John Maple was called to the scene from his Hampstead home, and told reporters that he reckoned the collapse had done £10,000 worth of damage, apart from destroying furniture he would value at £2,400.

In the shop of this corner house and extending a great distance to the rear of Tottenham Court Road, ran the newspaper report,

> there is an immense stock of valuable furniture of all descriptions which has fortunately remained uninjured. But in one of the houses that has fallen it is said that the furniture and other stock-in-trade was of the value of several thousand pounds.

John Maple announced he would at once raise a fund for the widows and orphans of the tragedy. At the subsequent inquest into the deaths of Mrs Driscoll and the others, the coroner chose to apportion no blame but deliver a verdict which merely 'stated the facts'.

If the store which was built in place of the one which collapsed in May 1857 in any way resembled the picture on the bill head of 1858, it was now ground floor plus four storeys. It was a whole floor higher than the building on either side. Gone was the Hen & Chickens sign, and in the centre of the Tottenham Court Road frontage high up between the third and fourth floor was MAPLE & CO instead of J. MAPLE, which denoted the formalisation of John's partnership with Henry Adams. The sheet was headed 'Bought of J. Maple & Co' however.

The new engraving emphasised the location of the store on a corner. The main showroom building of five floors (of which

145, 146 & 147 Tottenham Court Road in 1858 – 'Near the New Road'.

the top was doubtless the living quarters of the staff) turned round into Tottenham Place (now Beaumont Place?) for a distance of three windows. Attached to it, and half the height, were the workshops occupying nos 1 to 7 Tottenham Place which was wide enough to take a horse and cart.

'Wholesale & Export Warehouse' read a sign on part of the wall of the main building in Tottenham Place. So the activity of supplying furniture and furnishing to customers overseas, which became so large a part of their business, had already begun. The two-year Crimean War which ended in 1856, in which Britain had sided with Turkey against Russia, may have hampered John Maple's ability to secure all the Turkey carpets and Russia sheeting he required, though to compensate he probably won War Department contracts to supply army blankets and for his upholsterers to make tents. But the first seven years of the eighteen-fifties saw a phenomenal increase in the amount of goods which British manufacturers sold overseas. It was a time of global boom. The value of British exports to Turkey and the Middle East, for instance, rose from £3½ million in 1848 to £16 million in 1870. In 35 years, as E J Hobsbawm pointed out in *The Age of Capital 1848–1875*, 'the value of the exchanges between the most industrialised economy and the most remote and backward regions of the world had increased about sixfold'.

J Maple & Co of London, at the centre of the world's first and most successful industrial nation, fed on the general prosperity, gratifying the demands of the increasing number of people both at home and abroad whose priority was not only to accumulate wealth but display it.

Wealthy John Maple's own lifestyle was comfortable but, if

entries in his 1858 Bank Book are anything to go by, hardly ostentatious. He was investing money in 'safe' railway stock:

Shares in Edinboro Perth & Dundee Rly paid £18 – 13 – 8 dividend to 31 Jan 57	£250

Shares in LGOC [London General Omnibus Company]
& GWR [Great Western Railway] of Canada

He was buying pictures (or photographs?):

Cash paid by Mr Constable of Brighton	£1-17-0
A/c for Likenessess Do.	£6-6-0
P.O. order to Mansfreto for Portrait	18-0

He may by now have acquired his estate at Salfords in Horley, for he would have been unlikely to have wanted the Shooting Licence, which cost him £4 2s, in Hampstead. And was the Coach House which he had paved for £1 15s in town or in the country? He paid 15s for Excursion for Porters, and 17s 6d for Tickets to Crystal Palace. The bill of Taylor his tailor amounted to £1 9s 6d.

A separate account showed his outgoings for his wife:

Mrs Maple

1 Feather Bed	£2-8-0
Paid for cab	1-6
Print Dress	3-8
1 Robe (silk)	£3-0-0
1 Silk Umbrella	11-9
Wardrobe	£7-19-0

And he was obviously not going to indulge his children:

Harry's trousers	10-0
Boats for Blundell	10-0

Blundell was now a boy of 13. When he was ten his father had sent him to a private school at Maidenhead called Crawford College. There he showed a natural aptitude for mathematics. After only two years he sat for, and passed, the examination of the College of Preceptors, and in 1858 became a pupil at the school in London connected with King's College in Somerset House.

He had great faith in mathematics, he recalled to an interviewer from *The World of Commerce* many years later.

> Euclid to my mind is the basis of all our commercial thinking. It enables a man to go straight to an idea. Mathematics give him a reason for everything he does. He is able to avoid cross courses which lead, as a rule, to blunders and disappointment.

A good, sound, practical education was what England wanted. But no one should suppose for a moment that it would turn out a ready-made Lord Mayor.

> At school I worked more for a commercial career; I took almost passionately to mathematics. At eleven I had crossed my Ass's Bridge – my *pons asinorum*. At thirteen I had conquered my Euclid.

He would have two types of school in England: classical for the study of dead languages, commerical for the study of living languages. To the one he would send the parsons-in-future, to the other Dick Whittingtons to come.

A parent may send his son to college because he wishes to make a gentleman of him, but when the youth enters the paternal counting-house his knowledge of Greek hexameters avails him very little with the China trade in grey shirtings. He has it all to learn. Whatever failures we may meet with in City commerical life are due, I am persuaded, to the lack of true commerical education at school, which is the groundwork of the man of business.

Blundell's father had made good by 20 years hard slog and a firm belief in the effectiveness of the Big Store Movement of which he was a leader. He proclaimed his gospel through advertisements in the quality London newspapers and upper class magazines such as *The Illustrated London News*. No more dressing up in white top hat and fancy waistcoat to shout at passers-by. He had shed the market-boy image and was aiming up-market at the Man of Property – and his wife.

J Maple & Co, he told potential customers through the small print of his ladders of classified announcements, was

> the largest and most convenient furnishing establishment in the world

> Families from the country particularly will find it is a great advantage to be able to purchase every requisite in the same house

With the kind of upper-class clientele he was aiming at he knew he ran no risk in sending them goods On Approval – and they liked a tradesman who felt he could trust them. He made full use of the postal system which had been created the year he started business, and of the steam trains which now ran on a network of railway lines covering almost the whole kingdom.

> Samples and patterns post-free

> Sample parcels containing two 8-4 Damask Cloths, two Tray cloths, one dozen Napkins to match, and one pair 2½ yards wide Linen Sheets sent free to any railway station in England on receipt of an order for £2.

Marketing had spread very much further than Tottenham Court Road. John Maple's business had already become very much more than just a shop.

He played on the snob value of giving his Dining Room and Drawing Room Furniture romantically grandiloquent names:

> The Eugenie Easy-chair, price 25s
> The Prince of Wales Chair, price 32s
> The Vienna Easy-chair, price 35s
> The Paragon Couch, price 3 guineas
> The Prince of Wales Couch, price 3½ guineas

And in 1860 he never hesitated to address the market he considered worthy of his merchandise direct:

> TO NOBLEMEN, GENTLEMEN AND CONNOISSEURS
> John Maple & Co respectfully announce that they have on view a Grand BARONIAL SIDEBOARD. Price 125 guineas, not a quarter its real value.

He was well aware however that he should not rely merely on rich individuals purchasing goods for a private house:

J Maple & Co's advertisement in the Illustrated London News *of 1860 – 'Established Twenty Years'.*

> Hotel keepers and all large consumers will find
> an immense advantage.

By these advertisements he hoped to entice readers to come to his store's entrance at 145 Tottenham Court Road, enter and see for themselves the 12-Guinea Drawing-Room Suites in solid walnut wood covered in rich silk or Utrecht Velvet.

To those unable or unwilling to do so he would post them a copy of

> J MAPLE and Co's NEW ILLUSTRATED CATALOGUE
> containing the prices of every article required for
> completely furnishing a house of any class, post-free.

Harry Maple was only ten in 1861, but there was no holding back his 16-year-old brother Blundell from plunging into the sophisticated enterprise of his father's making, and immersing himself in it with the exuberance and bonhomie that was to characterise his whole commercial career.

> I went into my father's factory (he told *The World of Commerce*) straight from King's College and studied detail, from an envelope to a ledger. I grounded myself in prices – the prices and sources of woods of every description, from the battens of Sweden to the satin-woods of South America, and a hundred other varieties which are used in cabinet-making.

It was an early start, but in his long run-up to maturity the young Blundell gave himself the knowledge and the confidence to take the family firm into a second gear that, to the astonishment of his contemporaries, surpassed even the achievements of his pioneering father.

'Fifty years ago,' wrote a correspondent in *The Times*, looking back on the Maple & Co of the eighteen-fifties, 'the shop was not to be distinguished from the ordinary "goods-on-the-pavement" type which was at that time common, and is not yet extinct, in the Tottenham Court Road; and it remained open till 9 o'clock, doing much of its business with small people who came to buy household furniture after their own shops were closed. Somehow or other John Maple the elder gradually came to secure some richer customers, and early in the sixties he had contrived to enlarge his borders to make his business well known by advertisement and to take his place as one of the leaders of the new commercial movement – the movement for big shops where the owner of a house, however large or small, could come and find all the furniture he wanted on the premises.'

At 56 John Maple was at the height of his powers in 1861. At the outbreak of the American Civil War he made a shrewd deal in buying up all the calico he could lay hands on. He was well into his stride and there was no question of his relaxing his grip, withdrawing into the background with a view to be shortly 'handing over' to his son and heir. His half-brother Henry Adams was still his commerical partner, but the close association of John and Blundell Maple which could be said to date from 1861, was the beginning of a new era.

∂ᴠ∂ 2 ∂ᴠ∂

Blundell Maple Confounds His Critics 1861–1891

THERE were two faces to London's 19th-century furniture making industry – the 'honourable' West End section to which J Maple & Co of Tottenham Court Road belonged, and the 'dishonourable' or 'slop' East End section. In the West End, furniture making was a craft carried on by highly skilled craftsmen who had acquired their skills through serving disciplined apprenticeship stretching over a number of years. Each man prided himself on being able to craft a complete piece of furniture of high quality with one pair of hands. He was able to apply a variety of skills and thus see the job through from start to finish.

While very little division of labour was to be found in the large furniture factories of West End establishments such as Maple & Co, the slop manufacturers with small workshops in Bethnal Green, in Curtain Road and Hackney Road employed untrained, unskilled and badly paid men able to do one aspect of the work only – turning, carving, or french polishing, say. Production of a reasonably sophisticated piece of furniture was the work of many hands. Or else a workshop stuck to one product, became a specialist in, say, ladies' writing tables or wardrobes, in glove cases, pistol cases or jewel boxes, in chairs or upholstery. It specialised too, probably, in one of the rival styles which competed with each other in the first half of the century – Grecian, Gothic, Elizabethan, Italian Renaissance, French Rococco and the rest.

When John Maple set up in Tottenham Court Road with James Cook in the eighteen-forties and began adding furniture to his basic stock of drapery and carpets, the East End furniture trade was on a comparatively small scale. But in the next 20 years it expanded very rapidly so that, as Pat Kirkham says in *Furnishing the World*, 'by 1870 the East End outstripped the West End as the main furniture producing area in the capital' both in terms of workshops and workers. The demand which large stores such as Maples had created through their imaginative retailing had become greater than they could supply solely with products of their own manufacture.

West End and East End together strove to satisfy the Victorians' appetite for clutter.

> The Victorian home, like the Victorian female body, was well covered, and like the Victorian female mind, it was filled to overflowing with small superfluities. Sweeping window curtains, three deep heavy portières, long lace curtains to adorn

> folding doors . . . elaborate fringed draperies over the mantel-
> piece to match the heavily fringed tablecloth of sombre hue,
> draperies behind the piano, over the screen. (Irene Clephane,
> *Our Mothers*)

Every room was overfurnished. Over the dining-room fireplace a huge 'chimney glass' framed in massive mahogany. On
the drawing-room mantelpiece an enormous clock in white
marble flanked by heavy vases, bronze figures, stuffed birds,
wax flowers under glass domes, a walnut grand piano, horse-
hair sofa, stools, firescreens, cabinets. It was all grist to Maples'
mill.

It was not only the fashion of filling every corner but of
constantly changing the arrangement, throwing out what had
become too familiar and bringing in new pieces, which
maintained the flow of orders to Tottenham Court Road. And
not only from their mainstream upper class customers, but
from royalty.

In 1863 John Maple, along with most of his competitors, sent
all his account customers a souvenir card to mark the marriage
of Queen Victoria's son and heir to Princess Alexandra of
Denmark. Inside the card's decorative border was an oval
photograph of the royal couple, him seated and she standing
over him. Above it was the Prince of Wales crest of three
feathers and his motto Ich Dien. Below was the inscription
'Married at Windsor 10th March 1863'. At the very top was the
royal arms with a Danish flag and a union jack. Beneath the
border:

J. Maple & Co
Upholsterers, London

Prince Albert had died two years previously and the Queen
had gone into mourning, from which she never felt able to
emerge. It put a damper on the social life of the capital and the
shires – and spending. But entertaining and the old frivolity
returned with the marriage of the popular Bertie, whose
uninhibited Marlborough House Set enjoyed a glittering lifestyle in stark contrast to the gloom of the widowed Queen's
sombre circle.

Fashionable life was back to normal by 1870 when Maples
received orders for much of the furniture and furnishing of the
royal residence in Richmond Park called White Lodge.

Prince Teck, an Austrian, later made Duke of Teck, and his
wife Princess Mary Adelaide, a granddaughter of George III
and mother of George V's Queen Mary, were at first given
apartments in Kensington Palace. But, worried about losing
his status at court, Teck persuaded Queen Victoria to give him
also a mansion house of his own in the form of the substantial
White Lodge. At Kensington Palace, according to James Pope-
Hennessy, His Serene Highness 'kept the furniture in what
might be termed a permanent state of flux, preparing surprises
for anniversaries and snatching at any opportunity for an
almost neurotic rotation and change'.

On her 37th birthday the Princess was led by her husband
Francis for the first time into the drawing room at White Lodge
where, she wrote to her sister,

> the bright red cretonne curtains and loose covers were my first
> pleasant surprise; and then into the blue morning-room which,

Wimbledon Common from White Lodge.

Princess May's Sitting Room

Princess May's Balcony.

A Shady Seat.

White Lodge.

Holland Trincham.

White Lodge, Richmond Park in 1893, home of the Duke and Duchess of Teck.

had the carpet arrived in time, would have been quite ready for use, thanks to dear Francis. The blue parrots on the buff ground of the cretonne curtains and covers are deliciously pretty.

The whole order for these and other fabrics from H S H Prince Teck, White Lodge, Richmond Pk, are set out on page 565 of Maple & Co's ledger.

But of course it was not the Prince's style to leave well alone. The furniture and drapery were re-arranged and re-arranged continually over the next five years until the end of 1874. In another letter Mary Adelaide, now the Duchess of Teck, told a friend how pleased she was with the way everything had finally been placed.

> After dinner I was taken into the blue boudoir to be *agreeably* surprised which I *most certainly* was, for never have I seen a room more improved! The new corner sofa by good luck chanced to be too short for the corner it had been originally ordered for; so Francis put it between the windows . . . for which corner it seems made! The cabinet he removed to the wall under Mamma's picture, where it looks beautiful & its place under the 3 chicks' portraits is filled by the large sofa. In the corner by the cabinet stands an easel with Swinton's sketch of Francis on it & in front of this the round blue leather table making a back to the small *chaise-longue* which is placed cornerwise to the fire, with a small table in front of it.

His Serene Highness had been making another of his frequent visits to Tottenham Court Road.

> Behind the armchair, which takes up the opposite corner of the fireplace, now stands the little black Japanese *whatnot* from the Green Corridor; to be ultimately replaced by the new black cabinet ordered of Maple for my Christmas by Francis. The high whatnot, which used to be in the corner between the windows, now fills up the space between the sofa & the door into the dining room. The whole effect is most perfect & so delighted me . . . most snug & *cosy*! (quoted by James Pope-Hennessy in *Queen Mary 1867–1953*).

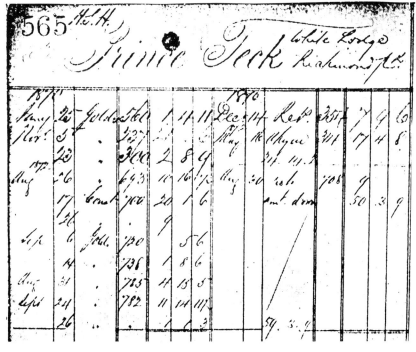

It was to be hoped that Maples got their money. Their invoices were headed with the words 'All goods must be paid for on or before delivery'. But the notoriously extravagant Duchess of Teck lived well beyond her means and owed money to almost every retailer in London. Eventually the Tecks had to flee to the continent to escape their creditors.

John Maple and his sons Blundell and Harry, whom he made partners of the firm in 1870, must have been prepared for Bad Debts. Surprisingly however they were not properly prepared for Fire. When fire destroyed buildings and stock to the value of £45,000 at the beginning of December 1871, they found they were not fully covered by insurance.

Fire started on the ground floor in the department for furniture, silks and damasks. It penetrated to the bedroom furniture department on the first floor, and again to the second floor on which they kept their chair frames, upholsterer's fittings etc. Among goods destroyed on the first floor were 80 fine wardrobes. The whole of that block was destroyed.

Maples' premises, reported *The House Furnisher & Decorator*, covered an immense area and were divided into blocks with substantial interior brick walls. The communications between the divisions were closed at night with double sets of iron doors placed a foot apart.

> To these doors Maples attribute the preservation of the other portions of the premises. Could the fire had extended laterally, nothing could have saved the whole property. As it is, great has been the loss, but a small portion of the entire building has been destroyed, and such are the resources of the establishment that scarce a check was given to the course of business.

The builders' men were at work before the embers of the fire had died out, and the premises were contracted to be rebuilt by the first week in February. The £45,000 which the fire cost them went mainly on rebuilding nos 145 to 149 Tottenham Court Road, for the cover they had on stock, for which they paid the London and Lancashire Fire Insurance Company an annual premium of ten pounds, in the new policy they negotiated after the fire, only amounted to £4,000. The wording on the policy was:

> On Stock in Trade their own in trust or on commission Utensils and Fixtures in their Warehouses Showrooms and Offices situate aforesaid Brick Built communicating with each other by double and single iron doors and more particularly described in plan lodged in this Office.

The year after the fire nos 141 to 144 Tottenham Court Road 'in the occupation of Messrs Maple, Swingler [Rebecca the flour factor] and Good' were sold by auction, along with the 12 shops nos 259 to 281 on the south side of Euston Road, the one time New Road, and houses in Southampton Court, Beaumont Place and Tottenham Place. – the huge island site which was soon to be occupied almost entirely by Maples showrooms, workshops and warehouses, timber yards and stabling.

Tottenham Court Road was in transition – and so was the whole of London's furniture trade. Standards were dropping; few London firms were bothering to take in youngsters and teach them the skills of the craft. *The House Furnisher* deplored what it called 'the decadence in the disuse of apprenticeship'.

Too little training was being undertaken by the trades unions and City Guilds. As a result, there was a shortage of first-class cabinet makers and too much was left to 'garett-men' from whose attic workshops 'but indifferent hands are turned out'.

Blundell Maple, who was 25 in 1879 and been through every department of the family store, took a particular interest in the cabinet-making branch where he made sure that the employees were top-class craftsmen and trained others to follow in the same tradition. He could have no influence, however, over the way the East End 'slop' manufacturers went about their business, on whom he was increasingly dependent as a retailer to maintain his stock. But if Maples were to excel as cabinet-makers, he considered they should also be timber merchants, and in a few years Maples became one of the largest consumers and converters of hardwood in Britain.

It was typical of Blundell Maple's all-or-nothing approach. His devotion to the needs of the family store was equally whole-hearted. In 1871 he turned down an invitation to stand as Parliamentary candidate for the old borough of Marylebone. A shopkeeper in the House of Commons? It was a height he might scale later – even to become the first retailer to join the Carlton Club – but it could wait. He declined too the offer he received from American businessmen to manage their company for three years at an annual salary of £10,000.

He reserved his energies not only for his workpeople and his customers, but also his neighbours. He took the trouble to ensure that all Maples carts and vans were loaded out of sight and without holding up the flow of traffic along Tottenham Court Road and inconveniencing the public who walked its pavements.

Tottenham Court Road had become more accessible – and more busy – since the Metropolitan Railway Company had built its cut-and-cover railway under the streets of north London from Paddington to Farringdon Street – the world's first 'Underground' line – in 1863. They had placed a stop on it within a few hundred yards of Maples front entrance. They called it Gower Street Station – and as Euston Square Station still serves Tottenham Court Road and Euston Road 128 years later.

Accessible and busy maybe, but Tottenham Court Road – or rather its shopkeepers – still suffered from an inferiority complex when it came to comparing it with the more westerly West End establishments. *The House Furnisher* welcomed the decision of draper James Schoolbred & Co to branch out into cabinet-making, upholstery and the decorative trades in 1873 – so long as they *made* at least some of their furniture and bedding themselves. The writer did not sympathise with the too prevalent tendency of certain large drapery houses to engross and absorb all other businesses. Such attempts were too apt to degenerate into mere 'slop-dealing', which in the cabinet trade above all others had done a great deal of harm.

> Your true upholsterer is a man of the most varied and important qualifications, and is often as necessary and as trusted an agent in many houses as are the family lawyer and doctor. We venture to welcome with hope the advent of the new houses. There is room, ample and to spare, for all fair and honest traders; and although it may be long before the Tottenham Court Road rivals

Blundell Maple.

New Bond and Oxford Street, we may hope yet to see the locality redeemed from being a by-word among streets. (10 June 1873)

There was no place for defeatist talk such as this, no thought of being in second place where John and Blundell Maple were concerned. It had been superlatives all the way since the eighteen-fifties, and they still settled for nothing less. Maple & Co's Furnishing Establishment, they still proclaimed at the head of their column of small classified advertisements in 1874, was the *largest* and *most convenient*, not just in the West End, or London as a whole, or even Britain, but *in the world*. The address they gave showed Maples now covered not only 145 to 149 Tottenham Court Road, but further down Tottenham Place – 1 to 15 – and 2 to 6 Grafton Street East.

A house *of any magnitude* could be furnished from stock in a few days – an immense advantage to Country Customers, for Merchants and for Exportation. Families who studied economy with durability and elegance should pay the easily accessible Tottenham Court Road a visit before giving orders. Maples supplied *every* requisite for house furnishing including linens, ironmongery, glass, crockery, bronzes, and every description of ornaments, either for dining or drawing room or for Christmas and wedding presents.

They had 5,000 brass and iron bedsteads to choose from, 'manufactured on the premises and all warranted'. They had a hundred bedroom suites of various designs in enamelled Siberian Ash, Satin-Wood, Hungarian Ash, Oak etc. It was the *largest* assortment of Bed-Room Furniture in London.

All carpets were sold at wholesale prices, the largest choice, the *finest* and *best* designs: old-pattern Brussels, Aubusson, Kidderminster, Felt, Turkey, Indian. An importation of extra-quality carpets had just been received by the ship *Red Gauntlet*. They had too a large stock of Persian, Turkey and Foreign Rugs from 17s (85p), 'some very curious in make and design'.

Maple & Co had a stock of the fashionable material Cretonne Chintz in all the usual patterns, but also in the Magnificent Designs drawn and manufactured especially for them, superior in taste and manufacture to any ever offered before.

And the greatest novelty of 1874? 'The Beaufort' Bed-Room Toilet Ware manufactured expressly for Maple & Co, new in shape and design, elegant, colours very choice. The ideal wedding present for anyone setting up house like Blundell Maple and Emily Merryweather who were married at Clapham in October 1874.

However Maples employees gave the happy couple a silver tea and coffee service 'of very chaste design and pattern' accompanied by a congratulatory address upon vellum. Furniture manufacturers associated with Maples – the slop traders of the East End? – presented the newlyweds with 'a most elegant dessert service of which the value', stated the local newspaper, 'was reported to be something fabulous, as the quantity was so extensive and the quality so excellent'.

Emily's home was Clapham House on Clapham Common, where her mother gave the reception – her father Moses Merryweather was dead. Blundell's parents, John and Emily Maple, came over from Horley, and the workers on their estate and the servants in their house, Petridge Wood, sent a handsome tobacco box inscribed with Blundell's initials. With it

**MAPLE and CO.,
TOTTENHAM-COURT-ROAD,
LONDON.**

FURNITURE.   FURNITURE.
FURNITURE.   FURNITURE.
FURNITURE.   FURNITURE.

MAPLE and CO.'S NEW ILLUSTRATED CATALOGUE, containing the Price of every Article Required in Furnishing, post-free. Foreign and Country orders punctually and faithfully executed on receipt of a remittance or London reference.

MAPLE and CO.'S FURNISHING ESTABLISHMENT is the largest and most convenient in the world. A house of any magnitude can be Furnished from Stock in a few days, an immense advantage to Country Customers, for Merchants, or for Exportation.

MAPLE and CO. supply every requisite for HOUSE FURNISHING, including Linens, Ironmongery, Glass, Crockery-ware, Clocks, Bronzes, and every description of Ornaments, either for Dining or Drawing Room, or for Christmas and Wedding Presents, in separate Departments.

MAPLE and CO. — DINING-ROOM FURNITURE.—Sideboards, in Oak, Mahogany, and other woods, from 5 gs. to 100 gs. Fine Oak and Mediæval Dining-Room Furniture. Tables, from 3 gs. to 70 gs. An immense assortment of Clocks, Bronzes, and other Ornaments.

MAPLE and CO. — DRAWING-ROOM FURNITURE, the largest assortment in London ; an endless variety of Cabinets, from 2 to 60 gs , many quite new in design ; a large assortment of Buhl Furniture, as well as Black and Gold; 100 Easy-Chairs, from 1 to 10 gs ; a very extensive Stock of Clocks, Bronzes, and Fancy Ornaments; 500 Chimney-Glasses, from 2 to 80 gs ; Console Tables, as well as Girandoles, from 1 to 20 gs.

FURNITURE. — DRAWING-ROOM.—The largest selection in the world to select from. Some handsome Drawing-Room Suites, in Silk, from 30 gs ; in Rep, from 10 gs. 500 Easy-Chairs in various shapes. Eugénie Easy-Chairs, 28s. 6d. ; Vienna Easy-Chairs, 38s. 6d. Couches to correspond.

FURNITURE.—MAPLE & CO.—Families who study economy with durability and elegance should visit this establishment before giving their orders. A house of any size furnished complete from stock in three days. An Illustrated Catalogue post-free.—145, 146, 147, 148, and 149, Tottenham-court-road, London.

**MAPLE and CO.,
TOTTENHAM-COURT-ROAD.**

BEDSTEADS.   BEDSTEADS.
BEDSTEADS.   BEDSTEADS.
BEDSTEADS.   BEDSTEADS.

BED-ROOM FURNITURE. MAPLE & CO.

BED-ROOM FURNITURE. MAPLE & CO.

BED-ROOM FURNITURE. MAPLE & CO. For BEDSTEADS in Wood, Iron, and Brass, fitted with Furniture and Bedding complete. Suites for Bed-Rooms, from 10 gs each. See Illustrated Catalogue.
MAPLE and CO.,

BRASS and IRON BEDSTEADS.—Five Thousand to select from. From 12s. to 30 gs. Handsome Brass Bedsteads, 5 gs. Bedding of every description manufactured on the premises, and all warranted.

BED-ROOM FURNITURE.—100 Suites, of various designs, to select from, from 10 gs for Suite complete Bed-Room Suites, enamelled Siberian Ash, Satin-Wood, Hungarian Ash, Oak, &c., from 15 gs.—MAPLE and CO., 145, 146, 147, Tottenham-court-road.

BED-ROOM SUITES in SOLID ASH, from 30 gs. to 50 gs. Bed-Room Suites in Black and Gold, very choice and handsome style, from 40 gs. to 80 gs. The largest assortment of Bed-Room Furniture in London to select from.

**MAPLE and CO.,
TOTTENHAM-COURT-ROAD.**

CARPETS.   CARPETS.
CARPETS.   CARPETS.

MAPLE and CO. for CARPETS. Families Furnishing should inspect this Stock before deciding. They will find a considerable advantage in price, besides having the largest choice to select from, including some of the finest and best designs ever offered. Patterns sent on receiving a description of what is likely to be required. All Carpets at the wholesale prices.—Maple and Co., 145 to 149, Tottenham-court-road.

MAPLE and CO.'S NEW CARPET SHOW-ROOMS, entirely for the display of British and Foreign Carpets of every description, are now open. Goods will be sold at the smallest remunerative profit. All the new, choice patterns for 1874; also 500 pieces of old-pattern Brussels, to be sold cheap. Kidderminster, Felt, Dutch, Turkey Indian, and, in fact, every description of Carpets, at the wholesale price.—145, 146, 147, 148, 149, Tottenham-court-road ; Nos. 1 to 15, Tottenham-place; and 2 to 6, Grafton-street East.

TURKEY CARPETS.—An importation of extra-quality CARPETS just received by the ship Red Gauntlet. Prices from 5 gs. to 40 gs. Axminster Carpets also in stock, from 6 gs. to 30 gs., especially suited for dining-rooms and libraries. Indian Carpets and Rugs in large quantities. Aubusson Carpets for drawing-rooms and boudoirs of every size. A large stock of Persian, Turkey, and Foreign Rugs from 17s., some very curious in make and design. The trade supplied.
MAPLE and CO., Tottenham-court-road.

CRETONNE CHINTZ.—Messrs. MAPLE and CO. beg to call particular attention to their Stock of this most Fashionable Material, which comprises, besides all the Patterns to be obtained elsewhere, a large assortment of Magnificent Designs, drawn and manufactured especially for them. These goods are superior in taste and manufacture to any ever offered before.
Tottenham-court-road.

CRETONNE CHINTZ.—Just received from Mulhouse, a Manufacturer's Stock of about 1000 Pieces, at prices varying from 10d. per yard. These goods are about half the price they were.

THE BEAUFORT BED-ROOM TOILET WARE, the greatest novelty of the day, new in shape and design; elegant, colours very choice. The Ware is manufactured expressly for Messrs. Maple and Co., price from 15s. 9d. to 5 gs. the Set. The trade supplied.—MAPLE and CO., Tottenham-court-road.

CRETONNE CHINTZ.   MAPLE & CO.

CRETONNE CHINTZ.   MAPLE & CO.

CRETONNE CHINTZ.   MAPLE & CO.

CRETONNE CHINTZ.   MAPLE & CO.

THE LARGEST STOCK of this New and Fashionable Material in London; some new and exclusive designs just received; not to be obtained elsewhere. Those who study taste should see these Goods before ordering. Patterns sent into the country on receiving a description of what is likely to be required.—MAPLE and CO.

MAPLE and CO., 145, 146, 147, 148, 149, Tottenham-court road; 1, 2, 3, 4, 5, 6, 7, 8, 9, 10, 11, 12, 13, 14, and 15, Tottenham-place; 2, 3, 4, 5, 6, Grafton-street East, London.

The largest stock of Cretonne Chintz, 'the new and fashionable material', in the London of 1874 – from the Illustrated London News Christmas Number, 1974

went a letter from George Carpenter, John Maple's game-keeper.

John and Emily Maple's daughter Clara had been married the previous summer (1873) at Horley to James Wharton. On that occasion Clara's parents had given an out-of-doors enter-tainment to all their estate workers and their families at Petridge Wood. But October was no month for garden parties, and indeed Blundell's wedding day was wet and cloudy. So on the following Saturday everyone on the estate was invited to Petridge House for a grand presentation of gifts of money, produce and drink. Every married man received a gold sover-eign, 12 pounds of beef and two gallons of beer, plus a new dress for his wife. John and Emily gave each single man 15s, eight pounds of beef and one gallon of beer. The carter boys got five shillings, five pounds of beef and a pot or two of beer. They gave their house servants similar gifts.

Blundell's father had reputedly returned to no 145 for an afternoon's work immediately after marrying *his* Emily 30 years earlier, but after a country wedding there was no tempta-tion for Mr and Mrs Blundell Maple to do other than what was expected of them, and go off on their honeymoon.

Blundell was not all *that* dedicated. Genial, hail and hearty, bon-viveur and showman, his concern to stay with the furni-ture trade was not as a cabinet-maker, or indeed as a connois-seur of furniture or decoration. He made no claim to have himself an eye for good design or good taste, only, as a businessman, for what sold. He would have been perturbed by the commercial depression of 1877, but untroubled by Charles Eastlake's attack on Britain's textile art as only fit to cover the floor of Madam Tussaud's Chamber of Horrors. A reviewer of Charles Eastlake's book *Hints on Household Taste in Furniture* in a February 1878 issue of *The Cabinet Maker & Upholstery Advertiser* said most wallpapers in England struck a person of good taste as fit only for the interior of lunatic asylums. It was likely however that those on the walls of the Royal Station Hotel at York, for the furnishing of which Maples received a contract from the North Eastern Railway Company in 1878, were more decorous.

The East End versus the West End controversy was at its height. The reporter whom the *Hackney Express* sent to the exhibition of East End Furniture in Bethnal Green in Septem-ber 1878 called it 'cheap and nasty'. By far the greater portion, he said, was wretchedly bad and unfit for wear and tear. The art of veneering, used as a cloak to hide bad materials and workmanship, was now carried on to its fullest limits, making thin pine and deal carry the appearance of solid work in mahogany. And much of it was being passed off by deceitful salesmen in West End stores who tried to persuade their genteel customers that the price was high because it was *not* a despised East End product.

> In the West End it is of everyday occurrence that salesmen and furniture dealers run down East End furniture while they them-selves actually go down to Curtain Road to replenish their stocks. (*The Cabinet & Upholstery Advertiser*, 13 October 1877)

Blundell Maple knew his market, the one his father had aimed at from the start, from which he had no reason to depart. It was not for him to be seen to be condemning carte blanche the products of Bethnal Green, so much of which, selected and approved by his buyers, he was dependent upon. Nor was he equipped to enter the Battle of Styles, nor considered it relevant to Maples' trade.

As Joan Evans pointed out in her introduction to *The Victorians* (1966),

> The aristocratic houses were so magnificently endowed from the Georgian era that most of them needed no change beyond greater comfort in the bedrooms of a kind easily bought in the Tottenham Court Road; only a few . . . acquired splendid and expensive 'artistic' carpets and curtains from Morris & Co. The upper middle classes had no such patrimony and were thankful for the artistic productions of Morris, and for the commercial comfort provided by Mr Maple.

John Maple had given each of his two sons a quarter share in Maple & Co in 1870, and kept half for himself. Seven years later Blundell also had half. His brother Harry went out duck shooting with his father at Redhill the last weekend of November 1879, contracted what he thought was a bad cold which turned out to be typhoid fever. He died within a week (December 3). He was only 28. After the funeral in St Peters Belsize Park and burial in the family vault in Highgate Cemetery, some 1,500 mourners assembled at Bedford Lodge, John and Emily Maple's house in Haverstock Hill, Hampstead. Almost half of them were Maples staff. Most of the shops at the top end of Tottenham Court Road partially closed the morning of the funeral, including Shoolbreds. The tragedy of Harry's early death was relieved by the birth the following year of a son to his sister Clara – Stanley Wharton.

Harry Maple never married and left his share in the family enterprise to his brother Blundell. Father and son were now equal partners. At 64 John Maple was as dynamic as ever, but Blundell took the helm and was universally regarded as the governor who became responsible for transforming a many-layered large-scale business into something even vaster.

His private life also burgeoned. Blundell had been rich; now he was very rich. In 1883 he made good his aspirations to be a country squire and join the ranks of the landed gentry who were his customers in Tottenham Court Road by buying an estate in the Hertfordshire village of Childwick (pronounced Chillick) called Childwickbury Manor. The place had a history which could be traced back to Saxon times. With his tongue in his cheek, he was known to tell visitors he was descended from Blondel the ministrel friend of King Richard Coeur de Lion. When Richard heard the minstrel singing outside the castle in which he had been imprisoned by Leopold of Austria on his way back from the Crusades, he told his wide-eyed listeners, Richard cried out that Blondel was calling him; 'Blondel m'appelle.' The minstrel's family, he said – *my* family – took the name, and it has been corrupted into Blundell Maple.

At Childwick Blundell indulged himself in what, in tandem with developing the store, became the grand passion of his life. 'Neither music, bric-a-brac, curios nor pictures have a greater charm for me than a well-formed living animal,' he once told an interviewer. Uncharacteristically shy, or perhaps just uncertain as to the effect it would have on his credibility in Tottenham Court Road, he started breeding and racing horses as 'Mr Childwick', and it was some years before this person's true identity was discovered.

He built up Childwick Stud Farm into the largest horse breeding establishment in Britain. He had some 220 boxes at Childwick and came to own more mares than any other raiser of thoroughbred stock in the country. He lashed out money on horses – £6,000 for one he called 'Childwick', the largest sum ever paid for a yearling, £15,000 for the Derby winner 'Common'. In 20 years he won £183,000 from flat racing – his colours were white and gold stripes and a claret cap. But none of his horses ever won a major event such as the Derby, the Oaks or the St Leger. None of them ever ranked in the first class.

The estate of some 850 acres had good coverts for shooting. He won many cups for his farm produce and for his shire horses. He delighted in driving a team of bay-browns harnessed to a fine dark-blue coach from St Albans railway station to the gates of Childwick Park in 20 minutes. 'You enter the glades of Childwick shaded by mighty elms and bright with blue bells,' recollected one of his guests.

> Mr Blundell Maple whirls you rapidly past the Jacobean house of his steward, a picturesque cluster of model cottages, a Gothic chapel, a village forge, a cricket-ground, a roofed well and a double avenue of limes.

His social position, and his wish to attend to the affairs of the store personally whenever the other calls on his time allowed, demanded a town house too. The boy who had been born over the shop in the less fashionable part of Marylebone moved to the more salubrious part of the borough on the Outer Circle round Regents Park, and acquired the remainder of a 99-year lease, dating from 1823, of the fine Adam mansion Clarence House in Clarence Terrace, together with stabling in Clarence Mews for his coach and horses, coachmen and stable boys.

Falmouth House, where Blundell Maple ('Mr Childwick') entertained his friends for the Newmarket race meetings.

Soon he was buying more land out of London, another 800 acres or so at Harpenden, four miles north of Childwick. It was on the Common at Harpenden that 'Mr Childwick' won his first horse race, with Charlie Wood up, in 1883. But for his serious horse racing activities he bought the 40 acre Falmouth House estate at Newmarket. The house had just come on the market in somewhat tragic circumstances. It had been built by Fred Archer, the champion jockey, in 1883. He had named it after Lord Falmouth for whom he had ridden many winners. He had just become engaged to Nellie Dawson, who the following year however died in childbirth. Two years later Fred Archer committed suicide.

Blundell paid £30,000 for Falmouth House with its pleasure and kitchen gardens, tennis courts and hacking stables for seven horses. The estate included Pegasus House in which he put Willie Waugh his trainer, brother of Alec Waugh, his Stud Manager at Childwick who sent the best of the animals he bred for training to Newmarket where, for some reason, Blundell was known as 'Mr Birdseye'.

There were training stables for 43 racehorses and a 32-acre private training ground, giving a 'tan gallop' of six furlongs. Accommodation for his jockeys and stable lads included bedrooms, reading and recreation rooms. He spent another £10,000 on buying the adjoining Zetland Lodge with its eight acres of land, 23 loose boxes and ten stalls. When Willie Waugh told him he needed more galloping space, Blundell bought another 82 acres adjoining the famous Lime Kilns Training Ground.

The mammoth Childwick Stud Farm/Newmarket Racing Establishment operation impressed all but his wife and daughters who took no interest in horse breeding or horse racing. But it gave the wealthy retailer real satisfaction to move up to Suffolk for Newmarket race meetings and regale his friends with lavish entertainment at Falmouth House. It was of a kind equalled only by the opportunity which his wealth gave him to ease the lot of those less fortunate than he.

His philanthropy began with those nearest to his homes and his workplace. In 1883 he chartered special trains to take some 1,800 schoolchildren of St Pancras to St Albans for a summer excursion to Childwickbury Manor. Awaiting them in the grounds were steam merry-go-rounds, swings and coconut shies, and a sumptuous Tea. He repeated the exercise the following year for Marylebone children. At Christmas he gave dinner to 270 poor people of St Albans in the Assembly Room of the town hall, followed by a musical entertainment which included songs by The Clarence Minstrels, a group composed of Maples employees.

He took considerable pains to raise money for the large hospital at the back of his Tottenham Court Road store. When the University of London (later University College London) was founded in 1826, it was the first to be established in England after Oxford and Cambridge and the first to admit students regardless of class or religion. Two years later a University Dispensary was opened at no 4 George Street, and in 1833 was founded what became University College Hospital. It was to raise funds for this that Blundell had collecting boxes placed in pubs and 'coffee restaurants' (cafés). In this

The new Constitutional Club in Northumberland Avenue – furnished by Maples in 1885.

way the Maple or People's Fund raised around £700 a year for UCH. He also appealed to his rich friends who subscribed another £900.

Obviously he could be a more effective philanthropist, could bring greater relief to working people, if he could also be a politician with a say in the conduct of both local and central government. He prepared the way with his usual precision. He joined the City Conservative Club, became a Livery man of the Fanmakers Company, a Grand Councillor of the Primrose League. He later got elected to the London County Council (created 1889), but first made a bid in 1885 to enter Parliament as the Conservative candidate for the new constituency of South St Pancras which had been carved out of the old borough of Marylebone for which he had declined to stand in 1871.

He held no brief for Free Trade. Calling himself a Fair Trader, he advocated imposing tariffs on the import of luxuries which could be manufactured in Britain and revive trade. 'Consolidate the Empire and shut out the foreigner!' He denounced those who grumbled at the cost of maintaining the royal family – 'a mere fleabite'. With the Marquis of Abergavenny he was the prime mover in the creation of the Constitutional Club which had first opened in Regent Street, but in 1885 were about to move to spacious new premises next to the Grand Hotel in Northumberland Avenue off Trafalgar Square. The style of decoration was not to everyone's taste. One member complained about the 'useless, ugly little pendant tabs' on the top of the chairs. Nothing more commonplace could be conceived, he told the committee, but he admired the tiling of the lavatories. If such criticism ever came to the ears of Blundell Maple, whose firm supplied the furniture and carried out the decoration, he will have taken it in good part.

The 60,000 population of South St Pancras were a mixed lot consisting of 'gentlemen of independent means and professional men in the squares, well-to-do shopkeepers and the working classes'. Some 1,500 of them had signed a requisition inviting him to stand, which said a writer in the London *Evening News* testified to his popolarity.

> Mr Blundell Maple's commercial position and his influence with the shopkeepers give him an advantage with which his opponent will find it difficult to contend. As the fight is likely to turn on trade issues Mr Blundell Maple has a further advantage in that he is a local man and knows the wants and desires of the local people. The fact that he is a large employer of labour will no doubt obtain for him a good many votes. Socialists have shown their enmity at his meetings. His opponent is Sir Julian Goldsmid, big landowner, capitalist and non-producer.

He told those who attended his meetings that he came before the electors as a shopkeeper in a nation of shopkeepers who had never yet been represented in Parliament. There must be work for the Workers, and he would strive to bring about a state of things in which that was so. He studied the working man's interest in everything. 'I will remedy the incidence of the taxation which is heaviest on the poor by transferring it to shoulders better able to bear it.' He would change the cry of Peace, Retrenchment and Reform to one of Peace, Work and Happiness for all.

In spite of his good claims for their support, the electors of South St Pancras gave 222 more votes to Liberal Sir Julian Goldsmid who was duly returned.

If many who called themselves Conservatives failed to vote for Blundell out of a dislike for his over-championing of the Working Class, many workers may have felt unhappy about having as their parliamentary representative someone whose treatment of his suppliers and employees, so it was rumoured, was greatly at variance to the fine phrases he used in his political speeches. Or was it just that his non-commercial activities left him too little time to supervise the conduct of his general manager Horace Regnart – the man who at 15 had been buried in the debris of the building which had collapsed in 1857 and risen steadily to so great a position of responsibility? Horace had first made himself an authority on bedroom furniture and the manufacture of bedding, and in recent years also on dining-room, drawing-room and library furniture.

Cabinet makers with small workshops who sought to do business with Maples found they could only deal with 'Mr Regnart'. There was no going to Blundell Maple, to his father or to his half-brother Henry Adams, who was a 'junior partner' along with Horace Regnart and his brother Henry, Frederick Lunnis, Edward Rayner, Robert Tubby and Robert Blundell (Mrs John Maple's brother?)

Regnart had the final word – the only word – on whether the craftsmanship of the bedroom suite he had ordered from an outside cabinetmaker met Maples standards. If he thought it

Blundell Maple, parliamentary candidate 1885 – a Moonshine *cartoon.*

inferior he rejected it, or paid less for it than the agreed sum – 'discounted' it, as they said. And with their own employees it was being said they had abandoned paying for piece-work, where a price was set before a man started the job and he was paid irrespective of how long he took over it, in favour of task-work by which he was paid so much an hour, and a more efficient man taking less time was paid less than an inefficient man who took longer.

To objectors Blundell insisted that it was all due to the sub-division of labour. 'Once upon a time,' he would explain, 'a man was an Upholsterer who stuffed chairs, cut a loose cover, made a blind, made a mattress. Today, in a big business like ours, a boy is taught only part of Upholstery, say stuffing, but as a specialist Stuffer he earns more than an old-style Upholsterer. Don't let anyone gull you into thinking Maples is a sweat shop.'

Maples was indeed big. 'One of the SIGHTS of LONDON to American visitors and others' proclaimed its advertisement at this time. 'Upholsterers by special appointment to Her Majesty'. In 1885 the Tottenham Court Road site covered an area that had been occupied by 200 houses. When the company applied to the St Pancras Vestry (local council) to close and appropriate the whole of Tottenham Place and part of Beaumont Place, both public thoroughfares, 'for their sole use and benefit', the Works Committee advised granting the application but the Ratepayers Alliance opposed 'this monstrous proposal'.

As timber merchants and direct importers of wood from Africa, Asia and America, from which they manufactured Cabinet Furniture 'by steam power', they needed all the space they could lay hand on. Their most fashionable novelty was Yew Tree Wood Furniture 'somewhat resembling mahogany in colour but much lighter and brighter looking'. They needed room for those 10,000 bedsteads cribs and cots 'specially adapted for mosquito curtains used in India, Australia and the Colonies'. They needed room to display the 500 Drawing Room Clocks which went for 400 days with only one winding, and for 'the largest and most varied collection in the world of Dresden, Sèvres, Worcester, Derby, Coalport, Minton, Doulton, Hungarian and Oriental pieces in their Clock, Bronze and

MAPLE & CO.,

TOTTENHAM COURT ROAD,

LONDON

THE LARGEST

FURNISHING ESTABLISHMENT

IN THE WORLD.

NOTICE.—DRAWING-ROOM CLOCKS to go for 400 days with once winding; a handsome present. Price 70s., warranted. MAPLE & CO. have a large and varied assortment suitable for dining and drawing room. Over 500 to select from. Price 10s. 9d. to 50 guineas. Handsome marble clock, with incised lines in gold and superior eight-day movement, 28s. 6d.; also bronzes in great variety.—Maple and Co., London.

POSTAL ORDER DEPARTMENT.— Messrs. MAPLE & CO. beg respectfully to state that this Department is now so organised that they are fully prepared to execute and supply any article that can possibly be required in Furnishing at the same time, if not less, than any other house in England. Patterns sent, and quotations given free of charge.

AUGUST 8, 1885.

Birds-eye view of Euston Road and Tottenham Court Road from Herbert Fry's London *in 1886.*

Horse-drawn vans take the name 'Maples' to every corner of Britain.

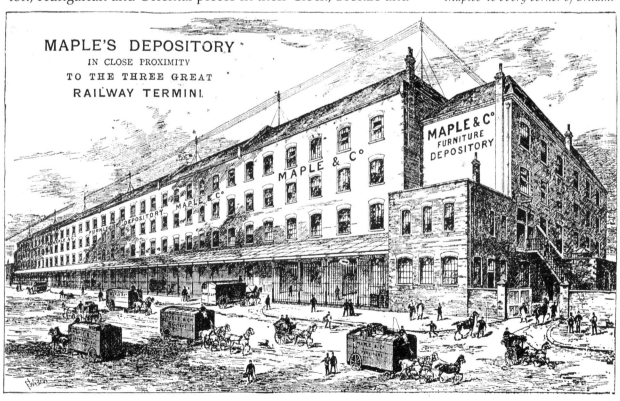

MAPLE'S DEPOSITORY
IN CLOSE PROXIMITY
TO THE THREE GREAT
RAILWAY TERMINI.

MAPLE & C°
FURNITURE
DEPOSITORY

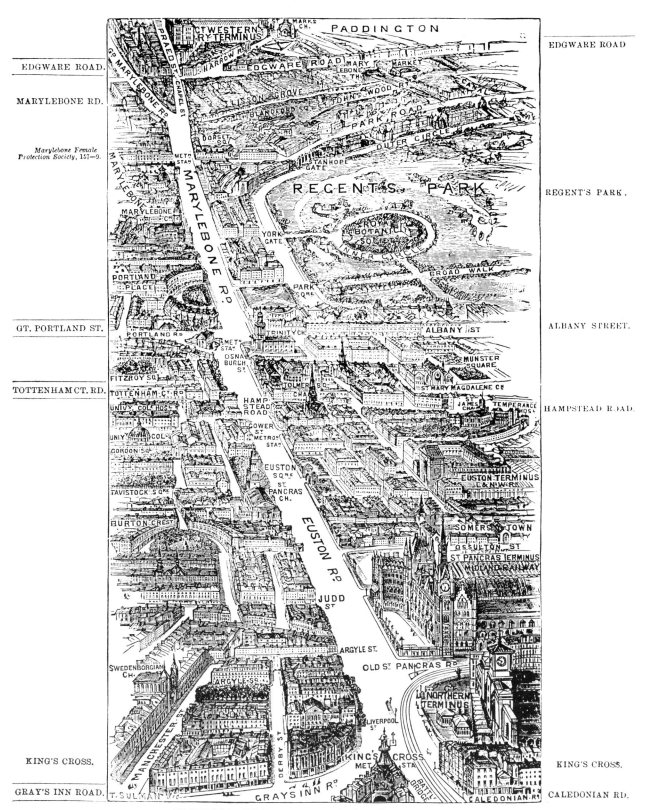

EUSTON ROAD AND MARYLEBONE ROAD,
KING'S CROSS TO PADDINGTON.

Ornamental China Department'.

For many years now the company's activities ranged much further afield than the manufacturing and retailing at Tottenham Court Road, however. Maples' horse-drawn vans set out every day loaded with carpets and curtains, light fittings and furniture for delivery to the houses of country customers, many of whom had stated their requirements to the Postal Order Department. Other vehicles would take members of the Decoration Department to fit gas fires and lay parquet floors under the instructions of the head of the department who was 'a thoroughly qualified architect assisted by a large staff of artists and skilled workmen'. Drivers were told to make sure they drove their van through the town's High Street before going to the customer's house, however much longer it made the journey, so that all could see the name 'Maple & Co' clearly painted on the side of the pantechnicon.

Londoners were similarly kept aware of the company's activities as contractors by seeing Maples vans delivering furniture to the nearly completed Grand Hotel at Charing Cross, the First Avenue Hotel in Holborn and the Holborn Restaurant, all of which they furnished in 1885.

The Grand Hotel in Trafalgar Square, Charing Cross – furnished by Maples in 1885.

Main dining room of the Grand Hotel.

The name was made familiar to people across the Channel too when Maples vans took goods to customers in France like Baron Edmund de Rothschild for whose chateau Mr Hughes of Maples made a fireplace and overmantel in October 1885. On the continent the company's name had entered many of the European languages. In Portugal in particular, a large well-padded armchair with upholstered arms was known as 'a Maple'. In Paris, where the company had an outpost in the Boulevard de Strasburg, indeed throughout France, *'les meubles Maples'* was the phrase they used to denote comfortable, stylish furniture; theatre audiences knew just what to expect when they read in their programmes that Act 2 was set *'dans un petit salon très Maples'*.

Maples furniture vans were never more in the news than when Blundell used them to convey voters to polling stations for the bye-election in the Dulwich Division of Camberwell in December 1887.

> Mr Maple's furniture vans (reported the *Daily News*) which were in considerable numbers for the conveyance of voters were cheered, hooted or laughed at according to the colours of the criers' politics.

Mr Maple had decided to have another try at entering the House of Commons as the Conservative candidate with the support of Lord Salisbury, but also of leading lights of the Liberal Party such as John Bright and Joseph Chamberlain. In his campaign speeches he called on the electors to work heart and soul to prevent Mr Gladstone ever coming into power because that would plunge the country into anarchy. Parliament needed to pass legislation to assist the working classes to find work. 'I am sure that many of those who recently congregated in the streets of London were men who desired work but could not find it.'

They did more than congregate on what became known as Bloody Sunday. When at the last moment the Home Secretary banned their meeting in Trafalgar Square and the police stopped them marching, they rioted. In Tottenham Court Road they threatened to attack Maples' timber yard. Blundell took command, opened his hydrants, connected his hose and laid his nozzles ready to sweep Tottenham Court Road the moment the mob rushed forward.

> It never assumed that aspect (reminisced a gossip writer in *The Pall Mall Gazette* some years later). The nature of the reception that awaited them somehow got known to the columns that were forming for attack in the Euston Road. The knowledge acted disintegratingly. They were not prepared to face such risks as these. They let Maples severely alone.

This time the majority voted for Blundell – 4,021 against the 2,609 of his opponent Henderson, a smaller majority than in the 1885 election by 282. But the election of the popular shopkeeper-horsebreeder was widely welcomed – and could not have been other than good publicity for Maples. The humorous weeklies made great play of his victory. *Judy* offered congratulations in verse:

> Dear Blundell Maple, let me grasp.
>   Your honest hand; for ev'ry section
> Of Loyal Britons will unite
>   To wish you joy on your election.
> Your friends, whose name is legion, smile;
>   Your foes with jealousy are yellow;
> But ev'ry true-born Englishman
>   Applauds you for a right good fellow.
>
> I quaff to you a brimming cup;
>   I clap you on the back my hearty,
> Because you thought a noble fight,
>   And loved your country more than party.
> In you the woods are well combined –
>   The smooth and bright, the strong and staple –
> You're Heart of *Oak*, my gallant friend,
>   And yet your name is Blundell *Maple*.

As a residence in his constituency Blundell Maple MP rented no 75 Crystal Palace Road, East Dulwich at a ground rent of £13 10s. He did not speak often in the House of Commons, and then sensibly only on subjects with which he was well acquainted. He successfully opposed a Cart and Wheel Bill which would have imposed taxation on horse vans, and attacked a Bill to introduce compulsory Early Closing, forming a lobby called the Early Closing Association to advocate voluntary action in this regard.

He would have been even more exhilarated by political triumph had it not been for the sadness brought about by the deaths of his two youngest daughters Winifred and Dorothy (in memory of whom in 1893 he established The Sisters Hospital at St Albans, the building of which he paid for on land he bought for the purpose, and then furnished and equipped at his own expense). It must have been distressing for him too that, especially as Harry had died a bachelor, he had no son to succeed him in the business. He and Emily

Right:
'Bloody Sunday' – the Trafalgar Square riot which overflowed into Tottenham Court Road.

THE NINETEENTH CENTURY

ART FURNITURE.
ADAMS DESIGNS.
CHIPPENDALE.

MAPLE
Tottenham

MAPLE & CO., Upholsterers by Special Appointment to Her Majesty.—The LARGEST FURNISHING ESTABLISHMENT in the World. Acres of Show Rooms for the display of every description of household requisites.

MAPLE & CO., Timber Merchants and Direct Importers of the finest Woods to be found in Africa, Asia, and America, and Manufacturers of Cabinet Furniture in various woods by steam-power.

MAPLE & CO.—YEW TREE WOOD FURNITURE. This is the most fashionable novelty, somewhat resembling mahogany in colour, but much lighter and brighter looking, and suitable for bedrooms. The price is about the same as for mahogany.

MAPLE & CO. — SEQUOIA, Oregon Woods, Circassian Ash, Hungarian Ash, Satin-Wood, and American Walnut, all made very strong and durable FURNITURE. These woods are all to be seen in their manufactured state.

MAPLE & CO.—Bass Wood FURNITURE is one of the novelties particularly recommended, being much harder than pine, and a prettier wood. 500 Bedroom Suites, finished in various woods, to select from. Prices from 5½ to 250 guineas. Many of these are quite novelties in shape and finish.

500 BEDROOM SUITES on Show to select from.
Established 48 years.

BEDSTEADS.
BEDSTEADS.
BEDSTEADS.

MAPLE
LOND

MAPLE & CO. have seldom less than 10,000 BEDSTEADS in stock, comprising some '00 various patterns, in sizes from 2 ft. 6 in. to 5 ft. 6 in. wide, ready for immediate delivery—on the day of purchase, if desired. The disappointment and delay incident to choosing from designs only, where but a limited stock is kept, is thus avoided. Catalogues Free.

MAPLE & CO.—300 BRASS and IRON BEDSTEADS, fitted with Bedding complete in Show Rooms, to select from. Strong Iron Bedsteads from 8s. 6d. to 10 guineas; Brass Bedsteads from 70s. to 40 guineas. 10,000 in stock.

MAPLE & CO. have a SPECIAL DEPARTMENT for IRON and BRASS Four-post BEDSTEADS, Cribs, and Cots, specially adapted for mosquito curtains, used in India, Australia, and the Colonies. Price for full-sized Bedsteads, varying from 25s. Shippers and Colonial visitors are invited to inspect this varied stock, the largest in England, before deciding elsewhere. 10,000 Bedsteads to select from.

MAPLE & CO. SPRING MATTRESSES.

MAPLE & CO. HAIR MATTRESSES.

MAPLE & CO. Wire-Woven MATTRESSES.

MAPLE & CO.—Spring Mattresses.—The PATENT Wire-woven SPRING MATTRESS. Such advantageous arrangements have been made that this much-admired Mattress is sold at the following low prices :—3 ft., 12s. 9d.; 3 ft. 6 in., 15s. 9d.; 4 ft., 18s. 6d.; 4 ft. 6 in., 21s. 6d.

POSTAL ORDER DEPARTMENT.— Messrs. MAPLE & CO. beg respectfully to state that this Department is now so organised that they are fully prepared to execute and supply any article that can possibly be required in Furnishing at the same price, if not less, than any other house in England. Patterns sent and quotations given free of charge.

MAPLE & CO., Tottenham Court Road, London,
And Boulevard de Strasbourg, Paris.

ADVERTISER, MAY 1886.

& CO. TURKEY CARPETS.
INDIAN CARPETS.
Court Road. PERSIAN CARPETS.

TURKEY CARPETS.—MAPLE & CO.
have just received large consignments of fine TUR-
KEY CARPETS, unique colourings, reproductions of the
17th century, being the first delivery of those made from
this season's clip.—MAPLE & CO., London, and 17 and 18
Local Baron Aliotti, Smyrna.

TURKEY CARPETS. — These special
Carpets are exceptionally fine, both in colour and
quality, while the prices are lower than ever known before.
Appended are a few examples of useful sizes, with prices.
The trade supplied :—
11 ft. 4 in. by 8 ft. 3 in. £6 10 0
12 ft. 0 in. by 10 ft. 6 in. 7 15 0
13 ft. 0 in. by 11 ft. 9 in. 8 10 0
14 ft. 9 in. by 11 ft. 0 in. 9 15 0
15 ft. 0 in. by 11 ft. 10 in. 11 15 0

WOODSTOCK CARPETS.—These are
inexpensive, but most artistic productions of the
English loom, woven in one piece, without seam, bordered
and fringed, suitable for reception and bedrooms. Can be
had in many sizes.   2-Ply   2-Ply
8ft. 0in. × 7ft. 6in. £0 18 4 | 12ft. 0in. × 10ft. 6in. £1 18 6
9ft. 0in. × 7ft. 6in. 1 0 8 | 12ft. 6in. × 12ft. 0in. 2 1 0
9ft. 0in. × 9ft. 0in. 1 4 9 | 13ft. 6in. × 10ft. 6in. 2 5 3
10ft. 6in. × 9ft. 0in. 1 8 11 | 13ft. 6in. × 12ft. 0in. 2 9 6
10ft. 6in. × 10ft. 6in. 1 13 6 | 15ft. 0in. × 12ft. 0in. 2 15 0
12ft. 6in. × 9ft. 0in. 1 13 0 | Rugs to match, 6ft. × 3ft. 6s 6
Several hundreds of old patterns at reduced prices. Each
Carpet is protected by the Trade Mark, 'Woodstock.' Can
only be had of MAPLE & CO., Carpet Factors. Purchasers
of Fringed Carpets should beware of imitations.

& CO. NEW SHOW ROOMS.
NEW SHOW ROOMS.
ON. NEW SHOW ROOMS.

MAPLE & CO.—The Specimen Rooms
are good examples of high-class DECORATIVE
FURNISHING, carried out in perfect taste, without extravagant expenditure. Every one about to Furnish, or rearrange their residences, would derive information by an
inspection.

MAPLE & CO.'S FURNISHING ESTA-
BLISHMENT, the largest in the World. Acres of
Show Rooms for the display of first-class Furniture, ready
for immediate delivery. Novelties every day from all parts
of the globe. No family ought to furnish before viewing
this collection of household requisites, it being one of the
sights in London. To Export Merchants an unusual advantage is offered. Having large space, all goods are packed
on the premises by experienced packers.

NEW ILLUSTRATED CATALOGUE FREE.

DECORATIONS, Artistic Wall Papers.—
Messrs. MAPLE & CO. undertake every description
of ARTISTIC HOUSE DECORATION, including gas-
fitting, repairs, parquet work, &c. The head of this Department is a thoroughly qualified architect, assisted by a large
staff of artists and skilled workmen. Coloured Drawings
and Estimates furnished.

MAPLE & CO.   400-DAY   CLOCKS.

MAPLE & CO. Dining-room CLOCKS.

MAPLE & CO. Drawing-room CLOCKS.

MAPLE & CO. — DRAWING - ROOM
CLOCKS to go for 400 days with once winding; a
handsome present. Price 70s., warranted. MAPLE & CO.
have a large and varied assortment suitable for Dining
and Drawing-room. Over 500 to select from. Prices from
10s. 9d. Handsome Marble Clock, with incised lines
in gold, and superior eight-day movement, 23s. 6d.; also
Bronzes in great variety.

THE CLOCK, Bronze, and Ornamental
China DEPARTMENT comprises a choice selection
of Dresden, Sèvres, Worcester, Derby, Coalport, Minton,
Doulton, Hungarian, and Oriental China. The largest and
most varied collection in the world.—MAPLE & CO., London.

however were comforted by the company of their very person-
able eldest daughter Grace.

And then there was the accusation that Blundell Maple was a
sweater – one that ground the faces of the poor.

In the corridors of power at Westminster he will have been
aware of the gathering momentum of Socialism and militant
Trade Unionism. He will have known about the Scottish miner
James Keir Hardie who had been convinced the Liberal Party
was incapable of helping the workers and formed the Independent Labour Party. He will have shared Members' alarm at
Annie Besant's ability in 1888 to call the Bryant & May match
girls out on strike. He will have noted with some anxiety how
the gasworkers under Will Thorne were agitating for an
eight-hour week, and the dockers under Ben Tillett for a
minimum wage of sixpence an hour and the abolition of
contract work which they considered the source of the worst
'sweating'. It was an ugly word and he did not like it being
applied to Maples.

For many years John and Blundell Maple had had to live
with the Alliance Cabinet-Makers Association and the London
Society of Upholsterers. But because there were so many they
could employ to maintain their enormous stock, they had had
no occasion to deviate from Horace Regnart's Take-it-or-
Leave-it regime, and no need to defend it – until they heard of
what witnesses were saying about Maples to the House of
Lords Select Committee on the Sweating System of the East
End of London who began their sessions in March 1888.

The main accuser was one Arnold White. 'This table,' he told
their lordships, pointing to one beside him, 'was sold to me for
6s 9d to-day. The man who made it sells it for 4s 6d to the shop
and out of that 3s 6d goes on materials, leaving him one
shilling [5p] for making it. The profit for the retailer who buys
it, however, is 6s 9d minus 4s 6d – 2s 3d [11p].' The sweating
system was aggravated, he said, by the practice in Tottenham
Court Road of deferring payment to outside workshops till
Saturday when banks were closed. These small manufacturers

JUDY'S CONGRATULATION.

DEAR Blundell Maple, let me grasp
   Your honest hand ; for ev'ry section
Of Loyal Britons will unite
   To wish you joy on your election.
Your friends, whose name is legion, smile ;
   Your foes with jealousy are yellow ;
But ev'ry true-born Englishman
   Applauds you for a right good fellow.

I quaff to you a brimming cup ;
   I clap you on the back, my hearty,
Because you've fought a noble fight,
   And loved your country more than party.
In you the woods are well combined—
   The smooth and bright, the strong and staple—
You're Heart of *Oak*, my gallant friend,
   And yet your name is Blundell *Maple*.

Such timber has a proud renown,
   There's nothing in the grove to match it—
It bends not to the ruffian blast,
   Nor falls before Gladstonian hatchet.
Long may you flourish, comrade brave,
   Like bay-tree by the running waters,
Since you have won a triumph grand
   For dear old England's sons and daughters !

*Elected at last – Blundell Maple
wins Dulwich for the Tories in 1887.*

could not pay their workers their wages except by having
Maples cash their cheques, a facility for which they charged by
discounting cheques presented in this way. Furthermore, he
said, Maples supplied these small men with wood and other
materials at prices higher than the market price. Henry
Waltham, secretary of the London Upholsterers Trade Society
testified that Maples & Co had always borne the reputation in
their own workshops of being a sweating house where the
foremen used vile language to the workers.

As soon as he read the assertions that were appearing in the
newspaper reports of the Select Committee's session, Blundell

Mr. Blundell
Maple came in well on
Thursday. He would
have polled even better
than he did; but his
opponent, Mr. Hender-
son, was an old resident,
and very Dulwich people
felt bound to do their
best for one of them-
selves.

[DEC. 10, 1887.

Maple at once had his solicitors invite White to verify the truth of statements he considered slanderous. His accuser had refused to come and hear Maples' side of the question, Blundell told their lordships in the first of four days giving evidence.

> Who is this Arnold White that he should be allowed to traduce without cross examination my firm whose reputation for straightforward and honest dealing is respected and honoured throughout the length and breadth of the land?

As far as Blundell had been able to gather, White was publicly known as having been defeated in the Radical interest at Mile End at the last general election, and his public record was limited to that.

> I have been actively engaged in the business for 27 years, and my father originally established the business nearly 50 years since; and during all those years not one word has been breathed against the honesty of our dealings or the treatment of our employees.

They employed over 2,000 hands directly, paying them weekly or monthly wages. He was immensely surprised and astonished to see the slanderous statements made by Arnold White against his firm, creating a damage that no money could ever repay, damage caused by perjured statements to the honoured name of a man like his father who, throughout the whole of his career, both commercial and private, had done much to maintain the honour and straightforward dealing which an Englishman should ever try to emulate and by which he had always borne an unsullied name.

When one of the Committee, Lord Thring, asked Blundell if he proposed to bring an action for perjury against White or any other of his accusers, the chairman of the Committee, the Earl of Dunraven, said if he did, the privilege of the committee would not protect them. Blundell said that when he had produced all his evidence to the Committee and the country heard what he had to say through reading of it in their newspapers, it would be seen how Maples had been slandered. He believed also that their lordships would realise there had been a vile and foul conspiracy. He had proof that witnesses had been paid by Arnold White to make untrue statements. He would call his counting house junior partner to prove that Maples had never charged one farthing for cashing cheques. But he, Blundell, was intimately connected with his business and fully took the whole responsibility of the firm. Maples had been much maligned. He was prepared to prove perjury and bring actions against the perjurors. Arnold White, he said, had paid Henry Miller, real name Mueller, 50s a week to give evidence.

No firm throughout the world could boast of giving greater contentment to their workpeople, and of getting longer service from their workpeople in proportion to the number of employed than Maples. They employed 1,295 men and boys in their own workshops and the manufacturing portions of their business. They had 69 boys under the age of 18 working with carmen, porters, stuffers, cabinet makers, polishers and mattress makers. They had one boy attached to a gilder, two each with plumbers, joiners and carpet planners, five each with upholsterers and decorators. They employed another 391 girls and 365 salesmen and clerks. Average length of service was more than ten years. The total number they employed was 2,051. His father, though 73, was at Tottenham Court Road from 10.30 am to 6.30 pm.

> We manufacture all our bedding on the premises, although few others in London besides ourselves do the same. Gillow, Collinson & Lock and most of the old West End houses buy, if not all their bedding, some of it. Maples has made on our premises every single piece of bedding sold by us for the last 15 years. In 1887 we manufactured 24,298 mattresses and palliases. In that year we sold and delivered 15,208 bedsteads and 4,067 wire-woven mattresses. We manufactured, or caused to be manufactured, 2,823 bedroom suites.

It is true that they did not produce on their premises everything they sold. They did not manufacture carpets, nor curtains, nor bedsteads, nor linens, blankets, ironmongery, china and glass. Nor did they manufacture all the furniture they sold, though they were daily increasing their cabinet factories in Tottenham Court Road. They also had factories working for them exclusively in Islington where 144 cabinet makers, painters and polishers were employed. This was the firm of Rose, Gorwill & Day, which Maples themselves set up for the purpose.

In answer to the insinuation that Maples, through the labels they put on their goods, gave their customers false information, Blundell said that to bedsteads they fixed the words 'Manufactured for Maple & Co'.

'There has been a vile and foul conspiracy'– Blundell Maple.

DINING-ROOM FURNITURE.

MAPLE and CO., Manufacturers of DINING-ROOM FURNITURE. The largest assortment to choose from, as well as the best possible value. Three more houses have been added to this important department. Half a century's reputation.—Illustrated Catalogues post-free.

MAPLE and CO. devote special attention to the production of high-class DINING-ROOM FURNITURE that will afford permanent satisfaction in wear. The numerous recommendations with which Messrs. Maple and Co. have been favoured by customers who have used the furniture for years is a pleasing testimony to the excellence of the articles.

DINING-ROOM SUITES. The LICHFIELD SUITE, in solid oak, walnut, or mahogany, consisting of six small and two elbow chairs in leather; dining-table, with patent screw; also Early English sideboard, with plate-glass back, and fitted with cellaret, 16 guineas. Design free.

DINING-ROOM SUITES. The STAFFORD SUITE, comprising six small chairs, two easy-chairs in leather, telescope dining-table, sideboard, with plate-glass back and cellaret, and dinner-waggon; in light or dark oak, walnut, or ash, very substantial in character, 23 guineas.

DINING-ROOM SUITES. The TAMWORTH SUITE, in polished or fumigated oak, walnut, or mahogany, comprising six ordinary, two easy chairs, and handsome couch, in leather, extending dining-table and sideboard, with cellaret, 27 guineas; an excellent suite, at a medium price.

MAPLE and CO., Manufacturers of

BEDROOM SUITES, from 65s. 6d. 500 Bed-room suites, at from 65s. 6d. to 275 guineas. These comprise a great variety of styles, many being of a very high-class and distinctive character, novel both in construction, arrangement, and combination of woods.

BED-ROOM SUITES. The WEYMOUTH SUITE, in solid ash, consisting of wardrobe with plate-glass door; toilet-table, with glass affixed; washstand with marble top, tile back, towel rods at side, cupboard beneath, three chairs, £7 15s. Illustration free.

BED-ROOM SUITES. The WHITBY SUITE, in solid ash or walnut, consisting of wardrobe with plate-glass door, toilet-table, with glass affixed, washstand, with marble top and tile back, pedestal cupboard, and three chairs, £10 15s. Illustration free.

BED-ROOM SUITES. The SCARBOROUGH SUITE, in solid ash or walnut, including wardrobe with plate-glass door, and new-shaped washstand, £12 15s.; or with bedstead and spring bedding, £17 10s.

BED-ROOM SUITES. The BOURNEMOUTH SUITE, in solid ash, including 6 ft. wardrobe, with plate-glass centre door, £18 10s.; or with handsome brass bedstead and spring bedding, £25 17s. Design and full particulars free.

BED-ROOM FURNITURE.—MAPLE and CO., Timber Merchants and direct importers of the finest woods, manufacturers of Bed-room and other Furniture by steam-power and improved machinery, Tottenham-court-road, London. Factories: Beaumont-place, Euston-road; Southampton-buildings, Liverpool-road; Park-street, Islington, &c.

MAPLE & CO

Tottenham-Court-Road, London, W.,

THE LARGEST AND MOST CONVENIENT

FURNISHING ESTABLISHMENT

IN THE WORLD.

10,000 BEDSTEADS,

BRASS AND IRON,

IN STOCK,

From 8s. 9d. to 55 Guineas.

Illustrated Catalogues Post-Free.

"PATENT WOVEN WIRE MATTRESS."

The above BLACK and BRASS BEDSTEAD, with the PATENT WIRE WOVE MATTRESS, complete, 3 ft., 38s.; 3 ft. 6 in., 42s.; 4 ft., 49s. 6d.; 4 ft. 6 in., 52s. 6d. Price for the Patent Wire Wove Mattress, without Bedstead. 3 ft., 9s. 6d.; 3 ft. 6 in., 10s. 9d.; 4 ft., 11s. 9d.; 4 ft. 6 in., 12s. 9d.

NOVELTIES in Fancy DRAWING-ROOM FURNITURE, such as Brackets, Occasional Tables, Settees, Pouffe Ottomans, Gossip-Chairs, Card-Tables, Easels, Pedestals, Cabinets, Screens, Writing-Tables, &c., at most Moderate Prices. Special Catalogue. MAPLE and CO., London, Paris, and Smyrna.

FURNITURE for EXPORTATION. VISITORS, as well as MERCHANTS, are INVITED to INSPECT the largest FURNISHING ESTABLISHMENT in the world. Hundreds of Thousands of Pounds' worth of Furniture, Bedsteads, Carpets, Curtains, &c., all ready for immediate shipment. Having large space, all goods are packed on the premises by experienced packers; very essential when goods are for exportation to insure safe delivery. The reputation of half a century.

MAPLE and CO., Upholsterers by special appointment to her Majesty the Queen. The reputation of half a century. Factories:—Beaumont-place, Euston-road; Southampton-buildings, Liverpool-road; Park-street, Islington.

HUNDREDS of THOUSANDS of POUNDS' WORTH of Manufactured GOODS ready for immediate delivery. All goods marked in plain figures for net cash—a system established 50 years.

MAPLE & CO., London, Paris, and Smyrna. Catalogues Free.

SPECIMEN DINING-ROOMS.

MAPLE and CO.'S NEW SPECIMEN DINING-ROOMS, decorated and fully appointed with furniture in pollard oak, brown oak, Chippendale mahogany, antique carved oak, American walnut, and other woods, are now open to the public, and should be seen by all intending purchasers.

THIRTY SPECIMEN ROOMS.

THE SPECIMEN ROOMS at Messrs. MAPLE and CO.'S are good examples of HIGH-CLASS DECORATIVE FURNISHING, carried out in perfect taste, without extravagant expenditure. Every-one about to furnish or rearrange their residences, should by all means inspect these apartments.

THESE ROOMS are not only helpful as showing the effect of the furniture when arranged in an apartment, but also most suggestive as regards decorative treatment, as well as a guide to the entire cost of furnishing in any selected style.—MAPLE and CO., Decorators and Furnishers.

DECORATIONS.

EXHIBITION of DECORATIVE ART. EXAMPLES of ART DECORATIONS in Carton-pierre, Tynecastle Tapestry, Lincrusta, Japanese and Flock Papers, Silk, Tapestry, and Japanese Embroidered Panels, Cretonne, Eastern Rugs and Mattings, Hand-painted Friezes, and interior woodwork. Thirty Speci-men-rooms, constituting a unique exhibition of Decorative Art, are now open to visitors.

MAPLE and CO. CARPETS.

MAPLE and CO. BRUSSELS CARPETS.—MAPLE and CO. have always in stock Brussels Carpets made to stand the test of daily use, both as regards texture and colourings. In fact, their carpets for hard, street-like wear have become almost proverbial.

CARPETS for HARD, STREET-LIKE WEAR.—MAPLE and CO.'S No. 4 quality is an extra stout Brussels Carpet, suitable for rooms where there is constant tread, and woven with regard to dura-bility rather than elaboration of design. A bordered Carpet of this grade, 9 ft. by 9 ft., can be had for forty shillings.

CARPETS for HARD, STREET-LIKE WEAR.—The "Maple" Brand Brussels Carpet is a special extra quality, made of selected yarns, and in all the designs and colourings for 1889, including some most wonderful replications of famous Eastern Carpets. This quality cannot fail to afford permanent satisfaction in use

TURKEY CARPETS.

A TURKEY CARPET is, above all others, the most suitable for the dining-room, its agreeable warmth of colouring enhancing the effect of the furniture and decorations, and indicating alike the good taste and comfortable circumstances of its possessor.

TURKEY CARPETS.—MAPLE and CO. are the very largest importers of Turkey Carpets; and having a Branch House at Smyrna, the centre of the weaving district, are able to exercise close supervision over the whole process of manufacture, which is the only way in which excellence of colouring and workmanship can be guaranteed.

MAPLE & Co

Tottenham-Court-Road, London, W.
THE LARGEST AND MOST CONVENIENT
FURNISHING ESTABLISHMENT
IN THE WORLD.

COMPLIMENTARY AND WEDDING PRESENTS.

NEW SPECIAL CATALOGUES FREE.

Medicine Cupboard, in bamboo and China matting, extreme height 24 in. wide, 12s. 9d. This can be supplied in real Japanese paper instead of matting, at same price.

The Ethelred Chair, in brown or white wicker, seat 16 in. high .. £0 8 9
D.tto ditto with cushions and drapery £1 5 6

·CARPETS. CARPETS.

ORIENTAL CARPETS.—Messrs. MAPLE and CO. have just cleared an importer's stock, comprising several hundreds of antique and modern Persian, Indian, and Turkey Carpets, mostly medium sizes, which are being offered at about one third less than the usual cost. These are worth the early attention of trade and other buyers.

ORIENTAL CARPETS.—These real Indian, Persian, and Turkey Carpets, so justly famous for durability as for great beauty as regards sheen and colour, cost only about the same as the poor imitations sold under the style of Anglo-Indian or Anglo-Oriental Carpets.—MAPLE and CO., Oriental Carpet and Rug Warehouse.

CARPETS.—10,000 Pieces WILTON PILE, BRUSSELS, and TAPESTRY CARPETS, in all the latest Designs. Owing to the state of the market for English wool, Carpets and all woollen fabrics can now be had at lower prices than ever known before. Buyers would therefore do well to take advantage of the present unprecedented low rates: 500 pieces (25,000 yards) best Brussels at 2s. 11d. per yard; 450 pieces Tapestry Brussels, best quality, but old patterns, at 1s. 9½d. per yard, usually sold at 2s. 6d.

MAPLE and CO., London, Paris, Smyrna, and Bucnos Ayres.

BED-ROOM SUITES from 65s.

BED-ROOM SUITES. 500 Bed-room Suites, at from 65s. to 275 guineas. These comprise a great variety of styles, many being of a very high-class and distinctive character, novel both in construction, arrangement, and combination of woods.

BED-ROOM SUITES. The WEYMOUTH SUITE, in solid ash, consisting of wardrobe with plate-glass door, toilet-table with glass affixed, washstand with marble top, tile back, towel-rods at sides, cupboard beneath, three chairs, £7 15s. Illustrations free.

BED-ROOM SUITES. The WHITBY SUITE, in solid ash or walnut, consisting of wardrobe with plate-glass door, toilet-table with glass affixed, washstand with marble top and tile back, pedestal cupboard, and three chairs, £10 15s. Illustrations free.

BED-ROOM SUITES. The SCARBOROUGH SUITE, in solid ash or walnut, including wardrobe with plate-glass doors, and new shaped washstand, £12 15s.; and with bedstead and spring bedding, £17 10s. Design and full particulars free.

CLOCKS.

MAPLE and CO. have a large and varied assortment, suitable for Dining and Drawing-Room.

The Florence Chair, in plain wicker, with cushions and drapery, seat about 15 in. high £1 5 6

Handsome Polished-Brass Corinthian Pillar Lamp, £8 10s. With cut-glass container, Duplex burner, with extinguisher, cut tulip shade and chimney, complete.

BEDSTEADS. BEDSTEADS.

MAPLE and CO. have seldom less than Ten Thousand BEDSTEADS in Stock, comprising some 600 various patterns, in sizes from 2 ft. 6 in. to 5 ft. 6 in. wide, ready for immediate delivery—on the day of purchase if desired. The disappointment and delay incident to choosing from designs only, where but a limited stock is kept, is thus avoided.

MAPLE and CO.—300 BRASS and IRON BEDSTEADS, fitted with bedding complete, in Show-Rooms, to select from. Strong Iron Belsteads, from 8s. 6d. to 10 guineas; Brass Bedsteads, from 70s. to 40 guineas, 10,000 in Stock.—Tottenham-Court-road, London, and Paris.

MAPLE and CO. have a SPECIAL DEPARTMENT for IRON and BRASS Four-Post BEDSTEADS, Cribs, and Cots, specially adapted for mosquito curtains, used in India, Australia, and the Colonies. Price, for full-sized Bedsteads, varying from 25s. Shippers and Colonial Visitors are invited to inspect this varied Stock, the largest in England, before deciding elsewhere. 10,000 Bedsteads to select from.—MAPLE and CO., London, Paris, and Smyrna.

MAPLE and CO., Manufacturers of Bedding by Steam Power. Purity and intrinsic value guaranteed.

DINING-ROOM FURNITURE.

MAPLE and CO., Manufacturers of DINING-ROOM FURNITURE. The largest Assortment to choose from, as well as the best possible value. Three more houses have been added to this important department. Half a century's reputation. Catalogues free.

MAPLE and CO. devote special attention to the production of high-class DINING-ROOM FURNITURE that will afford permanent satisfaction in wear. The numerous recommendations with which Messrs. Maple and Co. have been favoured by customers who have used the furniture for years is a standing testimony to the excellence of the articles.

DINING-ROOM SUITES.—The LICHFIELD SUITE, in solid oak, walnut, or mahogany, consisting of six small and two elbow chairs, in leather; dining-table, with patent screw; also Early English sideboard, with plate-glass back, and fitted with cellaret, 16 guineas.

DINING-ROOM SUITES.—The STAFFORD SUITE, comprising six small chairs, two easy chairs in leather, telescope dining-table, sideboard with plate-glass back and cellaret, and dinner waggon, in light or dark oak, walnut, or ash; very substantial in character, 23 guineas.

The Frankfort Cane Chair £0 19 6
Ditto ditto with cushion and drapery: seat 17 in. high £1 17 6

Bronzed Pillar Lamp, with marble foot, cut-glass container, Duplex burner, extinguisher, fancy globe and chimney, complete, 12s. 9d.

CLOCKS.

MAPLE and CO. have a large and varied assortment, suitable for Dining and Drawing-Room.

Handsome Decorated China Duplex Lamp, with solid brass supports, loose container, best lever-action burner with extinguisher, ornamental globe and chimney, complete, £1 12s. 6d.

CLOCKS.

Handsome marble clock with incised lines in gold, and superior eight-day movement, £1 3s. 6d.

Genuine Turkey carpets from Maples' depot in Smyrna, 1889.

Ten thousand brass and iron bedsteads for sale in 1889 – among one or two other things.

We have woven into yards of carpets the name of our firm, guaranteeing thereby the quality of that special make of carpet; and we do stamp our name upon certain articles of furniture which, although not made by us, are made specially for us, and for which we are responsible. But your lordships must be aware that this is done by other tradespeople, by gunmakers, by china dealers, by cutlers, and by no end of other tradesmen. But, inasmuch as we make ourselves responsible for every article of furniture that we sell in Tottenham Court Road, and are prepared at all times and at all costs to put anything right that has not turned out satisfactorily, we think we cannot be blamed for so doing. The fact of our name being thereon must be considered, not in any way as representing that each identical piece of furniture was made by us, but as a guarantee to the public of the durability of the article.

If by sweating was meant long hours and bad pay, said Blundell, Maples' factories and showrooms did not open until eight o'clock in the morning and were closed every evening at seven – on Saturday two in the afternoon. The wages sheet would show that they paid per hour as much as any of the best firms. In fact since he, Blundell Maple, had commenced business, he had endeavoured on one notable occasion, and on others, to get for the workpeople of London higher pay.

In giving his evidence, Horace Regnart, who stated that he passed for payment the invoices from outside workshops, agreed with the Committee chairman that it was his responsiblity to obtain a satisfactory article, to get value for money.

There was no question of tendering. His experience told him where to place orders. There was very little competition between the various workshops, since each had its speciality. There were no longer many makers in Bethnal Green and Curtain Road; most of them were in Finsbury.

Harris Lebus told the Committee he specialised in cabinet manufacturing, bedroom furniture and office furniture. He employed 190 in his own workshop, of whom eight were unskilled lads for cleaning and running errands. He sold his furniture to Maples and was paid entirely by piece-work. Joiners and cabinet makers in Maples' own workshops at Tottenham Court Road, said James Corp their foreman, were paid ninepence an hour. He might pay a good workman 9½d, 10d or 10½d. Some he paid on Friday night, some on Saturday morning. He had never had any complaints about wages. He had been a trade unionist since 1864. Another trade unionist employed at Tottenham Court Road, Frederick Baum of the London Society of Upholsterers, had nothing but praise for the standard of workmanship but little for the size of their wage packet.

> On their Leather Floor Messrs Maples leather work would equal any work done in any upholstery shop in London. The work is of a most beautiful character, and is certainly equal to any I have seen in any shop in London; and yet, strange to say, they are the worst paid.

They had a large number of apprentices bound for years. They were a good class of lad, fairly well educated and generally sons of small tradesmen. They received a good wage, rising from 2s 6d a week in the first year to £1 in the last. But they learnt a part of the trade only; they did not become an all-round upholsterer. Foreman of Upholstery Stuffing at

'No firm throughout the world can boast of giving greater contentment to their workforce,' Blundell Maple told the Select Committee on the Sweating System in 1888. The following year he instituted The Clarence Athletic Club at Mill Hill whose Sports Day (above) attracted hundreds of employees every summer – in the dark suit and boater, right is Norman Andrews' father.

Tottenham Court Road, David Gardiner Imlay, now 36 years in the trade, 28 of them in London, said he was trained as a paper-hanger, which was once part of the upholstery trade. There were now two branches of Upholstery: the fixing of curtains and loose casing (covers); and the stuffing of furniture. But there was nothing recent about this sub-division; he had found it when he first came to London. he had now been with Maples for 12½ years. One of his men, George Bailey, testifed Imlay never swore at him.

Every shop floor in Britain had its sergeant-majors, but all ranks meeting socially at the events, and particularly the annual sports, of the Clarence Athletic Club, which Maples established in 1889, helped to relieve any tensions and foster the happy family atmosphere which every company hoped to create among its workforce. The club was named after Blundell Maple's house in Regent's Park, and had grounds at Mill Hill.

The 'conspiracy' to blackguard and expose Maples – if indeed one existed – did little to dent the reputation of the firm in the eyes of its upper middle class customers. It was, after all, an institution. Something more shocking would be needed to make them withdraw their accounts than the accusations of lightweights like Arnold White and his paid witnesses. Most of those who bothered to read the newspaper reports of the Select Committee inquiry would have dismissed the allegations as coming from representatives of the undeserving Lower Orders who envied the commercial success of people like Blundell Maple, and even more their wealth.

What did shock newspaper readers in 1889 was the story of the apparent double suicide pact of the 31-year-old syphilitic, morphine addict Rudolf, Crown Prince of Austria, son of the Emperor Franz Joseph, and his 18-year-old mistress Marie Vetsera, in the shooting lodge at Mayerling on the estate of his home, the Hofberg, the living apartments of which had been furnished by Maples. The mysterious tragedy was the subject of the famous film *Mayerling*, and a Kenneth Macmillan ballet. On Rudolf's death the succession passed to Franz Joseph's nephew Archduke Franz Ferdinand whose assassination by a Serb at Sarajevo in 1914 led to Austria invading Serbia and the start of World War 1.

Looking back on these times historians dubbed the years 1873 to 1897 in Britain the Great Depression. The Maple & Company which in 1891 celebrated its jubilee had dug itself into a position from which no Depression could easily shake it – the result of good management by its still active founder and his son, helped by their team of junior partners, who knew that both they and their customers wanted value for money.

However a partnership was too frail a form of management to bear the expansion that father and son were planning for the new century that lay just ahead. The time had come for financial restructuring.

๛ 3 ๛

Hotels, Palaces and High Society 1891–1901

Soon after the Sweating System inquiry closed, John Maple, now in his mid-seventies, decided to stop going into Tottenham Court Road every day and retire. Blundell Maple became sole partner of Maple & Co. 'I found,' he explained later, 'that I had the whole weight of the business upon my shoulders inasmuch as the whole concern belonged to myself. I thought it was right that I should then turn it into a large company, and let all those that had worked with me participate in the results.'

By a deed dated April 8, 1891 Maple & Co were incorporated as a private limited company. The Memorandum of Association referred to a verbal agreement for the purchase from John Blundell Maple of his business for one million pounds. It was described as upholsterers, furniture manufacturers, furniture dealers, carpet manufacturers (?), linen drapers, ironmongers, braziers, builders, decorators, timber merchants, 'Manchester warehousemen', paper makers, general house furnishers, picture dealers, furniture removers, furniture stores, house agents, auctioneers and valuers.

Blundell founded the private company 'not with a capital largely in excess of what the business was worth, but with a capital such as I should not have been inclined to have sold the whole concern for; and it was founded on such lines as would allow all the employees who were coming in to be able to participate'.

He created an Ordinary share capital of £500,000 in £10 shares, the holders of which were entitled to one half only of the profits after the payment of interest on the £1 million Debenture capital, of which one half was a First Mortgage bearing 4 per cent interest and the other half a Second Mortgage bearing 5 per cent interest; and after payment of the dividend on the £500,000 6 per cent Preference shares.

In addition he made a £200 issue of £1 Management Shares, the holders of which were entitled to the other half of the profits.

Thus investors who wished to take a participation in the company had clearly to understand that they would have no voice in the company's management or in the appointment of directors. The company's articles of association provided that Preference shareholders could vote at meetings on a show of hands, but could not vote at a poll. On the other hand holders of Management shares each had one vote, while the Ordinary

Sole partner of the newly formed private limited company, 1891.

shareholders only had one vote for each £5,000 shares. Thus Ordinary shareholders only had 100 votes as against the 200 of Management shareholders. The company's directors were appointed, and the company itself controlled, by Blundell Maple who designated himself 'Governor'. The stock-in-trade – that is the plant, machinery, fixtures, freehold and lease-hold properties, investment and goodwill – was declared at December 31, 1891 to be worth £1,651,67 12s 1d.

Blundell and his father held more than a third of the Ordinary share capital on which in 1891 they received a dividend of 11 per cent, and much more than two-thirds of the Preference shares. Blundell saw the Management Shares as altogether different from the 'founders shares' which other companies had. The freehold properties, which Maples owned quite separately from the stocks and book debts, were nearly equal in value to the £1 million Debentures. The Management Shares, however, did not belong to any individual. They were in trust to reward the directors. Without Management Shares, Blundell would explain, he would have to pay a larger amount in salaries. 'Instead of paying the interest on those shares, we should have to pay the salaries which are generally given to such gentlemen as the directors who work this concern. Founders Shares are shares that are given to people who assist in founding a company. They do not do any work. Moreover they can dispose of their founders shares. The interest in our Management Shares on the other hand is used entirely to reward the directors for their personal services which are supposed to be directed exclusively to Maples.'

The only exception was the lawyer Arthur Bird whom Blundell appointed as Chairman, himself taking the title of 'Governor'. The six directors of the private limited company of 1891 were erstwhile junior partners Robert Blundell, Frederick Lunniss, Edward Rayner who had been Superintendent of the Counting House since 1876, Horace Regnart, Henry Regnart and Robert Tubby. They met for the first General Meeting on June 20, 1891 at 14 Grafton Street described as 'Dr Williams Library'.

At 46 Blundell Maple was riding high. In June 1891 he joined the favoured few who became the subject of a Spy cartoon in *Vanity Fair*. 'His riches' ran the caption, 'his inflexible faith in the goverment of the masses by Gentlemen, and his deference to the chiefs of his Party, make him welcome at the Carlton. He is firmly convinced that workmen in London factories should be legally competent to travel only to and from their rural homes at the expense of the railway shareholders. He is known as "Birdseye".'

The Echo ran a piece on Mr J Blundell Maple MP which said he filled three characters, and each with creditable sufficiency – that of the man of business in an alpaca jacket; that of the legislator in fine raiment; and that of the sportsman with his establishment at Newmarket.

> He is however Mr Blundell Maple through all alike. Seen in the palatial showrooms in Tottenham Court Road, he is neither legislator nor sportsman, but the energetic, swift-moving, slightly imperious, successful capitalist eager to infuse into his subordinates the divine enthusiasm which the budding million-aire unconsciously distils.

MOONSHINE.—May 3, 1890.

THE SHOP ASSISTANTS' HOLIDAY BILLS.

Fictional Maple (to St. Liberon). "TAKE CARE, CLUMSY. DO YOU WANT TO SMASH THE WINDOW? YOU'RE A NICE PRACTICAL MAN TO GET HOLD OF A SHUTTER. YOU'D BETTER GO HOME AND LEAVE THE WORK TO ME."

Shopkeeper/MP.

It is a very wonderful place, Maples, and there is no mistake about Mr J Blundell Maple. Seen a few hours later in the Lobby of "The House", Mr Maple has curbed his transports, but is still all square life and bustle. Dulwich would seem a most exacting constituency; to be always "on" something, and to make its Member earn the honour it has bestowed upon him.

A burly, dapper, well-built, nicely-balanced man who might have been trained in youth to the more heroic exercises and who, dressed in the Queen's scarlet, would be spotted at once as the major of his regiment, Mr Maple looks the world half-genially, half-defiantly, in the eyes out of a round, ruddy, slightly chuffy face.

His general appearance, said the writer, was that of conscious physical and moral comfort; of a man who slept well o'nights, and all through the day knew what o'clock it was.

Perhaps the Tottenham Court Road store did resemble a palace. But the house of some of their customers was the real thing. As seen, Prince Teck had patronised Maples when told he and his portly wife could take over the hunting box which George I had built in Richmond Park known as White Lodge. They had had it furnished, as James Pope-Hennessy remarked, in the fashion of the day,

> that is to say, they were loaded with ottomans and sofas, draped with shawls, large tables covered with Turkey rugs, small occasional tables, elaborate inlaid chairs, ornamental stools with twisted legs and palms in pots; family portraits on varnished easels and eastern carpets on the floor. The larger pieces of furniture came brand-new from Maple's emporium. The arrangement of the room was the Duke's.

It was the home of the Duchess of Teck's daughter Princess May who left White Lodge to marry Prince George, Duke of York, who had been given York Cottage at Sandringham which now became the first home of the newlyweds.

In December 1892 Prince George had been over York Cottage several times with "Maple's man" and, assisted by his father the

Afternoon tea in the Maple-furnished White Lodge, Richmond Park for the Prince and Princess of Wales and the Duke and Duchess of Teck in 1897.

Prince of Wales [later King Edward VII], and by his eldest sister Princess Louise, Duchess of Fife, he had chosen patterns for all carpets and wallpapers. The furniture was also bought from Maples, and was very modern. Maple, who had supplied pieces of furniture for some of the main rooms at White Lodge, was a London emporium much patronised by English and European royalties: "We spent I don't know how many hours at Maple & Liberty!" the Crown Princess of Greece wrote to her mother from London in July 1896. "I screamed at the things to Tino's horror, but they were too lovely! No. These shops, I go mad in them! I would be ruined if I lived here longer! – Divine Shops!" (*Queen Mary 1867–1953*)

The Crown Princess of Greece was buying furniture for an English cottage she was having built in the woods of Tatoi above Athens.

So the new Duchess of York and future Queen Mary had no need to go to Maples for furnishing *her* new home; her husband had anticipated her in a well-meaning attempt, as Kenneth Rose says in his biography, to save her trouble by filling its rooms with modern furniture from the emporium of his father's friend, Blundell Maple. He also furnished York House at St James's Palace without consulting his wife.

The Librarian at Windsor Castle confirms that Maples furnished both York House and York Cottage for the Duke of York at the time of his marriage, and that there are references to this in his diary, without giving any detail.

> There are very slight passing references to Maples having furnished the smoking room at Karim Cottage, Balmoral, and for Ferdinand of Bulgaria, Varna Palace; but again no details are given of their work. Queen Alexandra's account books record several payments to Maples from the 1890s onwards, but there is no detail of what the payments were for.

(letter to author of September 11, 1990)

Certainly Maples were describing themselves as 'Upholsterers by Special Appointment to Her Majesty Queen Victoria' in

The palace of the Viceroy of India at Simla for which Maples cabinetmakers made furniture in 1892.

The Blue Dining Room in the viceregal palace in Simla.

1892, and it was a ritual at this time for those who attended Maples' annual Cabinet Salesmen's Dinner at the Comedy Restaurant in London to send a telegram of loyal greetings to Her Majesty. It was in 1892 that many of those cabinetmakers had been engaged on making the furniture for the palace of the Queen's Viceroy in India at Simla.

No part of the British Empire was too far flung for the crating and despatch section of Maples' Export Department, or indeed any country in Europe. The trade barriers in the form of tariffs which many countries imposed in 1892 were extremely vexatious however. In his speech at the third annual dinner of the Furnishing Section of the London Chamber of Commerce Blundell Maple lashed out at 'unfair and unjust' tariffs. In France there were regulations whereby even the packing case in which Maples sent out their goods were weighed, and a charge made according to the wood used. In the states of Victoria and South Australia Maples were charged 25 per cent on their goods; in New South Wales 10 per cent; at the Cape of Good Hope 15 per cent, while in Canada the duty was 35 per cent.

Tariffs were generally lower in Europe – 5 per cent in Holland, 8 per cent in Germany and 10 per cent in Belgium – but in Portugal the taxation was of such a character as to prohibit Maples exporting to it.

Within six months of that characteristic plaint by Mr 'Fair Trader' Maple came the announcement in the *London Gazette* from which Society learnt that the man from whom so many of them bought their furniture had been lifted one rung above them on the social ladder.

WINDSOR CASTLE, Dec 2 [1892]
The Queen was this day pleased to confer the honour of Knighthood on John Blundell Maple Esq., M.P.

But of course they did more than buy furniture, they looked to the cabinet salesmen at Tottenham Court Road to tell them of the latest trends, to point out what was now in fashion to guide them on matters of good taste. In the eighteen-eighties fashion and taste was changing, and Maples went with them. A writer in an 1892 issue of *The Cabinet Maker* mocked the fashion which suggested 'the delicately masked prison of the lunatic where everything is padded and made soft for fear he might dash his brains against it'.

Comfort was beginning to play a less dominant role. Folks in Britain, said the writer, had long since become accustomed to chairs and sofas padded out of all shape. It would be some time before they were persuaded that the most comfortable settees were not necessarily those in which most wood was apparent. That was reserved for a generation who imagined they were advanced in taste to cover the naked wood with stuff, even where there was no excuse of comfort.

'Maple & Co undertake to supply all that is required for a house of any character in perfect taste' the management told the Correspondents and Visitors for whom they wrote the introductory Address of their revised and enlarged 650-page illustrated catalogue of 1892. In their showrooms, which now stretched from 141 to 149 Tottenham Court Road and back from 1 to 32 Tottenham Place, would be found goods carried out in designs by some of the best artists of the day, and at prices far below those usually asked. They recognised the difficulty which people often felt when choosing new furniture and deciding on what mode of treatment or decoration to adopt. It was not always easy to visualise the final result. So Maples had fitted up several suites of rooms furnished and decorated in different styles. The Press had described these as successful examples of high-class Decorative Furnishing carried out in good taste with extravagant outlay. They had a Vestibule, a Library, a Billiard Room, a Japanese Room, and several Entrance Halls, Drawing and Dining Rooms, Boudoirs and Bedrooms. They showed examples not only of different fashions in furniture but also in wallpaper, chimney pieces, gas and electric fittings, blinds, curtains, portières, mosaic parqueterie.

Apart from supplying the furniture and furnishings, they undertook every description of Artistic Decoration, Interior Woodwork, Panelling, Painting, Electric and Hot Water Engineering and Sanitary Work 'on latest scientific principles'.

They re-emphasised the importance of paying the store a visit. 'To lessen the fatigue of reaching the upper floors, two grand Staircases of very easy ascent, also comfortable Passenger Lifts, have been erected.' Their warehouse was acknowledged to be one of the sights of London, and as such was constantly visited by distinguished tourists, travellers and others from all parts of the world. In 1891 they had had the pleasure of doing business with nearly 34,000 different families. Maples had the actual knowledge and experience in the manufacture of Cabinet Furniture and Upholstery Furniture of every class, which justified the confidence of the public.

> On no account should Stuffed and Upholstered Furniture or Bedding be bought from Firms or Co-operative Societies who do not manufacture, but have to buy, as it is impossible for them to judge of the qualities of hair and other materials used after the furniture is covered.

Knighted – from December 2, 1892 'Sir Blundell Maple'.

141. 142. 143. 144. 145. 146. 147. 148. 149. Tottenham Court Road, and 1 to 32. Tottenham Place, London.   583

GENERAL FURNISHING IRONMONGERY, FENDERS, FIRE-IRONS, ELECTRO PLATE, CUTLERY, TURNERY,
BRUSHES, CROCKERY, GLASS, GAS FITTINGS, LAMPS, GARDEN FURNITURE, &c., &c.

MAPLE & CO have again largely developed these Departments, and devoted considerable additional space to the display of the various goods, which will be found most conveniently arranged for inspection in communicating Showrooms.

The stock of Furnishing Ironmongery now comprehends every description of KITCHEN REQUISITES suitable for Mansion, Villa, Cottage, Club, Hotel, or any class of Residence. A detailed list will be found on pages 626 to 634. BATHS of every description; REFRIGERATORS, ICE SAFES, FILTERS, KNIFE MACHINES, and other labour-saving Appliances, &c., in all the best makes, in great variety. BATH ROOMS, LAVATORIES, &c., fitted up complete.

The Stove, Fender, and Fire Iron Department is complete with DOG STOVES, TILE SIDE PANELS, SLOW COMBUSTION STOVES, HOB GRATES, &c., fitted with TILES of various designs; TILED HEARTHS, KERB FENDERS, in Marble and Brass; FIRE IMPLEMENTS in Brass and Steel; COAL SCOOPS and CABINETS, FIRE GUARDS, &c., while a large assortment of MANTEL-PIECES, in different designs and varieties of Marble, fitted up complete with Stoves, Tiles, Fenders and Fittings, suitable for any class of House or Room, are always on view; prices range from 25s. to £40. ASHES PANS of every kind made to order, at from 10s. 6d. each.

The stock of Gas Fittings has been very much increased, and includes all the newest designs in CHANDELIERS, BRACKETS, and HALL LAMPS, with all the new colours and shapes in Glasses. MAPLE & CO also undertake all kinds of GAS FITTING and Fixing complete, at most moderate charges, either in town or country.

A new Showroom has also been set apart for the display of ELECTROLIERS and ELECTRIC LIGHT FITTINGS of the newest and best types. INSTALLATIONS are conducted upon the latest and most approved principles, under the supervision of thoroughly competent Specialists. Estimates submitted free of charge.

An additional Gallery has also been fitted up for STERLING SILVER and ELECTRO SILVER-PLATED WARES; also for CUTLERY. MAPLE & CO'S TRIPLE-SILVER-PLATED WARES are a speciality, having an extra heavy deposit of Silver, and will stand the hardest wear for years. A large assortment of the finest makes of TABLE CUTLERY always on show.

The China and Glass Departments have been much improved and extended, and include a very large selection of DINNER, TEA, BREAKFAST, DESSERT and COFFEE SERVICES, MINTON'S, WORCESTER, WEDGWOOD and other eminent Makers' productions, at most moderate prices. An extensive SHOWROOM is now exclusively devoted to the display of all kinds of TABLE and ORNAMENTAL GLASS, plain, cut, and handsomely etched, engraved, or otherwise decorated.

The Lamp Department has also received important accessions, and all the best designs in EXTENDING FLOOR LAMPS in Wrought Iron, Copper, and Brass, TABLE LAMPS, HANGING, BRACKET, and other LAMPS, fitted with all the latest improvements, are now on show. ARTISTIC LAMP SHADES are also an attractive feature in this section.

MAPLE & CO Issue a special Catalogue of GARDEN FURNITURE, including Tents, Flower Stands, Rustic Seats, Tables, Tennis Fittings, &c., a copy of which will be sent free to intending purchasers on application.

Persons furnishing will find these goods at least 15 per cent. lower than the prices usually charged for articles of similar superior quality by Furnishing Ironmongers, and will also save much time and trouble in selecting, as a large stock is always kept on hand suitable for any kind of house. MAPLE & CO respectfully solicit comparison of quality and price.

Much more than furniture in 1892.

There was no part of Household Furnishings, for the genuineness and value of which the public were more entirely dependent upon the practical knowledge and commercial morality of the vendors, than Bedding. Comparatively few upholsterers manufactured the bedding they sold, but bought it from wholesale makers in London and elsewhere, and so could only offer goods of whose contents they knew nothing. Drapers, Co-operative Societies and others who merely took orders for bedding for makers' price lists, because they had no practical knowledge of its manufacture in many cases just placed orders with the wholesale firms that offered them the largest discount.

Nor is this the only disadvantage their customers suffer; too frequently their bedding is supplied by small manufacturers who have neither adequate machinery to prepare the materials, nor suitable premises in which to carry on the work; indeed if the purchasers of the Bedding could see the conditions and surroundings of some of the manufactories, they would be most unwilling to allow it to enter their houses.

They invited customers to visit Maples' manufactories adjoining the warehouse in Tottenham Court Road and see the machinery in motion. In 1891 they greatly extended their manufacturing premises to cope with increasing demand for Maples beds and bedroom furniture. They introduced 'numerous improvements in machinery greatly reducing the cost as well as accelerating production'. But through the cost of raw materials had risen, the price they were charging customers was in many cases lower than previously quoted, with no lowering of the standard of excellence. Their stock comprised 600 designs in French, Italian, Half-Tester, Four-Post and Twin bedsteads. They sent free to anyone who applied an illustrated

Cosy glow for cosy corners.

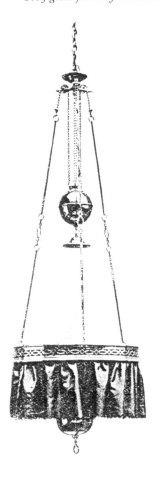

catalogue of Cots and Beds suitable for private families, schools, hospitals, public institutions, homes and asylums. For customers requiring fitted bedroom furniture they prepared and submitted drawings free of charge.

They warned customers not be deceived by illustrations of cabinet work which looked like the furniture they had seen at Maples 'but might represent goods fully 25 per cent lower in quality.

> This has found to be the case, some of these traders going so far as to issue Catalogues, the Drawings of which had been pirated from MAPLE & CO's book – notably a London Co-Operative Store, against whom an injunction in Chancery was obtained.

It would presumably have been easy to pirate one of the Artistic Cosy Corners 'decidedly English in their origin and conception and of original design' of which drawings appeared in the 1892 Maples catalogue. Alcoves and Turkish Lounges were very much in vogue in the eighteen nineties, copies of what were once seen 'in many an olden gabled and mullioned mansion.' At Tottenham Court Road Maples created a variety of Cosy Corners with 'Elizabethan' panelling, 'Moorish' arches, screens in 'Mishrabiyya', dadoes in oak and walnut, Tynecastle Tapestry, Anaglypta (low relief carving), 'Calcorion', 'Lignomur' and other fabrics in all the newest and best designs.

In the evenings they were lit by the cosy glow of an Antique Bronzed oil suspension lamp fitted with a patent self-extinguishing Duplex Burner.

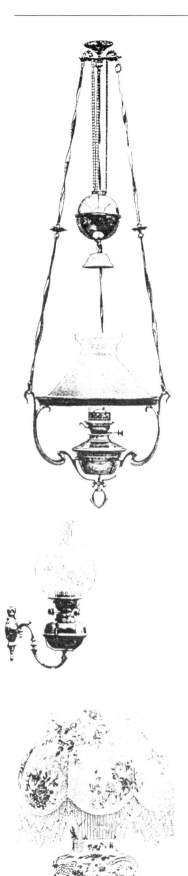

Bedsteads & Bedroom Furniture.

. . . .

THE continued enormous increase in these important departments point to the fact that while **MAPLE & CO.** hold by far the largest stock in the world of Bedsteads and Bedroom Furniture, they still give the best possible value. During the past year they have again largely extended their manufacturing premises, and introduced numerous improvements in machinery, greatly reducing the cost of as well as accelerating production, so that, notwithstanding advances in raw materials, prices will, in many instances, be found lower than previously quoted. At the same time, every care is still taken to maintain the standard of excellence, both as regards the quality of the materials and workmanship.

The Bedsteads seldom number less than **10,000**, comprising some **600** different patterns in French, Italian, Half-tester, Four-Post, Twin, and other styles, including Cots and Children's Bedsteads. A selection of representative designs will be found upon the following pages.

The stock of Bedroom Suites usually numbers from **700** to **1,000**, including every variety of style, and at prices ranging from **£3 10s.** to **500 Guineas.** The illustrations given represent various leading and favourite designs, all of which will be found of exceptional value, and **MAPLE & CO.** trust that they may be of assistance to customers unable to visit the warehouse. The collection of suites now on show comprises, besides the ordinary assortment, some magnificent specimens in inlaid rosewood, inlaid satinwood, pollard oak, cedar, and other woods. These suites are well worthy of the inspection of those in search of the very best class of furniture.

Original designs are prepared, as required, for fitted Bedroom Furniture.

Bedding of every description is manufactured on the premises, and guaranteed pure. Price Lists will be found on pp. 635-639.

In comparing prices of Bedding, as with all upholstered chairs, couches, settees, &c., it should not be forgotten that it is impossible to tell the value of the materials inside, as horse-hair varies from **5½d.** to **3s. 0d.** per lb., and wool from **2d.** to **2s., 3d.** per lb. Some firms quote lower for goods than they would cost, even if the raw materials were bought wholesale and manufactured by the aid of the most improved machinery. Again, with regard to furniture, somewhat of the same argument stands good. *Furniture can be produced to the same outline drawings fully 25 per cent. lower ; the way the article is manufactured, as well as the quality and quantity of the wood used, requires close observation and knowledge to detect the difference.*

MAPLE & CO. consider these remarks to be necessary, as certain traders have made it their business to copy the illustrations in their Catalogues, and have even gone so far as to issue Catalogues the drawings of which were pirated from **MAPLE & CO.'S** books ; inspections have been made of the goods so put forward, when they have been found to be base imitations in most inferior qualities. Against some of these traders, one being a London Co-operative Store, injunctions have been obtained in Chancery.

. . . .

Should the designs on the following pages not represent exactly what is required, MAPLE & CO. will always be most happy, on receipt of particulars, to prepare and submit special drawings, free of charge.

These burners being constructed upon thoroughly scientific principles do not cause the oil to become heated, so that an explosion is an absolute impossibility. The most nervous persons may therefore use a Lamp without the slightest fear of disaster.

They recommended using American Kerosene and water-white Crystal Oil as possessing the greatest illuminating power and perfect freedom from smell. Maples could supply it in original 40-gallon casks direct from the wharf.

Any over-nervous user of a cosy corner, or worried that an oil lamp cast too romantic a glow, could go along to Maples new showroom set apart for the display of Electroliers and Electric Light Fittings, and there choose a hanging that gave illumination of an unflickering, starker character but unlikely to explode – 'installed by a thoroughly competent specialist'.

New showroom space had continually to be found to display the latest household invention, every improvement, every novelty likely to take the public's fancy. There was no single reconstruction of Maples on the Tottenham Court Road island site, but by 1893, as the writer of the article 'The Influence of Commerce' in the *Illustrated London News* of June 17 observed, the once comparatively insignificant shop

has been amplified, extended and increased till it has developed into the handsome blocks of buildings whose ruddy tones give colour and warmth to the northern end of Tottenham Court Road and then, returning occupy the whole of the north and south sides of both Tottenham Place and Southampton Court, reappearing in the Euston Road, with the grand new red-brick elevation extending from Beaumont Place onward – breaking out again in Gower Street and with yet another long range in Grafton Street, where it includes the stately edifice so long the home of Dr Williams' library, while there are also, besides the great yards, where huge stacks of timber are ripening for use, numerous great factories and workshops fitted up with every modern labour-saving appliance.

MAPLE & CO
LIMITED
TOTTENHAM COURT ROAD, LONDON, W.
THE LARGEST AND MOST CONVENIENT
FURNISHING ESTABLISHMENT
IN THE WORLD

ESTABLISHED
HALF-A-CENTURY

Branch Offices for House
Agency:

CORNFIELD ROAD, EASTBOURNE,
AND
NORTH STREET, BRIGHTON.

CARVED OAK FURNITURE

MAPLE and CO are now exhibiting a remarkably fine Collection of Antique Carved Oak Furniture, including numerous reproductions of fine old specimens collected from ancient Baronial Halls, Castles, Mansions, Priories, &c., all of which are marked at purely commercial prices.

CARVED OAK FURNITURE

MAPLE and CO.'S Selection of Antique Carved Oak Furniture comprises unique and interesting specimens of Buffets, Dinner-Wagons, Chimney - Pieces, Book - Cases, Writing - Tables, Flap Tables, Cists, Coffers, Friar Anselm Benches, Corner Cupboards, Flower-Stands, &c. A handsome piece of Carved Oak Furniture is always an acceptable present.

CARVED OAK FURNITURE

MAPLE and CO have High-back Antique Carved Oak Chairs, for dining-room or library, at 14s. 9d. each, or with very handsome carved high backs, and seats upholstered all hair, in rich frieze velvet, £1 19s. 6d. each. Also a great variety of Elbow and Corner Chairs at most moderate prices.

DINING-ROOM FURNITURE

MAPLE and CO have now on show a Magnificent Collection of High-class DINING-ROOM FURNITURE in pollard oak, brown oak, and American walnut, as well as in the rich old Chippendale mahogany so much prized; while there are also a number of specimen dining-rooms, fully appointed and furnished, as examples of the different styles.

SPECIMEN DINING-ROOMS

MAPLE and CO.'S SPECIMEN DINING-ROOMS are good examples of high-class DECORATIVE FURNISHING, carried out in perfect taste, without extravagant expenditure. Everyone about to furnish or rearrange their residences would derive helpful information and suggestions by an inspection.

MAPLE and CO., Designers and Manufacturers of High-class ARTISTIC FURNITURE and DECORATIONS. The largest and most convenient Furnishing Establishment in the World. Established half a century.—141, 142, 143, 144, 145, 146, 147, 148, 149, Tottenham Court Road, London, W.

EXAMPLE OF A DINING-ROOM IN ANTIQUE CARVED OAK. Any article can be supplied separately. The Sideboard, £11 15s.; Dinner-Wagon, £4 17s. 6d.; Dining-Table, £6 18s. 6d.; Chairs, stuffed all hair, seat and back upholstered in Cairo Tapestry, £1 11s. 9d. each; Elbow Chairs, £2 19s. 9d.

The latter were regarded, he said, as the most convenient, well-lighted and appointed in London. With nearly 20 acres of premises, Maple & Co might safely and easily claim their right to their well-known designation as 'the largest furnishing establishment in the world'.

Some great businesses had been formed by the aggregate of a number of different trades, but in the case of Maples it had been simply the growth of the natural and legitimate constituents of house furnishing. To that Maples confined themselves, supplying, and in many instances manufacturing, every item, large or small, for the entire equipment of a home, and then decorating and furnishing it. That was no doubt an important factor in their success. For their customers recognised that they were dealing with men who had not only acquired a high commercial reputation but who, from their training and practical experience, were competent to advise upon every detail in modern furnishing. They were equipped to recommend what was appropriate as well as essential for the intial home-nesting of the young couple with a modest hundred pounds or so to spend, for the fitting up of a millionaire's mansion, an emperor's palace or a sumptuously appointed 19th century hotel.

The company did not merely enjoy a local celebrity. It was no extravagance of language to say that there was scarcely a town or village in the United Kingdom, on the continent of Europe or throughout the civilised world, where some of their productions were not in use. Nor was that all.

Still the largest and the most convenient after half a century – with house agencies outside London at Eastbourne and Brighton by 1893.

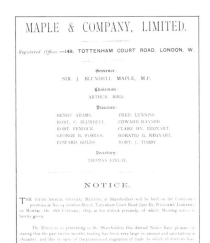

MAPLE & COMPANY, LIMITED.

Registered Offices:—149, TOTTENHAM COURT ROAD, LONDON, W.

Governor:
SIR J. BLUNDELL MAPLE, M.P.

Chairman:
ARTHUR BIRD.

Directors:

HENRY ADAMS.	FRED. LUNNISS.
ROBT. C. BLUNDELL	EDWARD RAYNER
ROBT. FENDICK.	CLARE HY. REGNART.
GEORGE B. FOSTEN.	HORATIO G. REGNART.
EDWARD GOLDS.	ROBT. J. TUBBY.

Secretary:
THOMAS FINLAY.

NOTICE.

THE FIFTH ANNUAL GENERAL MEETING of Shareholders will be held at the Company's premises at No. 14, Grafton Street, Tottenham Court Road (late Dr. WILLIAMS' LIBRARY), on Monday, the 18th February, 1895, at 6.30 o'clock precisely, of which Meeting notice is hereby given.

The Directors in presenting to the Shareholders this Annual Notice have pleasure in stating that the past twelve months' trading has been very large in amount and satisfactory in character, and this in spite of the pronounced stagnation of trade by which all interests have been affected.

The Hamilton Chair
A Chair much in favour, remarkably comfortable, with wide, deep seat, stuffed all hair, finished very soft, covered with handsome Tapestry and trimmed with deep fringe, £5 18s. 6d. If in Cretonne, without fringe, £4 18s. 6d. This Chair can also be supplied in Morocco or Saddlebags.

Examples of some
LUXURIOUS EASY CHAIRS

The Willoughby Chair
Exceedingly comfortable, with very deep and wide seat, stuffed all hair, and finished very soft in handsome Tapestry, trimmed with deep fringe, £5 18s. 6d. If in Cretonne, without fringe, £4 18s. 6d. This Chair can also be supplied in rich silk, trimmed as shown.

MAPLE & CO
LIMITED
Tottenham Court Road London
THE LARGEST AND MOST CONVENIENT
FURNISHING ESTABLISHMENT
IN THE WORLD.

EASY CHAIRS
LUXURIOUS EASY CHAIRS
MAPLE & CO enjoy a world-wide celebrity for really comfortable Chairs, especially for luxuriously soft Easy Chairs, Club Chairs, and Lounges. These are made in Maple & Co.'s own factories from specially selected materials by first-class upholsterers. Customers can pass from the Showrooms to the factories and see the various processes of manufacture.

EASY CHAIRS
COMFORTABLE EASY CHAIRS
MAPLE & CO have always an immense assortment of Luxuriously Comfortable Easy Chairs, Settees, and Couches, in different shapes and styles, upholstered in various fashionable materials, all ready for immediate delivery. The largest selection of comfortable Easy Chairs in the world.

EASY CHAIRS
COMFORTABLE EASY CHAIRS
MAPLE & CO being large manufacturers of Comfortable Easy Chairs, are not only able to offer their customers the widest range of choice from all the best shapes, but also to give the best possible value. Comfortable Easy Chairs will be found in the Showrooms at prices to suit all requirements at from 25s. upwards.

LIBRARY CHAIRS
LIBRARY EASY CHAIRS
MAPLE & CO have also on show all the most approved shapes in Reading and Elbow Chairs suitable for the Library or Study, or for the use of Bankers, Merchants, and others. Many of these are constructed so as to afford the maximum of comfort while occupying but a small space.

FURNITURE
ANTIQUE OAK FURNITURE
MAPLE & CO have, too, a remarkable collection of Antique Carved Oak, Elbow, Corner, and other Chairs in quaint and interesting shapes, well worthy the inspection of those who appreciate something out of the usual way. Antique Oak Chairs, upholstered seat and back in Penshurst Tapestry, 29s. 6d. each.

FURNITURE
ANTIQUE OAK FURNITURE
MAPLE & CO'S Selection of Antique Carved Oak Furniture also comprises unique and interesting specimens of Buffets, Dinner-Wagons, Chimney Pieces, Book Cases, Writing Tables, Flap Tables, Cists, Coffers, Friar Anselm Benches, Corner Cupboards, Flower Stands, &c. A handsome piece of Carved Oak Furniture is always an acceptable present.

MAPLE & CO., Designers and Manufacturers of High-Class Artistic Furniture and Decorations. The largest and most convenient Furnishing Establishment in the World. Established half a century.—141, 142, 143, 144, 145, 146, 147, 148, 149, Tottenham Court Road, London, W.

The Wellesley Chair
A delightfully comfortable roomy chair, very soft and restful, covered with handsome Tapestry, trimmed with deep fringe, and upholstered in best hair, £5 18s. 6d. If in Cretonne, without fringe, £4 18s. 6d. This Chair can also be supplied in Silk, and trimmed with fringe, as shown, or in Morocco, for club use.

A REALLY COMFORTABLE EASY CHAIR is always an acceptable present.

The Square Arm Divan Chair
A luxuriously comfortable Chair, stuffed all hair, finished very soft, and covered in handsome Tapestry, trimmed with deep fringe, £5 18s. 6d. If in Cretonne, without fringe, £4 18s. 6d. This Chair can also be supplied in best Morocco, or in rich silk, trimmed as shown.

Maples advertisements of 1893 describe the company as Designers and Manufacturers of High Class Artistic Furniture and Decorations. They were known all over the world for their really comfortable easy chairs.

Notice of the fifth annual general meeting for February 18, 1895 at which Sir Blundell Maple announced a 10½ per cent dividend for 1894.

From many a faraway forest come the floats bringing timber to be made into shapely and artistic furniture in their busy factories – scarce a vessel leaves Smyrna for England without carrying consignments of Eastern carpets for their customers – beneath sunny continental skies thousands of nimble fingers are deftly weaving dainty fabrics for the adornment of the houses of their patrons – it may indeed be said that there is no seat or centre of ancient or modern industry in connection with the furnishing and decoration of an English home whose productions do not find a market in the series of great warehouses and showrooms in Tottenham Court Road.

The climb to these heights had been at the cost of Sir Blundell Maple's health, and in 1893 he succumbed to serious kidney trouble which put him out of action for many months. On his return to business he was welcomed back with an illuminated address from 202 carmen and porters, 130 joiners, 400 decorators, 30 plumbers, 60 cabinet makers, 6 floor cloth cutters, 15 looking glass fitters, 31 gilders, 22 carpet porters, 15 cabinet porters, 211 curtain upholsterers, 20 bedstead warehousemen, 5 telephonists, 80 mattress makers, 16 furniture restorers, 240 carpetwork people, 17 bedroom furniture porters, 16 hardware porters, 34 removal men, 62 packers, 67 blind makers, 40 frame makers, 19 wicker chair upholsterers, 12 carton pieceworkers, 24 gas fitters, 105 polishers, 43 warehouse cleaners, 28 electricians, 65 domestic servants, 8 engine tenders, 176 furniture upholsterers, 49 stablemen and 9 timber porters, as well as sales and administrative staff. One person signed as the representative of each category. So much for his reputation of grinding the faces of the poor!

His energies fully restored, he applied himself to making the private company a public one. In 1895 the business became Maple & Company Limited. 'Lately,' he told shareholders at the first annual general meeting of the public company, 'I have thought it wise to invite the public to come in. Though the shares are to-day standing at an apparently large premium upon what they were issued at, you must remember that they were not issued largely to the public but only to the employees and those interested in the concern. Since I did not part with more than half the shares to begin with, the price at which they are standing now is what might practically be called the issue price.'

Under their articles of association they could not issue any more Ordinary shares; they were a fixed number. But they could increase the number of Preference shares. Every since the company had been formed it had never paid a dividend less than 10½ per cent, but all the time the market had been falling which was bad for companies like Maples who held large stocks. But now, said Sir Blundell, the market was rising, and the value of their stock of 30,000 beds for instance had risen. The profit in 1895 was £149,516. They paid a dividend on the Ordinary shares of 18 per cent. Their Reserve Fund, which rose as the Ordinary dividend rose, stood at very nearly £100,000. Since all their premises were freehold and made of cement, they had no need of a separate Depreciation Fund. A

The value of their huge stock of bedsteads increased – and now a picture gallery, too, offering paintings by 'T Gainsborough' and others.

398   **MAPLE & CO**   (Upholsterers to Her Majesty)

MAPLE'S DEPOSITORY.

IT is but a comparatively short time since MAPLE & CO completed the immense block of premises in the Euston Road, an illustration of which is shown on page 223. This building, it will be remembered, extends the whole length from Beaumont Place onward to the corner of Tottenham Court Road, and the vast upper floors were devoted to the warehousing of furniture and other effects. Large, however, as were these premises, they soon became totally inadequate to meet the ever-growing requirements of the Warehousing Departments, and MAPLE & CO then erected an enormous building at Camden Town, to which a yet further addition has just been completed. In the latter is an extensive range of Fire and Burglar-proof Safes, and Strong Rooms for the safe storage of all kinds of valuables. These premises, which are within a few minutes of the warehouses and showrooms in Tottenham Court Road, and in direct telephonic communication, as well as in close proximity to the three great Railway Depôts and Termini, have been built and fitted with all the latest and best appliances for the safe and careful custody of every description of household furniture, and personal property and effects.

The premises are lighted throughout by electricity, and are heated by a system of low pressure hot-water apparatus, so that a mild and even temperature is maintained, to the entire avoidance of damp or other influences prejudicial to the condition of the goods.

Powerful hydraulic lifts have also been fitted up, so that the furniture can be conveyed direct from the vans to the particular floor upon which it is to be stored. The risk of straining, or other damage in carrying is thus avoided, while the long and broad covered way extending the whole length of the building, will allow of the vans being unloaded in all weathers, without the slightest danger of the goods being wetted or otherwise injured in any way.

Intending depositors are invited to inspect the warehouses, which are open daily from 9 a.m. to 5 p.m.; on Saturdays, from 9 a.m. to 2 p.m.

Full details, plans, terms, conditions and other particulars as to the Removal and Warehousing of Furniture, Musical Instruments, Luggage, Carriages, Cycles, Plate, Wine, &c., Post Free on application.

MAPLE & CO
LIMITED
Tottenham Court Road London W
THE LARGEST AND MOST CONVENIENT
FURNISHING ESTABLISHMENT
IN THE WORLD

THE UGANDA SUITE, £10 15s
THE UGANDA BED-ROOM SUITE in Polished Hazelwood, consisting of Wardrobe with bevelled plate glass door, and large dressing underneath; marble-top washstand, toilet table with glass affixed; washstand with double tiled back, marble top, cupboard beneath, towel rods at ends; three chairs **£10 15s**

WEDDING PRESENTS
BIRTHDAY PRESENTS
COMPLIMENTARY PRESENTS
USEFUL PRESENTS
SPECIAL CATALOGUE 400 USEFUL PRESENTS POST FREE

MAPLE and CO. invite an inspection of their magnificent Collection of Ornamental and Useful Articles suitable for Birthday, Wedding and Complimentary Presents, which will be found to be the best and most complete in London. New Special Catalogue of Presents post free.

PICTURES, OIL PAINTINGS, and WATER COLOURS by rising artists; also Furniture, Decorations, and Photographic Frames, Statuary, &c, and, from the antique by celebrated Italian sculptors. A magnificent collection on view in the newly-added galleries.

A bedroom suite for £10 15s.

How the front of the Tottenham Court Road island site looked in the 1890s.

significant addition to their properties in 1895 was the large red brick furniture depository in Camden, North London, at the corner of Camden Street and Plender Street.

There were ten members of the Board in 1895: the six directors of the private company plus Edward Golds, George Foster, Robert Fendick and Sir Blundell Maple's half-brother Henry Adams. Solicitor Arthur Bird was chairman and Sir Blundell was Governor. Thomas Finlay was Company Secretary.

Britain was pulling out of the Great Depression. Maple & Co Ltd's total profit after meeting all management and other charges was £284,000 in 1896 compared with around £180,000 in 1893. Turnover was £265,000 up on 1895. Such an enormous increase in business was a phenomenal success, Sir Blundell told shareholders at the 1897 annual meeting. And it had not been made, he said, at the cost of their customers, but by spending less and being content with smaller profit margins. By increasing their capital they had gained another 1,294 shareholders whom he regarded as so many agents for the company. They were not issued with a balance sheet however, nor a profit and loss account, and the Press had to make an approximation of the state of the company's affairs from the dividends it paid and the sums it put to reserve. While so great a growth in business had doubtless been partly due to the reputation of Maples, commented *The Statist*, it had also been due to the general trade prosperity, and consequently any check to business would materially affect their profits.

The Stock Exchange was no guide to the success or otherwise of Maples since, to Sir Blundell's disgust, it did not as yet give the company an official quotation. This was because on some of its lines the construction of the company did not exactly correspond with what the Governor called their antiquated ideas.

Without any disrespect, he declared at the 1897 AGM,

In the 1890s not just retailers but manufacturers – the furniture factories in Southampton Court (left) and Tottenham Place (right).

I think that a concern which is as large as our firm where the shares are dealt in on the Stock Exchange every day, as are ours, the Committee of the Stock Exchange might enquire into the working, and if they found such a concern, representing as it does a value of nearly £4,000,000 of money, was thoroughly good and trustworthy, they might give a quotation, although we may not conform to the old, straightforward rules of the Stock Exchange.

A measure of the company's confidence in its future was the amount of capital it was investing in new building. In anticipation of increased volume of trade, more factories, workshops, stables, warehouses and strongrooms were added. And Sir Blundell told shareholders with justifiable pride how 'the handsome main frontage now extends from Beaumont Place to the corner of Grafton Street, while the Gower Street extension opposite the Metropolitan Railway extension is also completed'. On the continent too business was increasing to such an extent that they moved into larger and more important premises in Paris at no 5 Rue Boudreau near the Opera House, and bought some freehold land on which to build factories to enable them to meet the increasing number of large orders. This was in the Rue de la Jonquière.

The first big contract carried out in the new workshops was the redecorating and furnishing of the Elysée Palace Hotel in the Champs Elysées which was planned to be completed well before the opening of the international Paris Exhibition. 'I expect all the best people from all parts of the world will try and stay at the Elysée Palace Hotel, and the name of Maple will become more widespread than ever,' said Sir Blundell.

Hotel work became a major contributor to Maple's turnover. It grew from Sir Blundell Maple's association with a hotel developer, Frederick Gordon, and the two groups The Henry Fredericks Syndicate and Gordon Hotels Limited. Though Blundell was a director of both of these, Maple & Co had no financial interest in either of them. 'We in the Henry Fredericks Syndicate,' he explained to shareholders in February 1897, 'have some very large hotels in the process of building, and they will be decorated and furnished by Maple & Co. This work will be carried out on the same terms as the work which we did for all the Gordon Hotels. The same ratio of profit Maple & Co will have as we fairly charged to the Gordon Hotels Company.' That was at a small remunerative

The Hotel Cecil, overlooking the Embankment, completed in 1894 and since replaced by Shell-Mex House, for which Maples created several decorative schemes.

Frederick Gordon.

profit, but he was looking to the advertisement which Maples got and the increased business done through the hotels.

> In the case of these hotels it is not only the question of the order . . . these hotels increase the taste for furnishing. Having these hotels, provincial people and others that stay at hotels are in the habit of admiring the furniture, and assessing that it is better than that which they have in their own homes. They therefore patronised Maple & Co.

Frederick Gordon became a director of Maple & Co. in 1898.

Both Maples and their neighbours Shoolbreds were given contracts for the interior work of the magnificent new Hotel Cecil in the Strand (later replaced by Shell-Mex House), along with a newcomer S J Waring & Sons. 'The reputation of each,' reported *The Cabinet Maker*, 'will be greatly enhanced by the way in which the colossal task has been accomplished.' What the journal described as 'one of the most imposing decorative schemes in the hotel', the Restaurant à la Carte, was carried out by Maples – in 'Empire' style. The walnut woodwork had brass wreaths, swags and other enrichments; the chairs were of mahogany inlaid with brass. The curtains were rich in colouring, and the effect most stately and imposing. Maples were also responsible for the Empire Drawing Room whose enormous mantelpiece is shown overleaf.

The Hotel Cecil was on a grand scale, with a banqueting hall to seat a thousand and its own masonic temple. 'To-day London boasts a hotel which, not only in respect of magnificence but also in the matter of good taste, needs no comparison with any the world over. . . . The grand staircase springing from the level of the Embankment entrance and running up the centre of the southern block, has itself been compared to a palace – a palace of splendour and fairyland – and indeed the comparison is not an idle one.'

S J Waring became a more formidable rival when, the

FROM "EMPIRE" DRAWING ROOM AT THE HOTEL CECIL

The huge mantelpiece in the Empire Drawing Room of the Hotel Cecil which Maples created for this famous hotel.

following year, they joined forces with Collinson & Lock and with Gillows of Lancaster and Liverpool and began trading as 'Waring & Gillow'. They won the furnishing contract for the prestigious Carlton Hotel, and then the Waldorf and the Ritz. Maples had contracts however not merely for palatial hotels but actual palaces. At his 1897 AGM Sir Blundell announced that Maples had an order for a palace in Athens and 'been lately partly building and decorating two palaces in St Peters-

S J Waring's London shop in Oxford Street in 1898.

The Czar of Russia's Winter Palace in St Petersburg for which Maples received a furnishing contract in 1897.

burg, working for the Emperor of Russia'. Tom Alcock, Maples Clerk of the Works, posed for his photograph with a group of his colleagues before taking ship to Russia where the main contract was for the Czar's Winter Palace, the first of which had been erected by Peter the Great in 1711. The sixth and most

magnificent one, covering 400,000 sq ft, was completed in 1760. Gutted by fire in 1837, most of the rooms were restored however by 1839.

In the 1900 Czar Nicholas and Czarina Alexandra often stayed in the small Alexander Palace at Tsarskoe Seloe which Prince Felix Youssoupov (the murderer of Rasputin) says would not have lacked charm 'had it not been for the young Czarina's unfortunate improvements', replacing most of the paintings, stucco ornaments and bas reliefs with mahogany woodwork and Cosy Corners. Quoting the prince's comments in *The Last Days of Imperial Russia* (1976), Miriam Kochan writes

> New furniture by Maples was sent out from England. Alexandra however thought it delightful and was particularly fond of her opal-hued boudoir. Here, amid hangings of mauve silk, surrounded by vases of fresh roses she lay on lace-covered cushions on a low couch, a lace cover lined with mauve silk over her knees, beneath her favourite picture . . . Nicholas too liked this room and spent most of his leisure there.

Alexandra Fyodorovna, the 23-year-old girl whom Nicholas married in 1895, was a granddaughter of Queen Victoria and relished the prospect of redecorating a residence that would be entirely her own. 'She had tastes,' writes Laura Cerwinske in *Russian Imperial Style* (1990), 'that ran to bright English chintzes, light lemonwood furniture in the private quarters and upholstery in her favourite colour mauve. Her personal sanctuary The Mauve Boudoir had curtains, carpet, pillows and chaise longue in mauve.'

The Royal Palace at Bangkok which Maples furnished for the King of Siam at the turn of the century.

The throne room in the King of Siam's palace in Bangkok.

Surprisingly Sir Blundell did not refer to the work which Maples were doing at the Czar's Winter Palace at either the 1898 or 1899 annual meetings, and it is far from clear precisely what work the company did there. And what was the other palace in St Petersburg where he said he had a contract? The Winter Palace was bombarded by the light cruiser *Aurora* in the 1917 Bolshevik Revolution, without irreparable damage however, and today it is the Hermitage Museum.

The palace in Athens was for His Royal Highness the Duke of Sparta. Another palace which they were furnishing was for the King of Siam (Thailand), and at the same time one for his son the Crown Prince. A team went out from Tottenham Court

The Hotel Russell in 1900.

HOTEL GREAT CENTRAL
LONDON

Close to the Terminus of the Great Central Railway, enjoying all the delightfully fresh air of the Regent's Park and adjacent heights, yet within a few minutes of Bond Street, Great Cumberland Place, the Marble Arch, Hyde Park, Club and Medico Land, the Art World, and fashionable centres of the West End and principal Places of Amusement.

NOW OPEN

NOW OPEN

HOTEL GREAT CENTRAL, one of the Finest and most Luxuriously Appointed in the World, Decorated and Furnished throughout by MAPLE and CO. The Cuisine and Wines of the most delicate and dainty character, while the charges are exceptionally moderate.

NOW OPEN   SUITES OF APARTMENTS OR SINGLE ROOMS MAY NOW BE BOOKED, ALSO EN PENSION.   **NOW OPEN**
Telegraphic Address : "CENTELLARE, LONDON."

HOTEL GREAT CENTRAL

'Decorated and Furnished Throughout by Maple & Co'.

Road to India to decorate the palace of the Viceroy in Simla, and another to Constantinople to furnish the Austrian Embassy. Sir Blundell was particularly proud of the work they did on the Duke of Orleans' residence which he was convinced was one of the finest houses in England.

There was probably more money however to be made out of furnishing and decorating hotels with their large number of bedrooms and public rooms, lengthy corridors and staircases. In Paris, apart from the Elysée Palace Hotel, Maples were furnishing part of the Hotel Ritz in the Place Vendôme; in the

Inner main hall of the Great Central Hotel in Marylebone Road.

Ardennes a group were at work at the Palace Hotel; others at the Hotel Bristol at Beaulieu on the Riviera. In England the association with the Henry Fredericks Syndicate was bringing fat contracts outside London – for furnishing the Pavilion Hotel in Folkestone and the Metropole Hotel in Brighton – and in the capital, now entering a new era of prosperity, the Grand Hotel in Trafalgar Square, the First Avenue Hotel in Northumberland Avenue, the Hotel Russell in Russell Square and the Hotel Great Central in Marylebone Road.

The Russell was (and is) a big building of terracotta and red brick in 'German Renaissance' style, the interior full of dark-coloured marble. The Great Central, designed by R W Edis, the architect of the Constitutional Club, was also of bright coloured terracotta, but more restrained than the Russell with its balconies, arcading and armorial crests. It was to be the station hotel for the new London terminus of the Manchester, Sheffield and Lincolnshire Railway, linked to the Metropolitan Railway at Aylesbury – the Great Central Railway. The cost of having to put the final section of the line in a tunnel to meet objections to having it pass Lords Cricket Ground, left little money for building Marylebone Station and none at all for the proposed hotel. So the railway company sold the site to the Fitzroy Syndicate* who built on it what was originally to be

Fireplace in the Great Central Hotel.

called the Grand Central Hotel. It was indeed on a grand scale and in a grand style, with its Coffee Room (dining room) for 400, Table d'Hôte Room, Early and Late Room, Writing Room, Drawing and Reading Room with walls panelled in green silk and furniture upholstered in soft coloured silken fabrics and curtains of woven tapestry. The Smoking Room and Billiard Room for the men had chairs upholstered in dark padded leather – and a brass spitoon. The famous Wharncliff Suite had a main banqueting room ('the finest in London') and three smaller ones including a Honeymoon Room with an azure ceiling.

In their first advertisements the management invited guests to stay at

> HOTEL GREAT CENTRAL, one of the finest and
> most luxuriously appointed in the world,
> Decorated and Furnished throughout by MAPLE and Co.

It opened at the same time as the Carlton Hotel. It only had 40 years life as a hotel. It was requisitioned by the War Office at the outbreak of the Great War in 1914, opened up again after it, only to be taken over once more in World War 2. The last paying guest departed in 1939. After the war it became the headquarters of the British Railways Board. In 1989 it was acquired by a Japanese property company, Abe International Venture Corporation, who spent £150 million on restoring it to its former glory to the plans of architects S'International, with a view to re-opening it as a hotel under the management of the Atlanta-based Ritz Carlton Group.

The finance for *building* hotels, as opposed to decorating and furnishing them, came not from the shareholders of the public company Maple & Co but from the private funds of Sir Blundell Maple invested in bodies such as the Fitzroy Syndicate (which incidentally managed the Hotel Russell after it was built) and Frederick Hotels the company which in a sense competed with Gordon Hotels, though Frederick Gordon was persuaded by Sir Blundell to become its chairman.* Sir Blundell went out of his way to tell shareholders in February 1897 that 'Maple & Co have no shares whatever in any other undertaking'.

A large part of Sir Blundell's personal wealth was derived from these activities, as well as from Maples – he held eight times more Maples Preference shares than anyone else, worth hundreds of thousands of pounds. He could afford to be charitable and he did not hesitate to be so when a fitting opportunity arose. On seeing the diagonal plans which architect Alfred Waterhouse had made for a new University College Hospital, he was so impressed that he at once promised to provide the £100,000 which in 1896 he was told would cover the cost of rebuilding and re-equipping. When in the event it cost double that sum, he cheerfully agreed to pay the difference. At the laying of the foundation stone the Prince of Wales praised the great generosity of Sir Blundell Maple whose gift to the sick poor of London (that is, to those admitted to UCH) he compared with that of Mr Guy founder of Guys Hospital. In the hall of the hospital can still be seen the marble tablet engraved with gilded lettering which reads:

*see Appendix 1: *The Creation of Frederick Hotels* by Geoffrey Marsh

An 1897 advertisement for 'Maple & Co London' and 'Maple & Co Paris'.

The heading of the 1897 invoice, surmounted by the royal arms, proclaims Maples' wide spread of showrooms and factories, and operations in Paris and Smyrna.

MAPLE & CO

The Largest and Most Convenient Furnishing Establishment in the World

TOTTENHAM COURT ROAD LONDON AND PARIS

THE "DATCHET" DRAWING-ROOM SUITE

THE "DATCHET" DRAWING-ROOM SUITE, consisting of Four Small Chairs, Two Elbow Chairs, and Settee in finely inlaid mahogany, upholstered in rich silk, made and finished in the best manner ... ... 23 Guineas.
THE "SONNING" CHAIR, in Cretonne, can be had instead of one Elbow Chair if preferred at same price.
An immense variety of new models in Drawing-room Suites at from 10 to 100 Guineas.

MAPLE & CO LONDON

TRIPLE SILVER-PLATED CAFE NOIR SET, with 16 in. Tray, complete, £2 7s. 6d.

NOVELTIES FOR WEDDING PRESENTS

MAPLE & CO invite an inspection of their magnificent Collection of Decorative Furniture, Pianos, Clocks, Bronzes, Pictures, Ornamental Sterling Silver and Triple Electro-plated Wares, Indian Rugs, and other articles appropriate for Wedding or other Complimentary Presents. Everything marked purely commercial prices. Illustrations of 400 Presents post free.

MAPLE & CO LONDON

ORIENTAL CARPETS

The Largest Stock in the World.

| TURKEY | FROM | CARPETS |
| TURKEY | £5 | CARPETS |

The Largest Stock in the World

MAPLE & CO LONDON

SEAMLESS AXMINSTER CARPETS

Manufacturers' Accumulations at greatly Reduced Prices.

Ft. in. Ft. in.					£ s. d.
9 10 × 6 7	..	...	...	...	3 1 6
11 6 × 8 2	..	...	...	...	4 12 0
13 2 × 9 10	..	...	...	...	6 5 6
14 9 × 11 6	..	...	...	...	9 6 0

Several hundreds of these sizes in stock.

LARGE INDIAN HALL OR LAWN RUGS

10s. 6d. each. Illustrations Free.

INDIAN MUNG MATS

Special List of Sizes and Prices Post Free.

MAPLE & CO LONDON

MAPLE & CO LONDON

A SPECIAL PURCHASE OF

FINE COTTON SHEETS

of exceptional value   Top Sheet Hem-Stitched

About 72 × 117	*90 × 117*	*99 × 126 in*
10s 6d	11s 9d	13s 9d per pair

GOOD IRISH LINEN SHEETS

Smooth round thread, will wear well, and keep a good colour to the last.

About 72 × 117	*90 × 126 in*
18s 6d	21s 0d per pair

Both top and bottom Sheets Hem Stitched.

MAPLE & CO PARIS

BRITISH-MADE CARPETS

ALL KINDS AND SIZES

READY FOR IMMEDIATE USE

Largest Variety in the World

MAPLE & CO have thousands of Carpets of all kinds, as Axminster, Club, Nezbon, Wilton, Brussels Tapestry, Bosphor, Woodstock, and others, some being seamless in all the new patterns and in every variety of size, so that customers can see the complete effect and know the exact cost before purchasing as well as save much loss of time. The largest stock of English Carpets in the World.

MAPLE & CO LONDON

THE "MAYFAIR" BEDROOM SUITE IN MAHOGANY

THE "MAYFAIR" BEDROOM SUITE, made in specially selected Mahogany of rich and beautiful figure, and consisting of a handsome Wardrobe with broad fluted pilasters, champhered mouldings, and shaped bevelled silvered glass door; Toilet Table with elliptic top landscape glass affixed; Washstand with marble top and high tiled back, also towel rods at end; Pedestal Cupboard and Three Chairs, £23 15s.

THE "UNIVERSITY" SUITE IN CARVED OAK

THE "UNIVERSITY" SUITE, in solid carved oak, consisting of Six Chairs, upholstered in tapestry or stamped leather, finished brass nails, at 16s. 9d. each; Two Elbow Chairs 26s. 9d. each; Sideboard, £6 15s.; Dinner Wagon, £2 15s.; Extending Dining Table, with patent screw, £3 12s. 6d.; Overmantel, £3 7s. 6d. *The very best value obtainable.*

MAPLE & CO LONDON

BRASS BEDSTEADS

Largest Stock in the World

MAPLE & CO offer choice from many thousands of Brass Bedsteads in an immense variety of patterns at from **38s. 6d.** to **£50**, all bought before recent advances, so that buyers will effect a great saving. The largest selection of Brass and Iron Bedsteads in the World.

MAPLE & CO PARIS

ANTIQUE CARVED OAK FURNITURE

Largest Variety in the World

"ENGLISH MAKE"

QUAINT DURABLE INEXPENSIVE

MAPLE & CO (Ltd) are now showing an immense variety of English-made Antique Carved Oak Furniture, inexpensive and artistic, for Dining-rooms, Libraries, Sitting or Smoking Rooms. Specialities in Dining-room Chairs, at from **16s. 9d.** each. The largest, cheapest, and best selection in London. Illustrations of Carved Oak Furniture post free.

MAPLE & CO LONDON

THIS STONE WAS LAID BY
HRH ALBERT EDWARD
PRINCE OF WALES KG
Vice-Patron of the Hospital
on Tuesday June 21st 1898
as a memorial of the rebuilding of this hospital through
the generosity of Sir J Blundell Maple Bart MP

The upholsterer of Tottenham Court Road, already a knight, was one of the 14 people created baronets in Queen Victoria's Diamond Jubilee Honours. Others included the Lord Mayor of London, the President of the Royal College of Physicians and the Chairman of the Midland Railway. Commenting on those who had received honours, *The Times* of June 22, 1897 said, 'Sir John Blundell Maple, the head of the well-known firm, is an industrious Conservative member who shows a keen interest in many questions of importance to the working classes.'

As Colin Ford and Brian Harrison observed in *A Hundred Years Ago*, 'some old-fashioned stalwarts feigned shock when Sir Blundell Maple (of Maples stores) was made a baronet in 1897, but the wealth of the brewers and big industrialists could hardly be resisted at a time when the political parties needed money for their growing machines'.

It was a sign of the social fusion which marked the end of the century and of the old Queen's reign in Britain. Colonel F Dickins of Dickins & Jones was a dashing officer of the Victoria Rifle Volunteers. A word from Frank and William Debenham, it was said, meant admission to the political set of the Commercial Society.

> The interval separating the social life of retail traders from that of the professional classes had been largely bridged over by the rural hospitalities of others who, during business hours, stand behind their Bond Street counters . . .. Latter day Liberalism has found a notable supporter in Mr J Barker, head of a mammoth drapery firm in Kensington, now in Parliament and expecting a baronetcy. Mr C D Harrod has a hunting box on Exmoor and is visited by academics and parliamentarians. The daughters of Mr Whiteley of Westbourne Grove provide wives for Indian staff officers. (T H S Escott, 1904)

The Maple Almshouses and Convalescent Home at Harpenden – an Illustrated London News drawing made in 1897 the year they opened.

Sadly Sir Blundell had no son who could inherit his baronetcy. His daughter Grace Maple had just married a member of the German nobility, the 32-year-old Hermann Johannes Arnold Wilhelm Julius Ernst Freiherr von Eckhardstein. Known as Baron Eckhardstein, he was Kaiserlich deutscher Legationsrat in the German Embassy in London – 'First Secretary'. As Baroness Eckhardstein Grace lived it up in a grand house in Grosvenor Square which became a centre of London cosmopolitan society.

Of more direct concern to Sir Blundell Maple than the sick poor of London were the employees of the family firm for whom, after 20 or 30 years loyal service, the time had come to retire. In June 1897 he established, and with £150,000 endowed, a charity called 'Maple Convalescent Home and Maple Almshouses'. It was managed by a joint committee of Maples directors and Maples employees. On land he owned at Harpenden near his Childwickbury estate Sir Blundell had an almshouse built consisting of 16 one-bedroom flats, and beside it was a convalescent home. At the time of its opening the *Illustrated London News* described it as Almshouses or Homes of Rest for the aged 'or those of the employees and others of the great house in Tottenham Court Road who may have become incapacitated for business'. The Convalescent Home had accommodation for eight male and twelve female patents 'for whom cheerful reading and writing rooms and a well-appointed mess-room are provided, a steward and a matron being in attendance'.

> The Homes of Rest, like the Convalescent Home, are built in the Elizabethan style, from the designs of Colonel R W Edis FSA, the upper part being timbered, while a broad oaken verandah constitutes an important feature, and affords a pleasant shelter, under which the residents may sit or read or work, as they talk of the past and fight their battles of life over again; and each home may be described as a miniature flat.

Under the scheme introduced by the Charity Commissioners in 1931, a stipend was paid to each resident of £25 a year if unmarried and of £40 a year if married, plus between ten and

Van horses flee the fire that broke out at Maples Depository – a dramatic drawing in the Daily Graphic *of February 8, 1897.*

fifteen shillings a week to anyone in particular need. An almsperson and pensioner had to be someone of good character who needed assistance through being unable to maintain himself by his own exertions from age, ill health, accident or infirmity. He needed to have been with Maples for at least 12 years. His widow would be eligible so long as she was over 55.

The charity remained in being, and the almshouse occupied, for 93 years – up to 1990, when the building was put up for sale and bought by property developer Derek Tynan who converted it into what he advertised as 'Maples, Clarence Road, Harpenden' consisting of ten flats and maisonettes of varying sizes. All of them were quickly taken up by members of the public. Retired employees of the firm, or their widows, lived at Maples Almshouse under the care of the last warden Mrs Audrey Edgar, right up to the end. The last to leave was Mrs Louisa ('Loui') Watts, widow of George Watts who went to Tottenham Court Road in the nineteen thirties as a porter and by 1970, when he died, was Foreman of the Bedding Department. The funds of the charity are administered by the Trustees of the Maples Almshouses (chairman, John Gillum), and they pay for Mrs Watts, and the others moved out of the Harpenden Home of Rest, to live elsewhere.

The only event to mar the eventful year of 1897 was the destructive fire that badly damaged Maples' Camden Depository.

It started around midnight in a loaded van on the ground floor, caught the wooden ceiling of the first floor, spread to the roof, 'and then the whole crashed downwards furniture, pianos, candelabra and valuable goods of every description in one charred indistinguishable heap.'

> The fire burst out (*reported the local paper*) in a range of buildings four floors high, which covered a great area of ground, and had only been erected within the last twelvemonth. The huge structure was used as a furniture depository, and at the time of the outbreak was filled on all floors with a great masses of the most inflammable material.

Fire engines were called from as far away as Holborn and

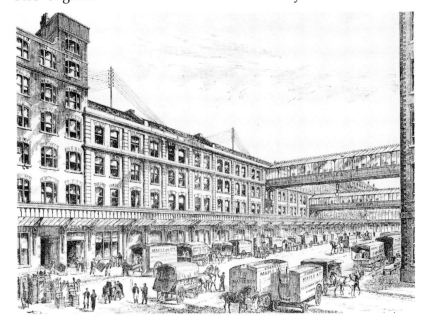

Prompt delivery of customers' orders from London to every part of the country was undertaken daily by a vast army of vans, drivers and horses.

The Riviera Palace hotel, Nice.

Scotland Yard, and then from Southwark south of the river. All the strongrooms containing depositors' jewellery were flooded. The flames could be seen for four miles around. People living in nearby houses were afraid of it spreading. The whole of one side, Block E, was destroyed, together with a coach house below the first floor roof used for four-horse driving. Another blazing van was pulled out but burnt to a cinder. The debris continued to burn all next day, and passers-by identified vases, dishes, plates and other valuables strewn on the ground. 'On the window sill of the warehouse was a large family Bible, almost the only article saved without injury from a van.'

The Camden Depository operation for the storage of other people's furniture which Maples collected from houses in horse vans, was separate from that of the Tottenham Court Road store whose stock of furniture for sale, but not on display, was held in other warehouses. There was a separate fleet of horse vans to deliver to customers' homes the merchandise they had bought at the store – and this was an important aspect of Maples' success. 'Depots with Stabling attached' shareholders were told in 1898, 'have been organised in the outer suburbs of the metropolis for the convenience of customers residing within these districts. Deliveries by the company's own vans are made free in all these neighbourhoods.'

In their Osnaburgh Street stables near Great Portland Street station they had 550 horses, and hundreds of others at stables in Lea Green, Hounslow, Kingston, Watford and Ware. When Stanley Wharton, John Maple's grandson, joined as Company Secretary in 1901 he was given the job of buying two horses a week from the Horse Buyer of the London General Omnibus Company.

Maples did not have their own cabs to deliver customers to their store, but rewarded the drivers of hackney carriages who did with a Cabby's Brass Ticket. The commissionaire on the front entrance gave each cabby, after he had discharged his passengers, what looked like an old penny, on one side of which was inscribed 'Maple & Co. Refreshment 3d'. On the other side was written 'Northumberland Arms'. On presenting

One of the many Dining Room Sideboards in Maples' Illustrations of Furniture of 1898.

it across the counter of the latter (still trading in 1991) the cabdriver could get either a pint of beer with bread and cheese or a half-ounce screw of tobacco. Artful cabbies would make a 'mistake' and put down a passenger, who had asked for Shoolbreds next door, at Maples, collect his brass ticket from the commissionaire and drive quickly away.

But there was no mistaking Maples' success. By 1899 their £100 Ordinary shares were worth £450. Sir Blundell reckoned the firm had grown 50 times since he joined his father in business in 1861. And John Maple still came down to Tottenham Court Road to see how things were going three or four times a week. Success did not come from large orders. It was not Maples' object to furnish only palaces and hotels, but to meet the wants of the smallest household in the Empire. However the railway companies were pressing to open the hotels they were busy building at their London terminuses. Maples had received contracts for the London, Brighton and South Coast Railway's Grosvenor Hotel at Victoria Station, and for the Great Eastern Railway's Station Hotel in Liverpool Street. They had furnished the London and South Western Railway's Station Hotel at Southampton. And there were orders for the Burlington Hotels in Dover Bay and Sunny Boscombe, Bournemouth, and for the Riviera Palace Hotel at Cimiez, Nice. Around this time too Maples had supplied all the furniture and fittings for The Savoy Hotel in the Strand 'specially manufactured with a view to the comfort and pleasure of the guests'; and The Coburg Hotel in Grosvenor Square described by *The Gentlewoman* magazine as 'the most beautiful hotel in London' and now The Connaught.

To cope with the surge of orders, in 1898 Maples bought what Sir Blundell called 'extensive freehold property' in Highgate Road, and started to build large factories on it with a floor area of more than 2¼ acres, to be fitted with 'the latest machinery for the manufacture of superior furniture and every description of high quality cabinet joinery.'

The huge variety and range of the superior furniture which Maples were manufacturing was set out graphically in the 400 pages of the 1898 edition of *Illustrations of Furniture*. Most were pen and ink drawings or engravings, but now there were also several pages of black-and-white photographs. Fully

THE HOTEL BURLINGTON, Dover Bay
,, HOTEL BURLINGTON, Sunny Boscombe
,, FIRST AVENUE HOTEL, Holborn
,, CONSTITUTIONAL CLUB, Northumberland Avenue
,, GOVERNMENT HOUSE, Simla
,, BURLINGTON HOTEL, Old Burlington Street
,, HOTEL VICTORIA, Northumberland Avenue
,, ROYAL STATION HOTEL, Hull (for North Eastern Railway)
,, GREAT EASTERN HOTEL, Parkstone
,, GRAND HOTEL, Brighton (new bedroom wings)
,, LIVERPOOL CLUB, Liverpool
,, VICTORIA CLUB, Jersey
,, WEST CUMBERLAND CLUB, Whitehaven
,, MALVERN HOUSE HYDROPATHIC ESTABLISHMENT, Buxton
,, CHARING CROSS HOTEL, new wing (50 bedrooms)
,, JOCKEY CLUB, Newmarket
,, DEVONSHIRE PARK PAVILION, Eastbourne
,, CREWE HOTEL, Crewe, for L. & N.W. Ry. Co.
,, DEVONSHIRE PARK THEATRE, Eastbourne
LIMMER'S HOTEL, Hanover Square
THE PUMP HOUSE HOTEL, Llandrindod Wells
,, SACKVILLE HOTEL, Bexhill-on-Sea
,, PLOUGH HOTEL, Northampton
,, GRAND HOTEL, Peterborough
,, GRAND ATLANTIC HOTEL, Weston-Super-Mare
,, GRAND HOTEL, Jersey
,, GRAND HOTEL, Lowestoft
,, ESPLANADE HOTEL, Seaford
THE COBURG HOTEL, Grosvenor Square
,, HOTEL MÉTROPOLE, London
,, HOTEL MÉTROPOLE, Brighton
,, GREAT EASTERN HOTEL, Liverpool Street
,, SAVOY HOTEL, Victoria Embankment
LE CERCLE D'ORIENT, Pera
LE CERCLE, Smyrna
LE CERCLE KHEDIVAL, Alexandria
LE CERCLE BILBAO, Spain
LE CERCLE DE RESIDENTES ÉTRANGERRS, Rosario
THE HELLENIC CLUB, Smyrna
,, HOTEL ST. GEORGE, Mustapha Superior
,, ROYAL STATION HOTEL, York
,, QUEEN'S HOTEL, Birmingham
,, COUNTY HOTEL, Newcastle
,, GRAND HOTEL, Northampton
,, BURLINGTON HOTEL, Eastbourne
,, PARK HOTEL, Preston
,, HOTEL CAROL Ire, Kustendjie, Roumania
,, SENATE HOUSE, Buenos Ayres
,, CENTRAL STATION HOTEL, Glasgow
,, FURNESS ABBEY HOTEL, Barrow
,, ROYAL LONDON YACHT CLUB, Cowes
,, ROYAL SPITHEAD HOTEL, Isle of Wight
,, L. & N.W. RAILWAY HOTEL, North Wall, Dublin
,, AVENIDA PALACE HOTEL, Lisbon
,, EASTBOURNE HYDROPATHIC ESTABLISHMENT, Eastbourne

Some of Maples' customers in 1898.

Maples did a large trade in pianos in the 1890s.

descriptive captions complemented the pictures: 'the *Tavistock* couch in saddlebags of rich Persian design mounted on velvet trimmed with a very handsome fringe.' There was a whole section on Furniture in Saddlebags and Velvet', the former presumably being imported from their depot in Smyrna – a kind of carpeting material used to make the saddle bags hung over camels in the East.

Gents Easy Chairs were different from Ladies Easy Chairs; couches came left-handed or right-handed. There were 30 pages of Dining Room Sideboards 'for well-appointed dining rooms', and 30 of Antique Carved Oak Furniture 'now so much in favour'. What they obviously did not also manufacture were 'the fine old examples of Chippendale, Sheraton and Hepplewhite furniture, while not new, of the finest quality and in excellent preservation'. 'Collected from ancient Baronial Halls, Castles, Mansions, Priories etc' were reproductions of old sideboards, buffets, chimney pieces, bookcases, writing tables, cabinets, doffers etc.' Furniture for offices included double-slope Clerks Desks with drawers and pigeon holes, safes, cash boxes, deed boxes. Furniture for Drawing Room and Boudoir which took up about half the catalogue, included Quaint Chairs, Occasional Chairs, Rocking Chairs, Folding Chairs, Ottomans, settees. There were 'Artistic' Cosy Corners, Japanese Cabinets, Turkish Lounges 'with richly embroidered Broussa Portiere'; furniture in the style of Louis XIII, XIV, XV, and XVI. There were pianos of all the well known makes, and by Ibach and Julius Feurach; and American Organs for schools and churches by Bell, Smith and Esty Organ Company priced at between ten and 250 guineas. There were grand pianos and overstrung iron-frame pianos in rosewood, walnut and mahogany at 37 guineas, and one 'with check repeater action especially adapted for hard wear or for use in extreme climates'.

Library and Board Room Furniture was to be found in the additional premises newly opened in Grafton Street and Gower Street – 12 designs of bookcases for studies and consulting rooms; Pedestal Tables (desks), bureaus and writing tables, and palm stands with copper linings; and for the Billiard Room saloon benches and Grog Tables. For the Drawing Room were

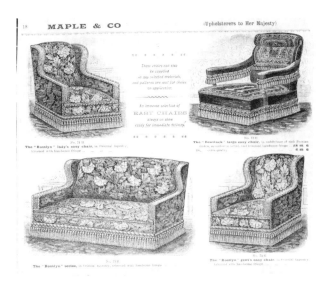

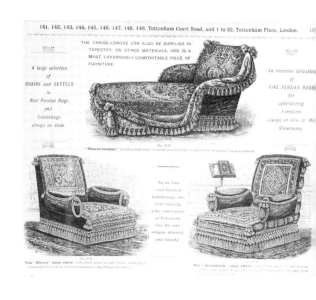

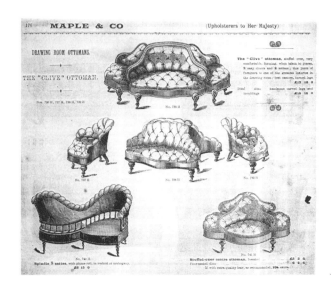

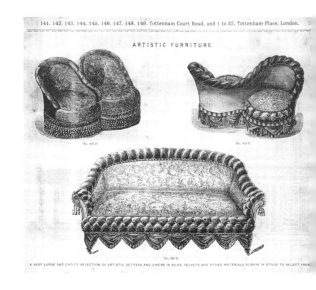

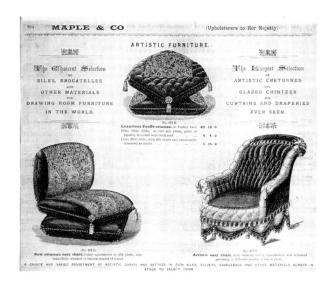

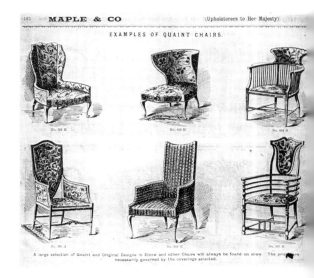

Chairs galore – easy, settee, ottoman, chaise-longue, artistic and quaint – from Maples 1898 Illustrations of Furniture Catalogue.

The Eighteen Nineties Look – specimen rooms in Maples Illustrations of Furniture *1898.*

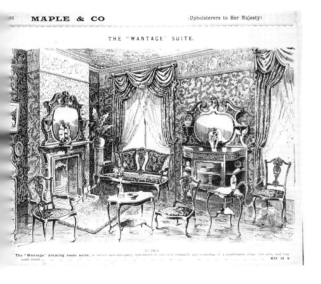

the cabinets, easels and tabourets (low stools without back or arms), and Chinese Furniture of 'curiously carved black wood with marble tops'; Japanese Screens, Oil Baize Screens, Louis XV Screens, Rod Screens; 'Fancy' easels, music stands, 'buhl' card tables, two-tier oval tables, three-tier whatnots, music cabinets and escritoires.

There was plenty of French Gilt Furniture: etagères (with shelves one above the other in stages for ornaments), jardi-nières (for plants), girandoles (branched supports for candles), pier-glasses (tall mirrors), curio tables. There were wicker, cane and bamboo furniture; ornamental arches and valances; inside and outside blinds; French Upholstered Bedsteads.

'To Facilitate Business,' pleaded the Post Room in an inserted sheet, please specify the articles and departments in your letters and telegrams 'rather than use general terms such as "My order" or "My things".

Whatever merchandise Maples offered for sale which they did not manufacture themselves, they bought in – and made a point of paying promptly for it *and in cash*. By paying ready

'French' was fashionable in 1898.

The heart of every comfortable home was a comfortable bed – from Maples.

money for everything and paying 'very close' – without waiting for what the Stock Exchange called accounting day – they saved themselves a good deal of money – in 1897 £35,000. In 1899 the advantageous terms they made with manufacturers for cash payment meant they received £5,000 more in discounts than the whole of the interest they had to pay on the Debenture Stock.

Much of the bought-in furniture came from France, a country with which Britain's relations had become strained over French ambitions in Africa – after protests from London, they had evacuated Fashoda. The infamous Dreyfus Trial also generated a certain amount of anti-French feeling. It was something that worried Sir Blundell.

> The lives and commerce of the two nations (*he said at the 1900 AGM*) are so interwoven, and especially in our case, where we have a house in Paris, that it is all important that we should try to make good friends of our French neighbours and ask them to make good friends with us. I know a great deal of the better class of the French people, and I can assure you that the insults that have been offered at times to the English – and which have been felt very acutely when they have been offered – do not proceed from the class we know as holding any responsible position in France.

Maples' house in Paris, he said, was highly appreciated by the French people and they came to it in large numbers. He hoped the English would not boycott the French, because then they might turn round and boycott the English. He looked to better feelings being established between English and French so that the French Exhibition would be a great success.

However that might be, there would always be a demand for furniture of every description. Britain's population was ever increasing and more and more houses being built. Maples were not engaged in a fanciful business of selling luxuries; it was a necessity of life to have a comfortable home and to have it furnished.

The Fashoda Incident did not lead to war with France, but mounting friction with the Boers in South Africa did, and the Boer War which broke out in October 1899 put a damper on social and commercial life for much longer than was expected. Volunteers for the South African War depleted Maples workforce which, so far from deploring, Sir Blundell Maple MP positively encouraged. To every employee who joined the Imperial Yeomanry Sir Blundell gave £50 out of his own pocket with which to equip himself and buy a horse. Witness to this patriotic gesture can be found in the many receipts for that amount still residing in Maples archives.

Never was it more important to have tight financial control at Tottenham Court Road, to insist on effective management. The 14 Maples directors formed a Consultative Committee of 19 heads of departments – 'the eyes of the directors in all parts of the concern' – to give their opinions to the Board. They were remunerated out of the Management Shares Fund and at no expense to shareholders or to the Reserve Fund to which another £57,000 was added in 1900. At an Extraordinary Meeting after the 1900 AGM the company's articles of association were altered to enable shareholders to elect the directors. Sir Blundell explained that when the firm came wholly into his

In 60 years John Maple's Hen & Chickens had spread round the corner into Euston Road (the one-time New Road).

hands in 1891 he formed a private limited company, asking his associates to become directors. 'It was agreed that I should have absolute power to select and get rid of directors myself.' The new articles transferred that absolute power to the share-holders, but so long as Sir Blundell was President, he was to retain the power of choosing from the Board of Directors those who would go on the Board of Governors.

The purpose of the alteration was to meet the rules of the

The End of a Century – it was Sunday Best all round for Maples employees and their families at the annual sports day of the Clarence Athletic Club on July 8, 1899.

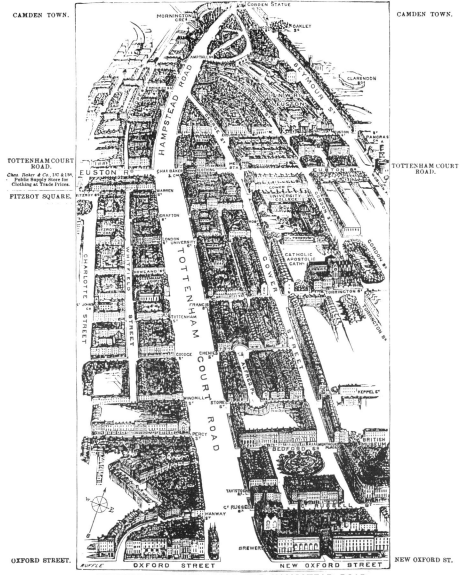

TOTTENHAM COURT ROAD AND HAMPSTEAD ROAD,

Stock Exchange, who thereupon gave Maples' shares an official quotation. The other stipulation, which the Board met, was from now on to give shareholders a balance sheet.

The shareholders and directors had gathered for the tenth annual meeting at Tottenham Court Road on Thursday March 1, 1900. Three days later, on Sunday March 4, John Maple died at Bedford Lodge, his house on Haverstock Hill, Hampstead, where he was highly esteemed, as *The Times* obituary notice observed, 'for his many acts of kindly benevolence, the postmen and omnibus employees of the district being among those in whose welfare he took an active interest.'

But his fame belonged to his founding of the House of Maple which he had lived to see grow from his small Hen & Chickens drapery business into the Largest Furnishing Establishment in the World covering the whole of the island site around the original shop at no 145. He was 85. He still had his Surrey estate at Salfords, Horley. He left £892,503 gross, £861,750 net, including 29,845 £1 Ordinary Maples shares, probably worth around £1 million. His wife Emily survived him, dying in 1904, also aged 85.

❧ 4 ❧

The Age of Extravagance
Ends with War
1901–1916

QUEEN Victoria died on January 20, 1901, and four weeks later Sir Blundell Maple was remarking to Maples shareholders that he viewed with pleasure the fact that His Majesty the King would no doubt, with his usual activity, be entering into the amusements of the people as soon as he possibly could. He hinted that Maples would have a share in working for His Majesty and for the Duke of Cornwall. He had to wait a couple of years however before the new monarch issued Maples with the royal warrant appointing them upholsterers, which he was not able to announce until the 13th AGM. But he received his due share of the work occasioned by the arrival of distinguished guests from the Empire for Edward VII's coronation. Maples received a contract for refurbishing the India Office on a lavish scale. On the first tier terrace they erected electric light fittings galore, hung the windows with rich silken

The Edwardians dine out in opulent style at the Maples-furnished Hotel Cecil in the Strand.

tapestries and decorated the balustrading with festoons of flowers. Over the Italian quadrangle they put a specially painted velarium (awning).

The Edwardian era, The Age of Extravagance, had begun. It was probably the last period in history, wrote James Laver, when the fortunate thought they could give pleasure to others by displaying their good fortune before them. A great part of that display was in furniture and furnishing, and in the house of the upper middle classes an increasing amount of it had been bought at Maples. 'Money seems plentiful,' wrote J W Benn in *The Cabinet Maker*, 'and certain household luxury has never, even in the Victorian era, reached the point at which it has now touched.'

The craze for over-furnishing every room was on its way out, but in Benn's view too slowly. In the fashionable salon

Over-furnished some Edwardian rooms might have been – but it was good business for Maples.

there still had to be something to startle: a blazing metal mirror or a fluffy floor lamp rich in pink or yellow millinery; a highly gilt Frenchified set of chairs, or upholstery overloaded with ornate fringes and flowers seeming to say, "Look at me, how brilliant and costly I am!" There was no denying the beauty of plush, and no desire to deny its effectiveness, but the practice of covering furniture with it entirely, even to the legs of tables which were encased in close-fitting trousers of the same, buttoned so to speak with gilt nails, was not to be encouraged.

In its review of the windows of the West End furniture stores *The Cabinet Maker* commented that Messrs Maple & Co commanded some of the best designing and producing talent in the trade, and their windows revealed some notable examples. 'To speak of all the things in the windows of this colossal establishment would take a volume . . .. Few, if any, places in Great Britain contain so comprehensive an exhibition of every phase and quality of our craft.'

It also contained, for a large part of each day, the Governor, immaculate in top hat and tails, standing in the entrance hall personally to welcome the ladies and gentlemen who were favouring him with their custom. Marylebone, wrote the anonymous 'Foreign Resident' * in *Society in the New Reign*,

*T H S Escott (1904)

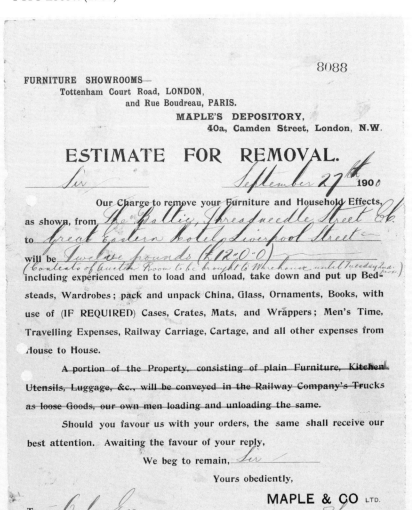

With rooms choc-ful of furniture, the decision to move from one house to another was not taken lightly; but entrusting the job to Maples ensured an efficient, inexpensive and anxiety-free operation – but first an estimate.

Lord Curzon's study in the Vice-regal Palace, Simla – carpets by Maples.

was one of the London districts whose shopocracy already rivalled that Society in which, so far, no retail trader had been admitted. On one occasion Sir Blundell, relates the author, was doing the honours of this establishment to a stately dowager shopping there in her son's company.

> 'I think,' naively observed the dealer, 'I had the pleasure of seeing your Ladyship at the opera last night.'
>
> Turning round to her companion, the lady of quality indignantly asked in an intentionally audible aside, 'What does this man mean?'
>
> 'That he will lend you his box whenever you want it; and if I were you, I should borrow it like a shot,' came the son's reply.

The western quarter of the town, says Foreign Resident, possessed many other tradesmen of as much social consequence in their way as was the first upholsterer converted by royal favour into a baronet. If Edward VII desired early and additional light on the subjects that interested him most, he might safely look for it, not to the managers of his own Foreign Office, but to the drawing room of Sir Blundell Maple's daughter Grace, the Baroness Eckhardstein. Grace, said Anita Leslie in her book *Edwardians in Love* (1972) was one of the few women, along with Rosa Lewis of The Cavendish Hotel, tolerated by Edward VII's mistress Agnes Keyser who founded King Edward's Hospital for Officers in Grosvenor Crescent.

Sir Blundell was well aware that nothing a fashionably dressed baronet could do by way of personal supervision could give his Tottenham Court Road emporium the superior reputation enjoyed by those in Bond Street, Regent Street and Oxford Street. But when the first Marquess Curzon of Kedleston, who was Viceroy of India from 1899 to 1905, seemed publicly to cast a slur on the quality of the goods sold in that street, the Governor was outraged.

Opening an exhibition of Indian Art in Delhi in 1903, the 44-year-old Lord Curzon made disparaging allusions to 'flaming Brussels carpets, Tottenham Court Road furniture, and cheap Italian mosaics', and advised maharajahs to abjure all such and furnish their palaces with Indian work. Whereupon he received a telegram from one maker of Tottenham Court Road furniture pointing out that Maples had furnished palaces for the Kings of Siam and Portugal, the Durbar Room of the Maharajah of Mysore, and supplied carpets and chairs for the Viceroy's own lodge in Calcutta. He might have added the work the firm did for the India Office at the time of the recent coronation, and the Viceroy's palace in Simla in 1888.

The next day Sir Blundell showed the reporter who had come to interview him for the *Daily Mail*, a letter headed 'The Viceregal Lodge, Calcutta' ordering carpets for Lord Curzon himself. One sentence read, 'I shall be obliged if you will consider order no 1 as a standing order to be supplied regularly every year.' Tottenham Court Road rejected with amused superiority, ran the article carrying the interview, the idea that it was entirely devoted to cheap goods for the multitude. The millionaire could be suited equally as well. Sir Blundell Maple held that English taste, as to form and colour and artistic effect of furnishing, had vastly improved in the last quarter of a century. Art schools and exhibitions had had an influence, and the modern artistically-furnished hotel had been an educative factor.

Sir Blundell Maple's daughter Grace, Baroness von Eckhardstein.

In a leading article the *Daily Mail* said Sir Blundell had made out an excellent case for his furniture.

> He points out that English wares are no longer cheap or rubbishy, but of distinct artistic merit. In fact British furniture now holds a proud place in the world, and is surpassed in durability and in design by none. It is perhaps just a little amusing to find the most august personages in India, and even Lord Curzon himself, go to Maples for the furniture of their houses and palaces.

In a two-page, well-argued article headed 'The Defence of Tottenham Court Road', *The Cabinet Maker* pointed out that the business of a businessman was to supply the requirements of the public at the price the public was prepared to pay.

> But apart from this side, everyone should know that in the Tottenham Court Road are to be found some of the finest examples of our craft and the work of some of our best and most skilled designers.

Indian princes were not such fools as Lord Curzon appeared to imagine, and those of them who possessed western refinement and education had, in scores, shown their good sense by coming to the great English emporiums for their furnishing and household equipments.

> One hardly expects consistency from an oratorical Viceroy at an Imperial Durbar, but it might have been well nevertheless for this distinguished gentleman to run over some of the headings of the bills he does not pay before indulging in these catchpenny phrases. Is Lord Curzon aware that the Indian carpet industry is

largely directed and capitalised from the Tottenham Court Road? Does he know that half the originality and vigour that many Indian arts possess today is supplied from the same contemptible source? If not, he might even spare an hour from a Viceregal polo match to look into these matters and become a little better informed before he so flourishingly attacks one of the great industrial centres of our country.,

The writer concluded however that Lord Curzon simply employed the words 'Tottenham Court Road' as a figure of speech and meant no disrespect either to the thoroughfare or its wares. 'None of the great firms there need tremble at the prospect of their business being doomed; in fact they have rather been "boomed" than otherwise.' Sir Blundell had come to the same conclusion when he referred to the incident at the 1903 AGM. It was plain that Lord Curzon did not mean anything at all derogatory about goods which came from Tottenham Court Road, but simply wanted to encourage work in India.

Sir Blundell took the opportunity of indicating that their own staff of designers and artists at Maples who were always producing new things, was as large as ever.

> I can assure you that anyone wanting anything special made will be gratified at the drawings which will be submitted, and will also see different designs here on the premises.

People who were having goods made for them could go to the factories with the designers and could see them in course of construction. Much of the manufacturing areas had now been moved away from Tottenham Court Road to give more space for showrooms in which to display all classes of goods and maintain at all times what Sir Blundell called 'an extensive exhibition of furniture'. The breadth of the range, catering for the lower end of the market as well as its higher end, had for 50 years been central to Maples' marketing. And to attract more of the former they now had a Hire Purchase Department – the first in Britain?

Sir Blundell called it Deferred Payment. Customers, he said, could come to the store, see furniture marked plainly with one cash price, and take it away on paying a very small commission in consideration of deferring payment of the full sum.

It was designed specially for those who were marrying and starting to furnish a house, and had a fixed income. It had been introduced as a two-year experiment in 1901. In the letter they now sent to customers confirming the service, they said they had been asked to organise such a department in connection with their old established 'ready money and small profit business' where goods could be obtained by deferred payment but at their usual marked cash prices. As it was impossible to alter their ready money prices, all goods being marked in plain figures for cash payments, a premium of five per cent was charged upon the total value of the goods supplied to offset the extra expenses. The conditions of the hire purchase system required the payment before delivery of one-fourth of the total cost of the goods in addition to the premium, and the balance according to agreement by equal monthly or quarterly payments spread over one, two or three years, with interest at the rate of five per cent per annum on the amount outstanding from time to time.

Obviously this rate of interest is not what traders as a rule expect to receive for the use of their money, but the exceptional financial position of Maple & Co enables them to offer special advantages.

Anyone settling an account within 12 months received back sixpence (2½p) in the pound of the commission paid, over and above the ordinary price of the goods. A shilling (5p) in the pound was charged in the first instance. The letter concluded with the words:

> This new departure has been greatly appreciated by a large number of professional and commercial men, as well as others, who have found it more convenient to furnish their homes on this system with first-class furniture, preferring to make the necessary outlay from their income rather than disturbing their capital.

Telling shareholders of the scheme at the 1903 AGM, Sir Blundell said he always contended that in England everyone was honest. They did not find any people coming to Maples to buy things with a dishonest intention to defraud the company. In the two years they had been running the scheme without announcing it publicly, it had been shown that the commission they were charging was quite sufficient to cover the extra expense and to cover any loss that might be made through any dishonest practice.

Hire Purchase has since become commonplace throughout the High Streets of Britain, indeed throughout the world. And if, as has been claimed, it was pioneered by Maples, it was something Sir Blundell could be proud of. Henry Labouchere ('Labby'), the editor and founder of *Truth*, the *Private Eye* of its day, said what he always admired in Sir Blundell Maple was that, far from being ashamed of the shop, he was always very proud of it.

> I have known him for years, and also his father. Often I had conversations with the son when he was looking after customers in the shop, and as a young man he was fond of telling of his political aspirations, at which his father would shake his head somewhat dubiously. When, later on, he got into Parliament, he still talked of the shop when discussing political issues.

Both father and son managed to generate the loyalty and admiration not only of their customers but their staff. Just how much was shown in the 20-verse farewell poem which a cabinet salesman called Thomas Seccombe, who joined Maples in 1863, wrote to his fellow salesmen on his retirement wishing them a prosperous new year 1902. He first recalled John Maple who had just died:

> Our late respected Governor, so famous at that time,
> The one you all knew so well, was only in his prime;
> No better man of business, I am certain ever breathed,
> And in making this assertion I feel sure that I'm believed.

> A kinder hearted Governor would be difficult to find,
> Though somewhat quick of temper, and prone to speak his mind
> To the men who shirked their duty or tried to take their ease,
> Or failed in hours of business their customers to please.

> But speaking as I found him, he was always good to me,
> One of the best I ever knew both generous and free;
> He took the keenest interest both in salesman or a boy,
> No matter what position he held in his employ.

The er—er—Membah for er—er—Dulwich.
Sir Bl-nd-ll M-ple.

Sir Blundell Maple.

Tom Seccombe was also genuinely impressed with the way young Blundell had turned out – in 1863 'full of health and strength from College just arrived.'

> He who now rules this prosperous house words fail me to
> describe;
> Should I attempt to do so, my efforts you'll deride.
> His splendid organising and finance just as grand
> Has made this house the envy of the trade throughout the land.
>
> A master mind was brought to bear when he took up the reins,
> Success attended all he touched, a height that few attains;
> And this I say with confidence, nor fear your contradiction,
> The progress which this firm had made you cannot say is
> fiction.
>
> It's forward gone by leaps and bounds, and staggered other
> houses,
> And well I know from what we hear their jealousy arouses;
> If we may guage the future by our progress in the past,
> I feel sure our reputation is likely now to last.

For at least ten years there had been Maples salesmen not only in London but outside it – but for selling houses not furniture. The company's advertisement for Carved Oak Furniture in the *Illustrated London News* of March 11, 1893 reproduced on page 52 carried the information:

Branch Offices for House Agency:

Cornfield Road, Eastbourne
and
North Street, Brighton

So it was in these South Coast resorts that Maples first planted outposts. The Brighton Branch in North Street is thought to have started selling furniture in 1900; and two years later in Bournemouth a small furniture showroom was opened in Old Christchurch Road with only one window and the entrance up a passage way which sold mostly cretonnes and lace curtains.

On September 30, 1903 Sir Blundell Maple received the highest honour the horse racing fraternity could bestow – membership of the Jockey Club. But he was too ill to attend any of its meetings. The incurable kidney trouble that had put him temporarily out of action ten years earlier had recurred, and on November 24 he died at Childwickbury, his St Albans estate, of what was diagnosed as Brights Disease. He was only 58. 'By his death,' wrote One Who Knew Him in *The Cabinet Maker*, 'the furniture trade has lost one of the most extraordinary personages that it ever possessed.

> Anyone meeting Sir Blundell Maple for the first time would be perhaps most struck by his bluff manner. Behind it however was great heartiness and a very genuine deposition. Looking, as I naturally do, at the man rather as a member of our craft than as a politician or a sportsman, I think one of his most notable characteristics was his intense love and pride in his business. The success of the business was sufficiently great to justify the son of old Mr John Maple in selecting any one of the professions he chose. Nevertheless he determined, in preference to all alluring offers, to take charge of the business in Tottenham Court

Road, and it is due to his intense pride in his work and immense capacity that Maple & Co is what it is to-day.

The name he had left, stated the *Pall Mall Gazette* in an obituary headed "A Prince of Merchants", would be remembered as a synonym of uprightness and fair dealing whether in business or on the Turf which was his hobby. 'He had to depend' commented the *Standard*, 'on the loyal and willing cooperation of a staff which included men of the highest technical attainments as well as simple wage-earners. In his relations with all he set an admirable example of consideration and generosity.'

When he died, the rebuilt University College Hospital which he had financed was nearing completion. At a meeting of the London County Council, of which Sir Blundell had been a member from 1895 to 1901 as the representative of South St Pancras, Lord Monkswell the chairman said Sir Blundell's interest in hospitals was almost unique. For Maples employees, as seen, he had established a Convalescent Home and Almshouse at Harpenden; for the people of St Albans he gave Clarence Park and Recreation Ground.

As the Member of Parliament for Dulwich from 1887 to his death, he created a great stir when in June 1901 he exposed the scandal of the excessive profits made by middlemen purchasing horses ('remounts') for the British Army from dealers in Budapest and Vienna. He suggested that the Remount Department of the War Office used the expertise of his stud man Alec Waugh who claimed he could buy 3,000 Hungarian horses at £30 each. He later brought upon himself the fury of Arthur Balfour the Tory prime minister for his criticism of the Sugar Convention. He had great admiration for Mr Gladstone the Liberal leader whose grandchild, Dorothy Drew, he once looked after when the Grand Old Man took the child's mother, his daughter, with him on a trip abroad for his health.

On the day of his private funeral at Childwickbury attended by his widow and his private secretary Edward Barnes – his daughter Grace, Baroness Eckhardstein, was herself too ill to attend – the cabdrivers tied black ribbons to their whips as they drove slowly down Tottenham Court Road past the store whose Governor had shown such concern for their welfare. A week later memorial services were held in St Albans Cathedral and St Pancras Parish Church. There were wreaths from 'The Factories, Highgate Road', 'Decorating Staff & Studio', 'Cabinet Factory (Mr Evans & staff).'

The newspapers all referred to Sir Blundell correctly as a multi-millionaire. It took some time to settle his estate in accordance with his will of November 1897, but by November 1904 accountants were able to put a figure of £2,403,349 in the left-hand column of the Capital Account. He appointed four friends as trustees and executors, and as guardians of his only surviving child, Grace, to whom they paid an allowance of around £1,500 a month. He left each of his three sisters £10,000: Clara (Mrs James Wharton), Emily (Mrs John Taylor) and Anne (Mrs Jeremiah Colman). His Childwick estate and his house in Regents Park went to his wife, plus a legacy of £10,000. His Harpenden and Newmarket estates were left to the trustees who were instructed to set apart £300,000 on his wife's death as a Settled Fund for Grace's children.

Sale of the late Sir J. B Maple's Horses in Training.

Mr. Somerville Tattersall disposed of the horses in training the property of the late Sir J. B. Maple on Wednesday and Thursday. There was a large company and competition was keen. The best prices were as follows :—

	gs.
Queen's Holiday, 3 yrs., Capt. Forester ...	4600
Newsboy, 3 yrs., Mr. W. T. Robinson ...	3500
Nun Superior, 3 yrs., Mr. G. Faber ...	3100
Simony, 5 yrs., Lord Chas. Montagu ...	2800
Premiere March, 2 yrs., Lord Westbury ...	2200
Nabot, 5 yrs., Hon. F. W. Lambton ...	1990
Divorce Court, 3 yrs., Mr. S. Joel ...	1600
Royal Lass, 2 yrs., Mr. W. Bass ...	1400
Pope, 2 yrs., Mr. C. Perkins ...	1050
The Czar, 2 yrs., Mr. C. Perkins ...	1000
Girton Girl, 4 yrs., Count Lehndorf ...	980
Vidame, 6 yrs., Mr. H. D. Paravicini ...	910
Ireland, 3 yrs., Mr. D. Fraser ...	910
Bowery, 5 yrs., Mr. L. de Rothschild ...	900
Petite Princesse, 2 yrs., Lord Westbury ...	850

The total of the two days' sale was 38,820gs.

Sir Blundell Maple's racehorses were sold for 38,820 guineas after his death in 1903.

Horace Regnart who became Vice-President of Maples on Sir Blundell Maple's death in 1903. His brother Henry Regnart took over as President.

To raise cash to pay the many legacies, the executors sold stocks and shares worth £130,000. They included investments in showmen Barnum & Bailey, Bovril and Elysée Palace Hotel company. In addition his 7,000 Maples £1 Ordinary shares realised £18,000; 20,000 6% Preference shares £29,000; 11,000 4% Debentures £110,000. His horses – blood and racing stock at Childwick and Newmarket – raised £102,000, less the cost of the sale and commission which came to £21,000. It took Somerville Tattersall two days to sell Sir Blundell's 15 horses in training for 38,820 guineas, the highest price being 4,600 guineas for the three-year-old Queens Holiday. The Newmarket properties, Falmouth House, Zetland Lodge and the private training ground were sold for much less than Sir Blundell paid for them.

There was now no Maple to run Maples. One of the four trustees and executors of Sir Blundell's will was General Manager (Clare) Henry Regnart, brother of Horace (Horatio Grece) Regnart, to whom Sir Blundell left £1,000 a year for two years provided he remained a director of Maples. Horace had come to London from Jersey, where he was born in 1841, in 1855. The following year, he was taken on by John Maple at the age of 15 as a shop assistant at no 145. When the building collapsed in 1857, as seen, he was rescued from the debris and, as *Vanity Fair* observed, 'came very near to providing an order for the undertaking department of the establishment'. And then 'by sleepless persistence he forced his way into the management of the company', becoming senior of the six 'Governors'. By 1903 he had been married for 33 years, but he had no children.

It was brother Henry Regnart (the father of five sons) who took over as President of Maple & Co Ltd on Sir Blundell's death. And Horace Regnart was elected Vice-President.

The new president saw the public of 1904, burdened with increased taxes, in no mood to buy luxuries. He steered Maples therefore further in the direction of what he called Domestic Furnishing. Young customers starting housekeeping would recommend Maples to their friends and so extend the company's connections. A large part of the 11,250 square feet of recently added showroom space was devoted to specimen one-bedroom flats (plus a servants bedroom). A young couple could buy *everything* they needed to turn the rooms into a home, from carpets and curtains, towels and sheets to coal buckets and fire tongs, pots and pans, lamps and umbrella stands. They could buy the whole lot on the three year deferred payment system.

Domestic furnishing gave the company liquidity, the ability to turn its capital over five times a year, whereas a large contract could be carried over from one year to another. Contracting business, and Maples' link with Gordon Hotels and Frederick Hotels, were adversely affected first by the death of Sir Blundell and then by that of Frederick Gordon which occurred shortly afterwards. But the new policy was obviously bringing dividends. In 1904 they had £182,000 cash in hand compared with £85,000 the year before; and the Reserve Fund stood at £307,000. The only luxuries which Henry Regnart tolerated were antiques, English and French. In their Antiques Department they had a large collection which they sold at what they considered purely commercial prices, 'in sharp contrast to some of our competitors who deal exclusively in antiques and who are compelled to obtain fancy prices'.

By re-arranging the loading and delivery offices and rebuilding two houses, they gave the store a central avenue consisting of 500 feet of unbroken showrooms and galleries. The directors were convinced that in no city either in Europe or America did there exist such a magnificent display of furniture and fabrics. By the acquisition of a new wing on the north of the site they created another spacious entrance in Euston Road. All this property was freehold and valued at around £2,440,000. They rented stabling on a very long lease. But the large block of factory buildings in Highgate Road were freehold.

The 10,000 6 per cent Maples Preference Shares with which Sir Blundell had endowed the Almshouse and Convalescent Home at Harpenden was yielding a larger income than that required to run the establishment – in spite of the latter being used in the summer by factory girls as a holiday resort. So, with the surplus money the directors granted a number of outdoor pensions to 'old and necessitous persons' who had

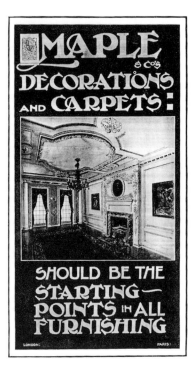

What Maples were offering in 1904 – functional furniture for flats (left), but still the Grand Style when needed (above). Note the new Art-Deco lettering.

been employed by Maples but owing to family ties or infirmity could not become Harpenden inmates.

Maples had had a branch in Paris for nearly 20 years. Up to 1905, both as regards capital and profits, it was treated as a department of Tottenham Court Road. In that year however, so they could apportion its profit and to save time and trouble with the revenue authorities, they established the Paris business on a separate footing. They created 'Maple & Co (Paris)' under the English Joint Stock Companies Act. Only directors of the London company were eligible for seats on its three-man Board. The London company held all its shares.

Customers were flocking to the showrooms they had built on their freehold land formerly occupied by the Eden Theatre. To meet demand for furniture storage in 1905 they built a fire-proof depository next to the showrooms. The original managers, Emil Moussu and Albert Moussu retired, and their places were taken by W G Golds and a Mr Tunstall.

The South of France was the setting the following year of the marriage of Sir Blundell Maple's widow Emily (neé Merryweather) to Montagu Ballard, chairman of The Royal Brewery, Brentford. The wedding, a small private affair, took place in March 1906 in the British Consulate in Nice. Lady Maple was given away by her daughter Grace, Baroness Eckhardstein. Mr and Mrs Montagu Ballard spent their honeymoon in Egypt. Maybe the event did cause a mild flutter in Society as the gossip weeklies reported. By marrying again, Lady Maple forfeited, they said, the £10,000 a year she received from Sir Blundell's estate, along with the use of, and the rental from, the house in Clarence Terrace, Regents Park, and Childwickbury, St Albans. But it did not stop Society buying their furniture from the family business. On the contrary, Henry Regnart was able proudly to claim that in 1906 'we have been honoured with more than our usual share of royal and distinguished patronage'.

> Many illustrious personages including our own Royal Family and several members of the Royal Houses of Europe have visited our establishment and graciously favoured us with orders. Our connection in the East, too, has been increased, and we have executed for Eastern potentates and others orders for some of the finest examples of furniture that our factories could produce.

Lady Maple (neé Emily Merryweather), wife of Sir Blundell Maple, after whose death she married in Nice in 1906 brewer Montague Ballard.

Gratifying though such patronage was to directors and staff, it was humbler folk who constituted the mainstream of custom that kept Maples in business. But in 1906 these middle class customers were seen to be satisfying their requirements 'with more regard to economy than perhaps was the case formerly'. Henry Regnart thought one reason was that the motor-car was diverting money away from ordinary channels of expenditure. Many a gentleman spent £1,000 or £1,500 on a motor-car which became a permanent charge on his income to an appreciably greater extent than horses and carriages ever did.

Merchants and cattlebreeders in the Western hemisphere as well as Eastern potentates looked to Maples of London for their furniture. One of the wreaths at the memorial service to Sir Blundell Maple bore a card inscribed (by a confused London florist?) 'Manager and staff of the Bueonos Aires establishment'. What the company had in Buenos Aires in 1903 how-

Not only royalty patronised Maples in 1906; most of their customers were humbler folk like Miss Gamble of St Helens.

The competition hots up in 1906 with Waring & Gillow opening a grand emporium in London's Oxford Street.

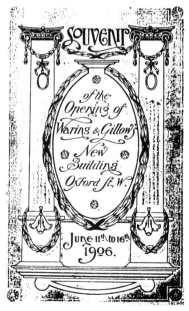

ever hardly merited the designation 'establishment'. Henry Regnart told shareholders in London in February 1907 that Maples had been doing excellent business in the Argentine Republic for 30 years. 'At one time we had an agency at Buenos Aires, but things developed so that we determined to open a branch directed from here.'

In the autumn of 1906 Horace Regnart sailed to Argentina with another director a Mr Stallabrass, to make the arrangements. Vice-President of Maples, he had just become Chairman of the £2 million Frederick Hotels. In 1907 he was knighted. Sir Horace Regnart established 'Maple & Co (South America) Ltd' in 1907 as a separate undertaking on the same lines as the Paris branch, with all the shares owned by the London company. Offices and showrooms were taken at no 326 Artes Street (in July 1909 moving to Carlos Pellegrini Street). An experienced member of Maples staff was sent out from London to act as manager. Furniture made at Tottenham Court Road was packed into crates, driven to London Docks and shipped across the South Atlantic to Buenos Aires.

'Our advent in Buenos Aires with our great reputation for work and goods of the highest excellence and artistic treatment,' said Henry Regnart, 'was bound to meet with ready appreciation, and we may congratulate ourselves that our expectations have been fully realised.'

La Ilustracion Sud-Americana of June 30 1907 carried a photograph of Maples steam traction-engines drawing trailers loaded with crates of furniture destined for Argentina about to depart from the loading bay in Grafton Street. This proved, stated the accompanying article, that in the great industrial cities of Europe, Buenos Aires was considered a worthwhile market calling for the maximum effort. The craftsmanship of the drawing room, dining room and bedroom furniture displayed in their Artes Street showroom was remarkable. The establishment of Maple & Co in their midst constituted a valuable source of cultural and artistic education.

> Maple & Co are famous not only for their great products, and for their financial and commercial strength, but also for the perfection elegance and strength of their furniture. We may judge this from their magnificent selection constantly on view in their Buenos Aires showrooms, where the merchandise is sold at the same price as in London except for the addition of freight and Customs clearance expenses. As is known, Maple & Co also have a branch in Smyrna in the Middle East, which is also a supplier of rich carpets and genuine oriental tapestry so very much appreciated by people of exquisite taste.

Maples largest overseas branch, the writer told his readers, was in Paris, the metropolis of good taste, and it greatly boosted Argentinian pride to see that the great London establishment had chosen to instal a branch comparable with that of Paris in the Argentinian capital.

Trading in faraway Argentina was far from plain sailing. In London and Paris goods were on sale only a few days after they left the workshops. But it took 12 weeks for furniture to find its way from London to South America. It was impossible therefore to turn over stocks as often as in London and Paris. But it was most encouraging to know, said Henry Regnart, that Maples' name was so well known in the South American Republics that the moneyed classes insisted on having Maples furniture and fabrics, and would not be put off with others.

The governing board of The Jockey Club in Florida Street, Buenos Aires, 'the centre of all the fashion and wealth of Argentina', were no exception. It was from Maples in November 1907 that they requested estimates for furnishing their large Empire dining room, other smaller dining rooms, smoking room and music room 'and when the work was completed the effect was sensational.' 'It is evident,' stated *La Ilustracion Sud-Americana*, 'that such splendid work cannot have been achieved by an ordinary decorator but by an artist with a profound knowledge of all the details of the styles of the respective periods.

> Even so, it would not have been sufficient for him to be acquainted with all the arts and sciences unless he had had at his disposal numerous specialised workmen as well as unlimited amounts of very special materials only available to the firm of Maple & Co of London, which was rightly chosen to carry out this beautiful work of art in accordance with the progress of our artistic education and social good taste.

Horace Regnart thanks Ambrose Heal for his congratulations on his knighthood, July 1, 1907.

Steam traction engines with crates of Maples furniture for Argentina leaving the Grafton Street loading bay in 1907.

There was a world of difference between selling beautiful pieces of furniture and that of furnishing, decorating and embellishing a great house with style and elegance. The latter was Fine Art open only to a few, among whom could be numbered the House of Maple, the result of years of study and experience in decorating the most outstanding mansions of the European capitals.

Henry Regnart was highly gratified that their work at The Jockey Club had been so admired by the whole of Argentina's Press, and more importantly by the committee appointed by the club to supervise the alterations. As a result Maples decided to build warehouses and workshops in Buenos Aires where they could manufacture Maples furniture for the Argentine market without having to ship it across the South Atlantic.

Regnart was able to tell shareholders in 1901 that the Buenos Aires business had not experienced the same vicissitudes as London and Paris. Argentina had youth on its side, and trade had not been influenced by the adverse economic conditions prevailing in Europe. To warehouses and workshops erected at a cost of £25,000, they now added other buildings costing £15,000 to house the larger stock they needed to meet the growing demand for Maples furniture. To pay for all this, and for new workshops and sawmills in Paris and enlarged showroom and repository, the directors increased the capital of Maple & Co of London to £2,000,200 consisting of a million Preference shares, a million Ordinary shares and a thousand Management Shares. They boasted 7,500 shareholders. From 1908 the directors once more had a member of the Maple family in their number; in that year, Stanley Wharton, John Maple's grandson and Sir Blundell's nephew, who was already Company Secretary, was elected to the Board. In 1910 Sir Blundell's daughter Gracie, who had just divorced Baron von Eckhardstein, married Sir Archibald Weigall who in 1920 was appointed Governor of South Australia. Till 1931 Sir Archibald and Lady Weigall lived at a house called Petwood in Woodhall Spa, and later they had a house at Englemere near Ascot and a town house in Ennismore Gardens. Grace fell on an icy pavement in 1928 and until her death in 1950 was confined to a wheelchair. Her daughter Priscilla became Lady Curzon and

The Jockey Club in Florida Street, Buenos Aires which was furnished and decorated by Maples (South America) Ltd in 1907.

Maples furniture in the Smoking Room of The Jockey Club, Buenos Aires.

later Mrs Coriat, and was the mother of four girls.

London's swiftest way of communicating with Buenos Aires was by sending 'cables' (overseas telegrams). It needed 20 to settle the matter of the re-engagement as manager (or sub-manager?) of a Mr Savry who had left them at very short notice and great inconvenience. With submarine telegraph cables, technology had introduced near-instant communication in place of the lengthy process of sailing ships, and then steamships, carrying mail across the oceans. And on land the automobile was revolutionising transport. At Tottenham Court Road the horse vans which had given Maples customers a free delivery service for 70 years were being replaced by motor vans capable of covering an area of 8,000 square miles.

No need to deliver to Brighton. In 1909 a Maples shop was opened at 109 Kings Road there.

Outside England the delivery area was the world. On November 18, 1910 the Foreign Section of Maples Shipping Department handled six consignments to Argentina; one to Austria; seven to Belgium; one to Brazil; five to Canada; four to Chile; one to China; two to Denmark; one to the East Indies; seven to Egypt; 18 to France; seven to Germany; one to Greece; eight to Holland; two to Hungary; one to Italy; and four to different parts of India. As one investor put it, 'the name of Maple is a household word wherever civilisation exists.'

Edward VII died in May 1910, and Maples were appointed Upholsterers and Decorators to his successor King George V – they had had his royal warrant as Prince of Wales. Queen Alexandra, the late king's widow, rented warehouse space at Maples Camden Depository at £25 a year.

The Depression lifted, and Maples embarked on a big programme of redecorating, installing new lifts and lighting, opening up even more floors of furniture including an under-

ground 200ft by 40ft showroom created by excavating beneath the street between the two halves of the island site. In 1911 Maples foreign trade was larger than it had ever been, in spite of high freights and tariff barriers.

The effect of the furnishing and decoration of the Empire Dining Room at The Jockey Club, seen here, was 'sensational'.

Progress indeed; but were Maples moving with the times as regards the kind of furniture they were offering?

Writers on Art and manufactures of varying eminence and opinion, said Frederick Litchfield in a history of furniture published in 1907, were unanimous in pointing out the serious drawbacks to progress which would exist so long as there was a demand for cheap and meretricious imitations of old furniture, as opposed to more simply made articles designed in accordance with the purposes for which they were intended.

> There is at the present time an ambition on the part of many well-to-do persons to imitate the effect produced in houses of old families where for generations valuable and memorable articles of decorative furniture have been accumulated.

The manufacture of furniture was chiefly carried out in large factories, so the sub-division of labour caused the article to pass through different hands in successive stages. Instead of furniture being the object of the craftsman's pride, it was the result of the rapid multiplication of some pattern which had caught the popular fancy, in which there was a good deal of decorative effect for a comparatively small price. Litchfield agreed however that the large furnishing firms had a strong case in their contention that the public would go to the market it considered best.

Gordon Russell who moved to the Cotswolds in 1904, deplored the dearth of progressive contemporary design in England and the practice of faking furniture in the styles of the 18th century. Ambrose Heal, another with a single-minded commitment to modern English design, considered himself immune from the whims of fashion, which were indeed ever changing. The style which in Britain was termed 'Quaint' and on the continent New Art, as *The Cabinet Maker* pointed out in 1903, had begun with extravagance which even the most leniently disposed could not tolerate. It was born of a desire to get away from traditional forms, away from Chippendale, Hepplewhite and Sheraton, and strike out on fresh lines. By the opening of the 20th century, however, it had become 'sedate and demure'.

Henry Regnart was well aware of the importance which the general public attached to 'Artistic' design, and what was being said about Maples' attitude to it.

> A genuine appreciation of artistic productions is no longer limited to a relatively small number. The everyday buyer of articles in general use, however trivial, is a keen critic of design. We may, as a firm, reasonably take credit for having been pioneers in this movement, as being among the first to recognise the growth of this artistic spirit, to encourage it in every way and to make adequate provision not for immediate needs alone, but for the future. (1912 AGM)

Maples were equipped to meet the highest requirements in that direction, he said. Maples welcomed the demand for a higher standard of design, as equally they welcomed the most severe comparisons of the qualities and prices of their manufactures. They had nothing to lose but everything to gain by fair and intelligent criticism.

> In architectural and colour decoration, in design, in furniture and the domestic arts, in textiles and metal work, our studios in London, Paris and Buenos Aires are in every respect representative and, we venture to think, more effectively and artistically endowed for the competition of to-day than any other existing organisation in the world.

With copies of the proceedings of the 1912 annual meeting they sent out a tiny booklet measuring five inches by three and a half entitled *A Few Suggestions for Easy Chairs*. It consisted of 14 pages, each with a photograph of an easy chair or settee. Loose covers for the 'Carnforth' Easy Chair at £5 10s in Marie Antoinette Cretonne were extra. The most expensive item in the booklet was the 'Stevenage' settee in Morocco at £23 17s 6d.

The extent to which Maples had kept up with modern trends in furniture design could be guaged from the 300 pages of the 1912 edition of *Illustrations of Furniture* set out under 250 headings. The writer of the introductory remarks was at pains to point out that they were illustrations of *modern* furniture.

> As much from the artistic side as from that of quality and workmanship they mark the advance in domestic furnishing so pronounced a feature of the present day, and to which the House of Maple had contributed such an important impetus . . . The supply of specially designed furniture adapted to the needs and requirements of small abodes is a prominent feature in the

business of Maple & Co, and suites of rooms, decorated, furnished and suitably equipped, are set apart in the galleries, which will enable the visitor to see at a glance how a small house can be furnished comfortably and artistically for a very moderate sum.

On the title page were pictures of the vast Tottenham Court Road island site with both horse-drawn and motor omnibuses outside; of the store in Rue Boudreau, Paris, and that in Calle Suipacha, Buenos Aires. It gave the telephone number '7000 Museum'. There was now, it seemed, a branch too in Monte Video, Uruguay, but no picture and no address. The Smyrna depot was at 17 Local Baron, Aliotti.

In 1912 Maple & Co were still 'the Largest and most Convenient Furnishing Establishment in the World'. The phrase, the reader was informed under General Information, by lapse of time had become a proverb. Visitors from all parts of the globe put Maples on their itinerary as a 'sight' on no account to be missed. The departments, immense in their range, omitted absolutely nothing in the scheme of modern furnishing, from the smallest domestic items to the rarest and most exquisite products of human skill. Those departments included Electric Lighting, Sanitary Engineering, Parquet Flooring, Cold Storage, Warehousing, Renovations, Removals, Estate Agency.

Maples had been honoured with the commands of King George V and Queen Mary, Queen Alexandra, the Czar of Russia, the German Empress, the Empress Eugenie of France, the King of Bulgaria, the Duke of Orleans, the Sultan of Zanzibar, the late King of Siam, and the royal families of Austria, Italy, Denmark, Belgium, Spain, Portugal, the Netherlands, Norway and Sweden. 'Notable orders have been executed for the nobility of all countries and for many embassies, clubs, officers' messes.' Maples were prepared and ever pleased on the shortest notice to confer with intending customers at the house it was proposed to furnish or decorate, either wholly or in part. Only expert representatives were sent, and all estimates were prepared and submitted entirely free. From the first Maples had made it a rule to sell for small profit and for net cash.

The 40-bedroom suites in white enamel, hazelwood, fumed oak and inlaid mahogany; the 24 designs of washstand and basin; the 44 bentwood, rush-seated fumed oak chairs; the 'thousand different designs' of upholstered easy chair in tapestry, cretonne and damask – all in 'traditional' design – were obviously to the taste of most of their domestic furnishing customers. There will have been a steady sale of the 'Sheraton' and 'Chippendale' clocks illustrated in the catalogue, and for the 7½ ft high Long Clock (grandfather clock) which cost £16 10s with a gong and 31 guineas with chimes; for the reproduction of Lord Nelson's 40-piece Tea Service at £1 5s and 67-piece Dinner Service at £3 5s; for the 'reproductions of handsome old Brocades with rich silken effects copied from Fontainebleau and other old palaces.'

Detail from the title page of the 1912 edition of Illustrations of Furniture *showing the Maples which had opened in Calle Suipacha, Buenos Aires.*

Plain and embroidered fabrics have during the last few years again come to the front. To those of refined and cultured taste materials of this character are so eminently adapted that Maple & Co have given eminent prominence.

TELEPHONE: 7000 MUSEUM
TELEGRAMS: MAPLE LONDON

GENERAL INFORMATION

"*MAPLE & CO—the Largest and most Convenient Furnishing Establishment in the World.*" The phrase, by lapse of time, has become a proverb. Visitors from all parts of the globe put MAPLE'S in their itinerary as a "sight" on no account to be missed. The departments, immense in their range, omit absolutely nothing in the scheme of modern Furnishing, from the smallest domestic items to the rarest and most exquisite products of human skill

Although assured that the present catalogue will fully prove its value, MAPLE & CO emphasize the importance of customers personally viewing the immense stocks, whenever possible, and taking advantage of the infinite choice awaiting them in all departments

Some of the more important departments are :—

FURNITURE	CURTAINS	ANTIQUES	CHIMNEY-PIECES	TIMBER YARDS	PIANOS
BEDSTEADS	BLINDS	DECORATIONS	INTERIOR WOODWORK	CLOCKS AND BRONZES	REMOVALS
BEDDING	CHINTZES	SANITARY ENGINEERING	PARQUET FLOORING	CHINA AND GLASS	WAREHOUSING
CARPETS	LINENS	ELECTRIC LIGHTING	SPECIMEN ROOMS	CUTLERY	COLD STORAGE
			ESTATE AGENCY	IRONMONGERY	RENOVATIONS

MAPLE & CO have been honoured with the commands of

HIS MAJESTY THE KING	H.I M EMPRESS EUGÉNIE	THE ROYAL FAMILY OF THE NETHERLANDS
HER MAJESTY THE QUEEN	THE ROYAL FAMILY OF AUSTRIA	THE ROYAL FAMILY OF NORWAY
H.M. QUEEN ALEXANDRA	THE ROYAL FAMILY OF ITALY	THE ROYAL FAMILY OF SWEDEN
H.I.M. THE CZAR OF RUSSIA	THE ROYAL FAMILY OF DENMARK	H.M. THE LATE KING OF SIAM
HER LATE MAJESTY QUEEN VICTORIA	THE ROYAL FAMILY OF THE BELGIANS	H.M. THE KING OF BULGARIA
HIS LATE MAJESTY KING EDWARD VII.	THE ROYAL FAMILY OF SPAIN	H.R.H. THE DUKE OF ORLEANS
H.I.M. THE GERMAN EMPRESS	THE ROYAL FAMILY OF PORTUGAL	H.H. THE SULTAN OF ZANZIBAR

Notable orders have been executed for the nobility of all countries and for many Embassies, clubs, and officers' messes

Mail Orders Provincial, Colonial, and Foreign orders—a large and ever-growing branch of MAPLE'S business—receive attention at the hands of a specially trained staff. The requirements and convenience of every customer by mail are studied with the same care as is given to personal orders, small orders equally with large

Delivery Goods are delivered free by MAPLE & CO'S own vans within a radius of fifty miles from the London Show-rooms and special distances on particular routes, and customers can utilize these vans to send up goods requiring renovation, of which advice must be sent in advance. Carriage is paid on all orders of £2 and upwards for furniture, earthenware, china, glass, ironmongery, and garden furniture to any railway station or port in Great Britain, or to any port in Ireland with direct steamship communication. Carriage is paid on *all* orders for carpets, curtains, lace curtains and linens to any railway station or port in the United Kingdom. The right of selection of route is reserved. Goods are packed free of cost, no charge being made for packing materials if they are returned in good condition.

Estimates MAPLE'S are prepared and ever pleased, on the shortest notice, to confer with intending customers at the house it is proposed to furnish or decorate, either wholly or in part. Expert representatives alone are sent, and all estimates are prepared and submitted entirely free of cost

Terms From the first MAPLE & CO have made it a rule to sell for small profit and for net cash. Their many years' experience and their command of capital have combined to secure them such a position in the world's markets as to enable them to give customers the utmost advantage. Thus it is that, while MAPLE'S stocks are largest, selection choicest, and variety greatest, their prices are beyond all compare the lowest. Special terms of payment can be arranged if desired

In first transactions by post or otherwise within the United Kingdom, a remittance should be sent or reference given to a banker or well-known London firm. In the case of orders from abroad, it is usual for a remittance to accompany the order

¶ Names and addresses should be distinctly written, and all correspondence relating to orders should specify particulars and the name and address of the customer to whom the goods are charged. As an aid to ready reference and quick despatch, the letter number should always be quoted

MAPLE & CO LTD, TOTTENHAM COURT ROAD, LONDON   PARIS . BUENOS AIRES . MONTE VIDEO

Maples in 1912 – still proverbially the largest and most convenient furnishing establishment in the world.

Fabrics for curtains included 'Plushettes', Jute, Tapestries, Art Serges, Silk Damasks, Reversible Silk Chenilles (of British manufacture), Brocades, Lampas Silks, Genoa Velvets, Moquettes, Utrecht and Frieze Velvets. Cretonnes with The Famous Indian and Bird Designs could once more be supplied, 'the blocks having been re-engraved at great cost'. They could only be obtained from Maples. In grey there were Ground and Black-Ground Cretonnes, Moire Ground Cretonnes and Plain Jaspe material (with the admired steel effect). English and Continental lace curtains came three yards long and 50 inches wide in ivory. There were Madras muslin 'Brise-Bise' materials for blinds. All-Bead Blinds (English) could be obtained from the Oriental Department, which also stocked Natural Colour Shantung and Tussore Silk, which Maples imported direct, and Best Quality Japanese Silk sofa, carriage or motor wraps. There were embroidered Kashmire rugs at 13s 9d (69p), and Canton Satin Embroidered Tables Covers at 39s 6d (£1.97).

Pure Ventilated Down Quilts in Old-Fashioned Turkey Red Chintz could be had from stock at 6s 6d (32p); any size of Printed Satin Down Quilt could be made to order in a few days. Of the eight classes of blankets the cheapest were 'stout, useful Witney blankets from strong but not fine yarn, suitable for secondary or servants beds or schools or public institutions'.

The assumption was that most Maples customers had servants. There was a whole section in the catalogue for 'Servants Bedroom Furniture'. A Servants Bedroom Set consisted of dressing chest and mirror, washstand, towel horse, cane seat chair and toilet ware (jug, basin and soap dish). It cost £2 2s 9d (£2.14) if 'grained as oak', and £4 18s 6d (£4 92) 'enamelled white'. For the nursery where Nanny and the children spent so much of their time there was the high chair, white painted chest-of-drawers, dwarf wardrobe, toy cupboard and medicine cupboard.

Servants' blankets, Class A, cost 5s 6d a pair, and measured 50 inches by 70 inches. Class H 'Elysium' was made from the finest and softest fleecy wool 'especially adapted to meet the requirements of invalids and others who could not bear a heavy cumbrous covering but need considerable warmth.' 'Nicely bound at each end with satin ribbon' the 78 by 96 inches size cost £2 18s 6d (£2.92) and the 104 by 120 size £4 18s 6d.

There were spoons and forks for every occasion: table spoons, soup spoons, table forks, dessert spoons and forks, tea spoons, egg spoons, mustard spoons, salt spoons, gravy spoons, as well as soup ladles, sauce ladles, sugar tongs and butterknives. It was the sign of the patrician to know which was the right spoon to use for what. However there could be no mistaking the other electro-plated table furniture to be bought from Maples: the glass jam jar, sugar bowl, sweet dish, cake basket, jam stand, biscuit box, butter dish, crumb scoop, cruet, pickle stand, salad bowl, salt cellar, pepper castor, toast rack, egg steamer, entree dish, sauce boat, souptureen, sugar basin, sardine dish, coffee pot, muffin dish or cream jug. A 'Bijou' canteen of cutlery suitable for bungalows, seaside cottages, shooting boxes etc could be had for only £3 18s 6d (£3.92).

A set of some 100 items of ironmongery, turnery, brushes and kitchen utensils were offered at £11 6s 9d (£11.34). There were sponge baths, hip baths and sitz baths – reclining baths. A 'Useful Equal-Ended Bath in Japanned Oak' was available for 13s 6d (67p). Madam could choose from a variety of Sets for Early Morning Cup of Tea, 'some on metal trays with indentations to keep the cups and other pieces from slipping while being carried out'. For her cook she could buy French Fireproof Porcelain 'used by French chefs, cleaner and better for all culinary purposes than copper, enamelled iron or tin, and more presentable than the common whiteware ordinarily substituted for copper'.

Her husband had a choice of 24 Sets of Table Glass consisting of 12 portwine, sherry, claret, champagne, finger and liqueur glasses, tumblers, soda tumblers, water jugs, quart decanters and claret decanters. The Arlington Service at £8 and the others could be found in the newly arranged Galleries for Glass on the first floor 'most attractive in point of magnitude and elegance'. There were Celery Glasses, Spirit Bottles, Ice Pails, Water Bottles and Glasses for bedroom use. Specialities suitable for complimentary wedding and birthday presents included hock glasses, espergnes for the centre of table, glass sets for dressing tables, ice plates and custard glasses, flower vases and punch bowls.

Made-to-measure bed draperies were the vogue in 1912 – but you had to take a lot of trouble over the measurements. Loops and tassels were extra.

There was a good selection of Electric, Gas and Oil Light Fittings and Floor Lamps – 'country house installations a speciality'. The services which Maples offered apart from selling furniture and furnishings from Tottenham Court Road were as various as ever. A principal one was Warehousing and Removals 'by trained and skilled workmen accustomed to handling valuable and fragile articles'. They had 'special facilities for continental removals and for packing and removal of costly works of art, collections of curiosities, valuable libraries'. The Furniture Depository in Camden Street was planned and constructed for the safe and careful storage of all kinds of household furniture, personal property and other effects. It was lit by electricity and maintained at a mild and even temperature. They gave special attention to bedding and furniture liable to damage from damp or dust. Plate and other valuables were stored in specially constructed rooms (still to be seen in the basement of the building now occupied by theatrical costumiers Berman & Nathan). Pictures, musical instruments and works of art were specially provided for. A commodious fireproof adjunct to the depository was Cold Air Storage for the summer care of furs and costly fabrics, carpets, rugs, mounted animal heads, woollens, curtains, velvets and tapestries 'ensuring immunity from the destructive ravages of moth and other deteriorating influences'.

Knife cleaners, linen presses, filters and 'Seltogenes' for the kitchens of a past age.

But most people knew of Maples through its emporium in Tottenham Court Road. In its annual review of furniture shop

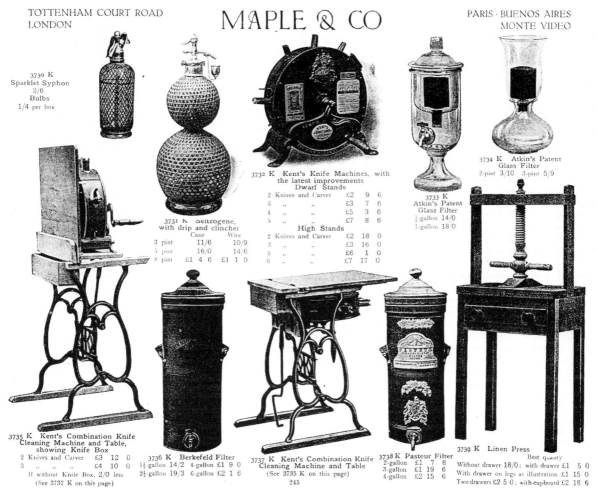

TOTTENHAM COURT ROAD LONDON

MAPLE & CO

PARIS · BUENOS AIRES MONTE VIDEO

3730 K Sparklet Syphon 2/6 Bulbs 1/4 per box

3731 K Seltzogene, with drip and clincher

	Cane	Wire
3 pint	11/6	10/9
5 pint	16/0	14/6
8 pint	£1 4 6	£1 1 0

3732 K Kent's Knife Machines, with the latest improvements

Dwarf Stands

2 Knives and Carver	£2	9	6
3 ,, ,,	£3	7	6
4 ,, ,,	£5	3	6
5 ,, ,,	£7	8	6

High Stands

2 Knives and Carver	£2	18	0
3 ,, ,,	£3	16	0
5 ,, ,,	£6	1	0
6 ,, ,,	£7	17	0

3733 K Atkin's Patent Glass Filter ½-gallon 14/0 1-gallon 18/0

3734 K Atkin's Patent Glass Filter 2-pint 3/10 3-pint 5/9

3735 K Kent's Combination Knife Cleaning Machine and Table, showing Knife Box

2 Knives and Carver	£3	12	0
3 ,, ,, ,,	£4	10	0

If without Knife Box, 2/0 less (See 3737 K on this page)

3736 K Berkefeld Filter 1½-gallon 14/2 4-gallon £1 9 0 2½-gallon 19/3 6-gallon £2 1 6

3737 K Kent's Combination Knife Cleaning Machine and Table (See 3735 K on this page)

245

3738 K Pasteur Filter 2-gallon £1 7 8 3-gallon £1 19 6 4-gallon £2 15 6

3739 K Linen Press

Best quality Without drawer 18/0; with drawer £1 5 0 With drawer on legs as illustration £1 15 0 Two drawers £2 5 0; with cupboard £2 18 6

TOTTENHAM COURT ROAD
LONDON

MAPLE & CO

PARIS · BUENOS AIRES
MONTE VIDEO

REMOVALS AND WAREHOUSING

REMOVAL DEPARTMENT

ALL removals are carried out by trained and skilled workmen accustomed to handling valuable and fragile articles, and every care is exercised both in packing and removal. The vans are of the most modern type and fully equipped, ample materials being always provided to ensure proper protection for the goods. The removal can thus be carried out quickly, safely and economically

MAPLE & CO have SPECIAL FACILITIES for CONTINENTAL REMOVALS, also for the packing and removal of costly works of art, collections of curiosities, valuable libraries, and other articles requiring exceptional care and attention

WAREHOUSING

MAPLE & CO'S Furniture Depository is open daily from 9 a.m. to 5 p.m. for inspection by intending depositors

The Depository, which has been specially planned and constructed for the safe and careful storage of all kinds of household furniture, personal property and other effects, is in close proximity to the leading London Railway Termini, is fitted with all the latest improvements, lighted by electricity, and maintained throughout at a mild and even temperature, to the avoidance of damp or other influences prejudicial to the condition of the goods

Special attention is paid to bedding and furniture liable to damage from damp or dust, while plate and other valuables are stored in specially constructed rooms. Pictures, musical instruments and works of art are also specially provided for

STRONG ROOMS AND SAFES can be rented on terms which can be had on application

The COLLECTION AND SAFE STORAGE OF VALUABLE WEDDING PRESENTS is also an important branch

COLD STORAGE FOR FURS AND FABRICS

MAPLE & CO invite the attention of their customers to the commodious fire-proof adjunct to their Depository at Camden Town, N.W.

Unrivalled facilities are now afforded in the new Cold Air Storage for the summer care of furs and costly fabrics, carpets, rugs, mounted animals' heads, household woollens, upholstered furniture, curtains, laces, velvets, and tapestries, thus ensuring immunity from the destructive ravages of moth or other deteriorating influences

Maples Depository in Camden Street, Camden.

windows, *The Cabinet Maker* reported that the displays made by Shoolbreds and Maples attracted great numbers of the public at Christmas 1912. Their window dressers however, in the opinion of the writer, did not attempt any very striking or original display, 'preferring, perhaps with good judgement from the business point of view, more conventional treatments'.

Conventional English furniture was certainly what Argentinians expected to find in the windows of the Maples in Suipacha Street, Buenos Aires. As Baron Clemens von Schey-Koromla, a lifelong observer of the Buenos Aires scene, has shown, it was a time when the Spanish colonial way of life was giving way to a more cosmopolitan style.

Maple & Co arrived in Buenos Aires at exactly the right moment to provide for the accompanying changes in architecture – the French *petite hotel* with high Mansard roofs in the city, the mock

'Conventional English furniture' of Before The War Mk 1.

Tudor villa in the suburbs. Matching furniture became a must: the long extendable dining-room table with twelve chairs and two matching sideboards for instance. *Arcones*, huge wooden chests, were replaced in bedrooms by wardrobes with mirrors and chests of drawers. As the English habit of writing letters spread into Argentine society, desks of all the well-known British designers were introduced (letter to author December 1990).

In 1912 Buenos Aires society were able to shop around for such furniture, with the establishment in that year of Harrods (South America) Ltd, wholly owned by Harrods Stores Ltd of London, who built an almost exact replica of the famous Knightsbridge store in the Argentine capital. They not only sold furniture but undertook building and decorating.

The man who had set up Maples (South America), Sir Horace Regnart, the company's Vice-President and chairman of Frederick Hotels, died in 1912, aged 72. The *Titanic* floating hotel sank on its maiden voyage, suffragettes were protesting,

Long extendable dining room table.

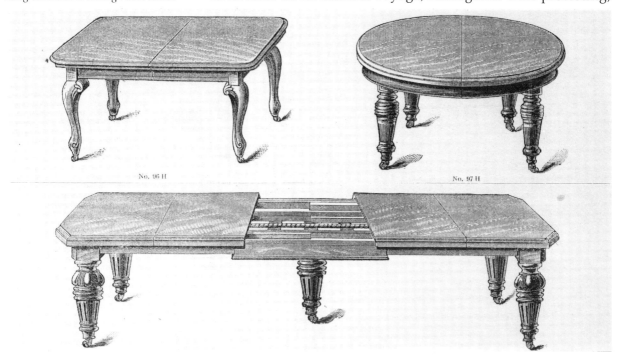

Every hotel has its writing room.

dockers were rioting, there was mob law in the East End of London, but trade was booming and furniture sales were higher than ever. There was war in the Balkans, and speculation of the likelihood that the fighting among the Russians and Bulgarians, Serbs, Turks and Greeks would affect anyone else. More worrying was the mounting size of the German Fleet and the martial posturing of Kaiser Wilhelm.

When the blow fell in August 1914, it seemed to Henry Regnart that the whole civilised world fell into some kind of stupor. The last thing anyone wanted to do was to buy furniture. With the outbreak of World War 1, although the gloom gradually lifted, Maples' series of annual profit rises ceased. A greater fall in turnover was prevented by the company receiving contracts from the Admiralty, War Office and the governments of the Allies who were with Britain in their fight against Germany, Turkey and Austria-Hungary.

> It appears to me (*Regnart told shareholders on February 25, 1915*) that under war conditions furniture and its accessories come to be looked upon as a kind of luxury. Even many of the matrimonial arrangements, I fear, have been either postponed or hurried thorugh without that due deliberation, marked and attended by the furnishing of the home, which is usual on these very important occasions.

But they must not be depressed. Maples was going forward with unabated confidence. Their customers were old and tried friends who would not abandon the company in its hour of trial. It had been a waste of time and energy to try to do anything with the business in Paris. The only department which was in any way flourishing was the Repository which

they had always considered of third-rate importance as a paying proposition. They had done a roaring business. The buildings were full to the roof with rent-paying furniture. It was therefore futile to push the ordinary business. No-one wanted more goods when they were rushing about Paris looking for places to store what they already had. Business in Buenos Aires too was no better than in London, if as good. Instead of completing the new workshops and warehouses, they were delaying the work as long as possible.

> The commercial interests of all countries are now so interlaced and bound up one with another that the war appears to have affected all alike, both in the Eastern and Western Hemispheres.

The army and navy contracts involved employing the mattress makers, stuffers, upholsterers and others stitching and assembling canvas, webbing, tents, groundsheets and the rest. In 1915 a team went down to Southampton to fix curtains, carpets and wall coverings in the Duke of Westminster's yacht which he was sending to Dunkirk as an officers' hospital ship. John

The lifestyle in tune with the grandeur of the Grand Salle of the Grand Hotel in Trafalgar Square, furnished and decorated by Maples, faded out in the wake of the slaughter on the Western Front in the so-called Great War. For most of Maples customers life in Britain was never to be quite the same as Before The War.

McGill, Maples' man in Hamburg, was still doing jobs in neutral Stockholm in 1915. On the ship taking him back to Newcastle from Bergen he heard on the radio that the Germans intended to blow up all enemy ships of any kind on sight. But John made it, and lived to spend the years 1919 to 1938 working for Maples in India.

Keep The Home Fires Burning sang Ivor Novello, and none were more anxious to do just that than Maples. Their customers may have been cowed by the sight of Zeppelins over London and the shrapnel in the streets, let alone the news from the Front. But, as they told themselves, life must go on. In spite of the President of Maples' fears, many did *not* postpone their matrimonial arrangements and, like Pam Haydon's parents, took due deliberation on furnishing their matrimonial home.

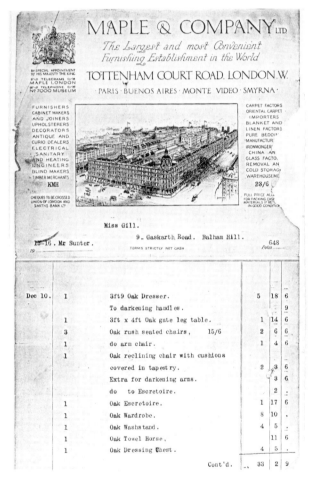

'By Special Appointment to His Majesty the King' (George V), in 1916 Maples could still describe themselves as Furnishers, Cabinet Makers and Joiners, Upholsterers, Decorators, Antique and Curio Dealers, Electrical, Sanitary and Heating Engineers, Blind Makers, Timber Merchants, Carpet Factors, Oriental Carpet Importers, Blanket and Linen Factors, Pure Bedding Manufacturers, Ironmongers, China and Glass Factors, Removal and Cold Storage Warehousemen.

To make no 9 Gaskarth Road, Balham Hill ready to move into after their wedding in 1916, Miss Gill and her fiancé went to Maples. Mr Sunter drew up an inventory of furniture, all in oak, carpets, curtains, kitchen utensils, fire tongs and the rest, and the bill came to £96.

In 1916 the establishment which John Maple had founded in 1841 had been trading for three-quarters of a century. The middle of the Great War, in which the Battle of the Somme had just accounted for 1,250,000 German and Allied casualties, was no time for public celebration. But for directors, managers, staff, shareholders and customers, the growth of the enterprise over those 75 years cannot have been other than a matter of the greatest satisfaction.

THE SECOND 25 YEARS

୨୦ 5 ୨୦

The Art of Comfortable Living at Home and at Sea 1916–1941

LONDONERS knew that the beginning of the end of World War 1 has come when in August 1918 they read in the *Evening News* of the Allied attack by a mass of 'tanks' on the Somme salient and on September 29 how the British 4th Army had broken through the Hindenburg Line. On November 11 they were out in the streets, up Whitehall and down the Strand, thronging Oxford Street and Tottenham Court Road to celebrate Armistice Day, dancing on the pavements, on the buses, on the lorries, singing, shouting and waving flags. As Big Ben struck, recalled Winston Churchill, the strict, war-straightened, regulated streets of London became a triumphant pandemonium.

A curtain came down on what people began to refer to nostalgically as Before The War. Maples had been a cherished part of that world, but because of its deep rooted place in the shopping routines – and indeed affections – of its regular patrons, it carried over into the new world of the Twenties. Maples' upholsterers returned to sewing blankets instead of canvas, and the store resumed its position as One of the Sights of London, as The Largest Furnishing Establishment in the World. It was still the choice of the Upper Crust whose conservative tastes were unaffected by the upheaval, who still knew what they liked and where to get it. At the beginning of the Twenties, as Andrew Barrow pointed out in *Gossip 1920-1970*, 'high society showed few superficial signs of the ravages of the ghastly war through which it had recently passed. Mayfair was still full of great town mansions occupied by the family who had built them and run by staffs of 30 or 40 servants'. These had been the mainstay of Maples' trade up to 1914 and continued to be when life returned to normal after all that emotion on Armistice Day. It was only a matter of reminding them that Maples were, and had been for 80 years, 'leaders and pioneers in artistic furnishing and decorating', and that their name had become 'the hall-mark of good furnishing in every quarter of the globe ... pre-eminent in the highest expression of artistic elegance and unequalled for quality, workmanship, design and value'.

There was no reason to break with the successful marketing strategy of giving their customers what they wanted.

> It is now universally acknowledged that the eighteenth century in the area of domestic technic design, comes first for beauty, for style, and for the application of both to the purpose of use and comfort. It will be no surprise therefore to find that the larger number of our best models bear the artistic imprint of the well-known masters of that epoch – Chippendale, Sheraton, Heppelwhite, Shearer and others.

It was Maples commending in a brochure their range of *Chairs, Sofas & Settees* which visitors would see on display at Tottenham Court Road. A complete history of the Seat or Chair would afford a fairly reliable record of development towards 'that "art of comfortable living" which is the last and best contribution of material civilisation in our age'. To demonstrate what they were talking about, there were the recreations of various parts of a house in the styles of different periods – what the Italians called *scenografia* . There was the Charles II Entrance Hall 'entirely carried out by Maple & Co's own factories', with 'Grinling Gibbons' carved fruit and flower

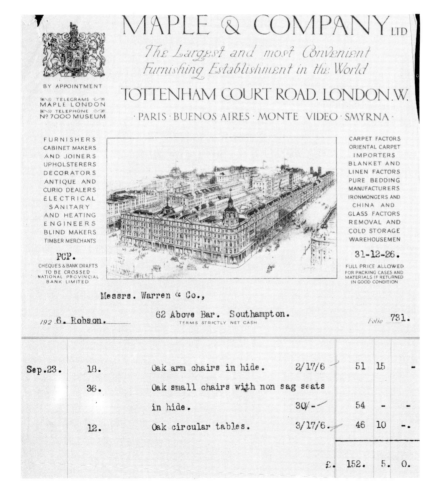

Chairs with non sag seats for 30s each in 1926. Same letterhead as 1916.

drops in Lime Tree. The proportion of the design and high quality of the workmanship, it was pointed out, was quite comparable with the examples of the 17th-century craftsmen. There was the 18th-century bedroom with furniture of Italian walnut with slight inlay of black and pear tree which had the soft flat curves of the William and Mary period. There was a Staircase and Hall in the Louis XVI style with 'an air of rich refinement and good breeding eminently suitable for a Town Mansion'. The effect of period lighting was sustained by 'walls in stone stucco relieved by solid bronze electric torches'.

There was an Adam style drawing room, and an English style dining room 'dignified and refined, which grew out of the Renaiscence contemporaneously with the growth of the comfortable house'. 'The "home" as an English ideal,' visitors were told, 'has now become a household word the world over.'

The bedroom in Deco Chinoiserie style had cream-and-gold lacquer furniture, Chinese wallpaper and window draperies, with blue ground matched from an old blue plate of the Kang Hi dynasty. The 'Art Deco' style introduced around 1910 was still in vogue until about 1925 but had passed its best. With its strong colours in contrast with the earlier and by now out-moded Art Nouveau, it made great use of glass, particularly mirror glass, combined with lacquer, ivory, shagreen, tor-toiseshell and mother-of-pearl.

'Bohemian' and exotic, its perpetrators were no exponents of the art of comfortable living. Maples realised that many wished to be 'modern' but comfortable. In *Chairs, Sofas and Settees* they declared

> The present day, which may with some justice claim to show a real renascence of taste and logic in design, contributes the single development of a new element – the stuffed or entirely covered furniture.

Confident that their workshops could rely on steady orders for furniture with the artistic imprint of the 18th-century masters, they had always been aware too of the demand for whatever was considered 'modern', the meaning of which changed with each generation. In their Twenties brochure *Modern Furniture for Modern Homes* the theme was

TASTE WITH ECONOMY

In it they showed how a house when furnished by Maples could be made artistic and comfortable at an extremely moder-ate cost. It contained a schedule of suggested suitable furniture for 'a compact modern house costing from £650 to £1,000 freehold' (given in full in Appendix 3, pages 170, 171 and 172):

A COMPLETELY FURNISHED HOUSE
for £145
A Home can be completely furnished at Maples with carpets, furniture, curtains and fittings, upholstery and bedding for £145; and every necessity such as blankets, bed and table linen, household linen, china and glass, cutlery and plate, kitchen ironmongery and turnery, clocks, ornaments, light fittings, also a two-valve Wireless Set supplied for an extra £50.

They must have had a very special wireless set in mind. The highest priced set illustrated in the catalogue was the Three-

TASTE WITH ECONOMY

THIS book is compiled with the object of illustrating how a house when furnished by MAPLE can be made artistic and comfortable at an extremely moderate cost, herein is suggested suitable furniture for the compact modern house, costing from £650 to £1,000 Freehold.

A COMPLETELY FURNISHED HOUSE

for £145

A HOME can be completely furnished at MAPLES with carpets, furniture, curtains and fittings, upholstery and bedding for £145; and every necessity such as blankets, bed and table linen, household linen, china and glass, cutlery and plate, kitchen ironmongery and turnery, clocks, ornaments, light fittings, also a two-valve Wireless Set supplied for an extra £50. On Pages 3 and 4 will be found a detailed list showing how the money can be expended.

MAPLE & Co invite those who desire to furnish a larger house to write for their General Catalogues, wherein will be found models taken from their very extensive and varied stock, and they emphasize the fact that every purchase has the MAPLE guarantee of satisfaction.

CARRIAGE is paid on all orders for carpets, curtains and linens, and orders for £2 and upwards for furniture, earthenware, etc., to any Railway Station or Port in the United Kingdom.

A CORDIAL invitation is given to visit the showrooms and inspect the quality of the furniture; it will be found that the exhibition of Furnished Homes will be of the greatest help and interest to all those about to furnish.

IF a personal visit is not possible, please write to the Mail Order Department stating your requirements, which will be carefully studied, and by return of post catalogues, patterns and all particulars sent enabling you to make pleasing selections.

MAPLE'S DEFERRED PAYMENTS

CUSTOMERS who do not wish to disturb their investments may avail themselves of these facilities, the terms of which are the best obtainable.

ALL furniture can be selected at the marked cash prices, and after payment of a deposit of 10 per cent., the balance, according to the total involved, may be spread over a period of one, two or three years. Interest at $2\frac{1}{2}$ per cent. per annum only is added for the desired accommodation. Full particulars will be gladly sent on request.

Valve Radio Gramophone, AC Mains Model 70 (Band-Pass) including valves and royalties at £23 2s. There was a "Beethoven" 3-valve set in a walnut cabinet at £14 14s; a His Masters Voice "Bijou" cabinet gramophone with an exponential tone chamber (?) at £7 15s; and a Marconiphone two-valve radio set at £4 19s 6d.

Another catalogue of the period *Inexpensive Furniture for Modern Homes* showed a Pye QAC 3 3-wave band 5-valve radio set with 'electric eye' tuning, in a light or dark walnut cabinet at 13½ guineas (£13.65), a Marconi battery set for eight guineas (£8.40), and a HMV AC/DC All-World Radio Gramophone in figured walnut at 25 guineas – 33 guineas with an automatic record changer.

Customers who could afford a fashionable radio gramophone on which they could listen either to Henry Hall on the BBC or Harry Roy on record, would have their own Austins or Rovers, and for them Maples now provided a Private Car Park off George Street. If they had driven up from Wimbledon or Putney to spend the day walking the floors at Tottenham Court Road they were able to rest tired feet for a sit-down lunch in an Up-to-date Restaurant on the third floor.

Inspecting the 128 designs of straight-back wooden chairs filling 16 pages of the Chairs and Sofas catalogue, and the 64 varieties of those with upholstered seats, to say nothing of the 137 entirely upholstered easy chairs and settees, would take at least a couple of hours to inspect. Father would covet a Gentleman's Deep Seated Easy Chair with a drawer for pipe and tobacco; Mother would browse among the bedroom furniture pondering the differences between finely figured mahogany, solid mahogany and mahogany inlaid, undecided about the lure of grey wood or white enamel, wondering whether the Magnificent Suites on 18th-century lines, but possessing all the essentials of present day requirements, would suit The Cedars in St Johns Wood; short-skirted thoroughly modern Millie would linger beside the solid oak cocktail cabinet covered with dark hide leather complete with decanters, tumblers, Y-shaped "Saywen" coloured cocktail glasses, ice bowl, shaker, salver and bitters bottle, all for £47 10s. The eye of their musical son would have been caught by the pine organ in the Music Department on which a grave man was playing Handel, and the magnificent grand piano of famous artist Sir Laurence Alma-Tadema which he had designed for his own use in the Byzantine style. Inside the lid was a parchment on which visitors to his house by the Regents Canal had signed their names. They included Tchaikovsky, Padereweski, Saint-Saens and singer Clara Schumann. When Alma-Tadema died in 1913, his effects were auctioned by Christies but the piano failed to find a buyer. Shortly after the end of the war however Henry Regnart bought it for £441 and put it on show at Tottenham Court Road. 'The piano,' writes Jeremy Cooper in *Victorian and Edwardian Furniture and Interiors* (1987), 'which King Solomon could not possibly have refused from the Queen of Sheba, remained on prestigious display in Maples showrooms until they, and it, were destroyed by a bomb in World War 2.'

Reassured by reading that they could have what they wanted at the marked prices, as they could Before The War, could put down ten per cent of the total as deposit and pay the rest up to three years at 2½ per cent interest, a family was hopefully persuaded that Maples Cash Prices combined with their liberal terms made

FURNISHING OUT OF INCOME
a most attractive proposition

Almost all they saw at Tottenham Court Road was either manufactured in one of the workshops on the same island site, in the Highgate factory, or by an outside manufacturer to Maples specification. Apart from the display areas, the 40 acres of the Tottenham Court Road complex included, as it had done before 1914, factories and workshops, stables and garages and, most importantly, their great timber yards which in the *Chairs, Sofas and Settees* catalogue they described as 'the most extensive in London'.

> Several million cubic feet of timber lie stored therein, seasoning slowly and surely in the oldest and best of fashions – the open air. Only when the wood is fully mature is it withdrawn for the purpose of manufacture. The hair for the stuffing, the springs, the coverings – in fine, the entire assemblage of materials is selected with the most careful attention to quality and condition.

The task of manufacture was carried out by craftsmen skilled in each particular branch under the most careful supervision 'in extensive workshops equipped with the latest appliances for economic and artistic production'.

One of the largest spaces at Tottenham Court Road was taken up by the Curtain Factory with its four enormous cutting tables at which women sat sewing net curtains, working at heavy cloth hangings, and making loose covers, seamstresses estimators, machinists, managers – more than a hundred in all. It had a high ceiling from which huge stage front-drop curtains would be suspended for days – Maples had always done a great deal of theatre work. Almost as much room was taken up by the Carpet Factory with its Chinese Room, Oriental Room for Persian carpets and the Turkey carpets imported from the Maples agent in Smyrna, and its English Carpets Room.

And of course furniture and furnishing was not only being manufactured on the Tottenham Court Road site but designed there. Maples' reputation attracted top designers of the calibre of Thomas Edward Collcutt (1840-1924), the architect of London's Palace Theatre in Cambridge Circus (still standing) built for Richard D'Oyly Carte in 1891, who designed furniture not only for Maples but Jackson & Graham, Collinson & Lock and Gillows.

Craftsmen and designers would have worked in vain however without people to sell what they created.

Maples spent as much time, trouble and money over finding suitable people to sell their merchandise and their services, and to train them to their own high standards, in the 1920s and 1930s, as they had ever done. Hunter Regnart, who took over as President of Maples on the retirement of his father Henry Regnart in 1926, was keen that there should be no slackening off in the tradition which had been a major factor in the retention of the custom of generation after generation of upper-class families – the personal friendly service on which John and Blundell Maple had laid so great a score.

'In those days,' recollected Stanley Darvill in 1991, meaning around 1927 when he was accepted as a trainee salesman at the age of 17, 'in those days Maples could pick and choose. Many young men came to London from the provinces intent on a

Burgoyne 5-Valve Receiver, in strong super-rex case (various colours), complete with five Mullard valves, Exide unspillable jelly accumulator, Drydex batteries
£5 . 19 . 6

" Melogram " Console Cabinet Gramophone, in Walnut, fitted with double - spring motor   £7 . 19 . 6

TOTTENHAM COURT ROAD
LONDON   MAPLE & CO   PARIS · BUENOS AIRES
                                               MONTE VIDEO

CARPETS AND FLOOR COVERINGS

MAPLE & CO'S Warehouse has for many years been the largest and most important centre for all kinds of Carpets and Floor Coverings, both of European and Oriental manufacture, and purchasers visiting the showrooms may always depend upon seeing what is most appropriate for the purpose required at the lowest London prices

ORIENTAL CARPETS AND RUGS

MAPLE & CO are direct importers of Oriental Carpets and Rugs, and thus avoid all intermediate profits—a saving of which their customers share the advantage. The stock comprises an immense variety of the finest Indian, Persian, and Turkey Carpets and Rugs, as well as some rare and curious Antique specimens. Prices cannot be given here, as Oriental Carpets and Rugs are not made in standard sizes like those of European manufacture ; but on receipt of requirements MAPLE & CO will be pleased to forward descriptions and prices of those in stock of suitable dimensions. The stock of Oriental Carpets amounts to over 4,000—the largest collection in the world

BRITISH CARPETS

In the sections for British weavings will be found all the best varieties of Axminster, Saxony, Wilton Pile, Brussels, Kidderminster, and Tapestry Brussels Carpets, both by the yard and in bordered squares, in the latest and choicest patterns and colourings. A few prices are given as a guide on the following pages

LINOLEUMS, FLOOR CLOTHS AND MATTINGS

The stock of these is the largest in the world at the most moderate prices

PATTERNS

Patterns of any kind of Floor Coverings sold by the yard will be sent on application, which should give full particulars of what is required ; or, when desired, MAPLE & CO will be happy to make a selection. They have been asked in very many instances to do this, and their great experience has enabled them almost invariably to make a satisfactory choice

MAPLE & CO have completed further important additions to the Carpet Department, and have added new showrooms for Seamless and Made-up Carpets, Linoleums, Mats and Mattings, which will largely contribute to the convenience of customers

"UNDER OUR FEET," a handy book giving much information on Floor Coverings generally, will be sent post free on request.

" Beethoven " 3-Valve A.C. Set, in Walnut Cabinet, internal frame aerial suitable for voltages 100 to 120 and 200 to 250   £14 . 14 . 0

Every Thoroughly Modern Millie had a wireless set and a cocktail cabinet.

His Master's Voice " Baby "
Portable, Model 99, Full Tone
£3 . 5 . 0

His Master's Voice " The Bijou "
Cabinet Gramophone, fitted
with a two-record motor,
No. 5a soundbox, exponential
tone chamber and automatic
brake. It is also equipped with
a record storage cupboard,
easily accessible and having a capacity for 50 records.
Model 145, in Oak, any
shade £7 . 15 . 0

Model 248 Marconiphone 2-valve
set £4 . 19 . 6

career in retailing for which no better apprenticeship could be found than with Maples.' Typical Maples trainee was Patrick Rowe, the 15-year-old son of the head of Mark Rowe & Sons, the Exeter furnishers. It was true to say you got the best training at Maples, said Patrick in 1991, 'but it was also true that it practically took an Act of Parliament to get you into Maples, and an Act of Parliament to get you out.'

Parents of successful young hopefuls who left homes in Yorkshire or Somerset wanted to be assured their boys would be in safe hands on their own in London. Maples had long been aware of their anxiety and had acquired a building near the store, 49 Grafton Street, which they ran as a hostel for the young men of 15 and upwards whom they employed as living-in, 'fed and watered', trainee salesmen. There were some 70 of them in The House, as it was known to them, when Stanley Darvill became a Maples junior salesman at the age of 17 in 1927. As such he was forbidden to meet customers, and was not allowed to sell them anything until he had been a junior for nine years. His starting wage was 27s 6d (£1.37) *a month*. After five years he became a Senior Junior, and a few years later Assistant to a Senior Salesman.

The training was nothing if not thorough. Everyone in The House had to take the National Association of Retail Furnishers course at the College of Distributive Trades in Leicester Square. It comprised basic Furniture Education and ended with sitting the examination for a Certificate in Retail Management Principles, which they were all expected to pass. The Maples training scheme was under the direction of William Knight and latterly of Hugh Scully. It was terminated, and the hostel at 49 Grafton Street closed and sold, in 1970.

The discipline and the training ensured high quality staff. It was tough however on those with little financial resources to fall back on, and many failed to last the course. But Stanley, who had answered an advertisement in the *Daily Telegraph*, felt he was lucky to be called for an interview with Walter Short, the company secretary, who tested his mental arithmetic, to have survived it and be taken on – particularly as none of his relations had been with the firm which was the passport which gained so many an interview.

John Maple's great grandson Gerald Holman became a trainee in 1925 – the son of Mildred Wharton, Clara Maple's daughter who married Dr Frank Kay Holman. Philip Wharton, son of Clara's son Stanley Wharton who had married Maria Negretti (of the Negretti & Zambra barometer family), started his training in 1931. Young Norman Andrews had no difficulty in being seen by Short in 1930. His father had been a Maples salesman for many years. To avoid confusion with the Mr Andrews already on the sales staff he had had to take a 'Shop Name' and had chosen 'Mr Strood' after the town in Kent his family came from. When Norman was accepted and reported for duty appropriately on St Pancras Day (March 14), he was told he too would have to find a Shop Name since the same Mr Andrews was still on the payroll. On the shop floor at Tottenham Court Road Norman Andrews had to get used to being called 'Mr Ackroyd' – same initial.

Patrick Rowe was only 15 when in 1933 he had to answer for himself before Walter Short. His father had been head of the furnishing business established in Exeter in 1834, Mark Rowe & Sons which he had sold in 1925 however. He had applied for a job with Maples and been appointed manager of their Bournemouth branch. There was little fear therefore of young Patrick not being granted an interview, only of not passing it. In 1991 Patrick remembered it was by no means a foregone conclusion.

The front door of The House was locked at 10.30 pm, and everyone had to be in by then if they were under 18; over 18 they could stay out till 11. Anyone waiting to come in later had to obtain a pass signed by the director. Late arrivals had to knock up the steward/housekeeper who in Stanley Darvill's time was a Mr Walkinshaw whom they called 'Stick'. Those who presented themselves after 11 and could not show a pass were reported to the director responsible for House discipline. Few had much money left, however, for many nights-out at the flicks or palais-de-danse after being paid their monthly 27s 6d, with seats at the Plaza or New Gallery being 1s 3d and 2s 4d. Most of those who had had enough of talking shop in the common room at no 49 spent their evenings at the London Central YMCA at the bottom of Tottenham Court Road. Maples director A B Cloutman was also a director of the YMCA and arranged free membership for Maples juniors. It was only a short walk away and left plenty of time to be back, before the door was locked, after an evening in the swimming pool, at the billiard or snooker tables, enjoying an entertainment in the St Georges theatre or a meal in the subsidised restaurant.

Juniors had nothing to pay for breakfast (8 am at The House), or for lunch, tea or supper in no 4 dining room at the Gower Street end of the store. They had a choice of beer, ginger beer or water. Those who cultivated the waiter and greased his palm on Friday evening secured second helpings. As they moved up the sales ladder, they were elevated to the next level of dining room. At the top was the Directors' Dining Room; no 1 was for Senior Buyers and Managers; no 2 for Shopwalkers and Cabinet Salesmen; no 3 for Senior Salesmen and Clerks; no 4 for all those not important enough for no 3, plus juniors; no 5 for all female staff irrespective of rank.

Every young man whom Walter Short accepted started his training in the Post/Correspondence Department. By delivering and collecting letters three times a day, to and from people in every corner of the vast establishment, he got to know his way around, who was who and what was where. If things were busier than usual, Stanley Darvill volunteered for Special Duties, which meant going over to the store before it opened to sort out the mail, for which he received an extra pound a week. Juniors spent weeks, perhaps months, mastering the geography of what Patrick Rowe was told consisted of 52 acres of showroom. Every day they walked several miles.

'As I found my way around the store,' recollected Patrick Rowe,

> I discovered the magnificent 'front shop' which contained the main entrance and where stood the two frock coated floor walkers, Mr Black and Lieutenant Colonel Alexander, ready to receive customers as they entered. These gentlemen were expected to recognise, and receive by name, all royalty, all titled

people and celebrities. They were extremely well turned out and very good at their job.

Behind a screen on the left of the main entrance door sat four cabinet salesmen in frock coats playing cards at a table with a box of snuff in the centre. When it became his turn to be called on by Mr Black or the colonel, the salesman in question put down his hand, brushed the snuff from his nose with a handkerchief, and appeared, as if from nowhere, to conduct the customer to the department he had asked for. 'All these cabinet salesmen were well educated, distinguished-looking gentlemen, of mature age and very experienced, capable in every respect of dealing with high class customers on the same level – Harry Creighton, Dan Waddon, Tommy Baker, Major Moody and the rest.'

The Correspondence Room on which all Maples juniors were based for the first few months of their training was on the top floor at Tottenham Court Road. In it the director in charge – for Patrick Rowe it was a Mr Watling – read through the letters which salesmen had written out in hand, checked the spelling and punctuation, made sure they opened correctly with 'Dear Madam' or 'My Lord' as suited the addressee, and generally edited them to his liking. He gave his revised version of all out-going letters and internal memos to a junior to take to the Typing Pool. When he got them back, he himself signed the letters from sales staff, and sent those by departmental heads to them to sign.

When a vacancy occurred, a junior embarked on the next stage of his training, which was to be assigned to a department, attached to the Buyer. 'Most of the furnishing and soft furnishing departments were under the control of a Governing Director, assisted by a Buyer, at this time,' remembers Patrick Rowe, 'and the remainder of the staff were young trainees – mostly living in at no 49, and thus the cost of staff overheads were reduced to a minimum.'

Norman Andrews went to Soft Furnishing. There were two separate soft furnishing departments each with a Buyer. There was a large Damask or Woven Fabric Department for velvet, silk, brocade, tapestry, embroidery and cushions on the ground floor, with a large store room in the basement; and there was a Printed Fabric Department with a Lace and Net Curtain section and a section for Blinds – there was a small blind factory at the top of the building. It was in this department on the first floor surrounding an ornate well overlooking the Front Shop that Norman spent his first two months as a junior salesman proper – without officially of course being allowed actually to sell anything if a Senior Salesman was available. 'But often we jumped the gun. Life was hard and very competitive at Maples in the nineteen thirties. Poaching other salesmen's customers led to accusations of being a "mogue". Lord knows how the name arose. The way to make the grade was to contact anyone who could officially bring you customers. Such people were known as "uncles".'

All salesmen were on commission. In Soft Furnishing they had to put in small chits giving details of the sale, which were signed by the Buyer and sent to the Counting House, who checked them and paid the commission every two weeks – a system known as Premiums or 'Spiffs'. As an incentive the

Buyer would increase the rate of commission on special lines and specially on 'Cold Pigs' – stock which had stuck for some reason, was left over from a cancelled order, or had to be shifted at any cost.

Because of this two-week delay in the payment of commission, management accepted a certain amount of unofficial advance payment. It was up to the Chief Cashier to accept or reject an IOU presented for a modest sum, which would be deducted from the commission when it became due. It all depended on the mood the cashier was in. Some went to his office, the left pocket of their jacket bearing an IOU for a small amount, the right-hand one for a larger one, and submitted whichever they thought, from the way they were received, had the best chance of being cashed.

No-one was allowed out of the building in shop hours without a Pass-out Chit signed by a director or manager, which had to be shown to the watchman on the door. All such passes were always granted and easy to obtain, and made the recipient 'officially absent'. But there were always unofficial dashes across the road, and the risk of being spotted and reported. Old hands kept a list of pub telephone numbers, and could be relied upon to make an urgent call to The Northumberland Arms asking the landlord to request the truant's instant return.

Pranks abounded. In Norman Andrews' day there was a running dare among the juniors to bring a customer over to the fiery tempered Mr S ten minutes before closing time, when he always sat down to change his shoes so he could make a quick dash for his train on the stroke of six. The prize went to the person who caught him with one shoe on and one off, while the others watched him trying to control his embarrassment and his fury at the thought of missing his train.

After two months in the Cretonne Section, Norman was made a 'City Matcher', which meant visiting suppliers in Paternoster Row and Old Bailey for samples and patterns to match designs. After 18 months as Outside Representative, as he preferred to call himself, he was promoted to Junior Soft Furnishing Salesman in dark short coat and striped trousers, black shoes, white shirt, stiff collar and 'business tie'. Anyone seen walking through the front hall on a Saturday morning wearing a sports tie was sent away to change it. 'Young man!' Stanley Darvill was told when he wanted to be quick off the mark for his journey to Clarence Sports Ground, 'this is a business house; go back to The House and put on a business tie.'

Patrick Rowe had an 18-month assignment in the Second Hand and Antique Department after his six week stint as postman in the Correspondence Department (the Corrie). This was controlled by Tam Adie, a Governing Director who was also in charge of the Bedroom Furniture and Bedstead Departments. Patrick's time was now spent in the basement attached to Mr Cranley, buyer of second-hand furniture, and Mr Ashenhurst, buyer of reproduction furniture. He had daily encounters with Mr Adie of course – 'a short stocky man of Scottish extraction, with an extremely short fuse'.

> He had a habit of standing square in front of you, legs apart, with his thumbs tucked into the armholes of his waistcoat. He would

look up at you with his eyes glittering through his rimless spectacles. He had a remarkable turn of phrase, and was capable of making the tallest man feel very small.

As the day approached I viewed the prospect with much trepidation. Arriving in Tottenham Court Road, I looked up at the magnificent premises with the dome at the corner and the impressive entrance with the large oval bed of hyacinths in the centre, the gilt walls and decorated ceiling. As I hurried past the entrance I caught a glimpse of the tall distinguished-looking gentleman in the frock coat lurking inside to receive customers.

Beside him was the stone tablet, erected in 1929, carved with the somewhat inaccurate Latin inscription to mark the rebuilding operations of that year, in English: "If beautiful things please you, if exquisite furniture, all that you may desire our shop contains. Our house was founded when the Queen was reigning her second year – the King not yet twenty, it was restored." 1839 – 1929

At the staff entrance Patrick was received by an elderly doorman who had been with the company for very many years, been transferred from heavy work to lighter and lighter duties until he found himself inside a little glass box at the staff entrance. He was escorted to a stone staircase with white tiled walls and taken in a goods lift to the fourth floor. Passing

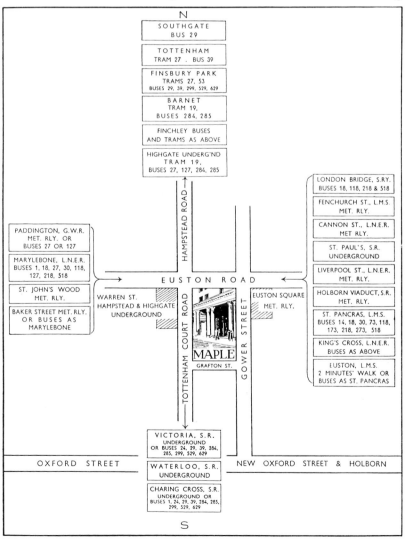

Most of Maples customers now came to Tottenham Court Road by public transport.

through the Counting House he saw clerks on high stools, some of them wearing black cravats with gold tie pins, and women in black overalls, all poring over thick, heavy ledgers in which they entered customers' accounts in fine copper plate handwriting. His ancient guide handed him over to a lady in the company secretary's outer office, where he waited the few minutes before the precise time of the appointment and was ushered into the inner sanctum.

> Walter Short was of average height, grey haired, rather thin on top and received me with a rather limp handshake. His office was utilitarian rather than luxurious. He instructed me to sit down, and subjected me to a long penetrating stare. He had cold blue eyes which seemed to pass through my head to the wall behind. The palms of my hands began to moisten and I had the distinct feeling that we were not going to like each other. "Well sonny," he said, "tell me about your schooling and your achievements so far."

And then, to Patrick's horror, Short proceeded to the routine he had followed with Stanley Darvill.

'Now I'm going to give you some mental arithmetic to do and see how quickly you can provide the answers. Add these two five figure numbers together.'

Patrick's nerves sent his mind into a complete blank. 'Come along sonny, you'll have to do better than that.' Quick calculations needing substraction and division followed, which Patrick would have found difficult with pencil and paper never mind in his head, and he could see his dream of a Maples training receding fast.

> He fixed me with his penetrating blue eyes again and said, 'Well, sonny, we will see if you can spell, since you do not seem to be able to do simple arithmetic.' I felt some relief. I was not good at arithmetic but I could spell, and my confidence returned. He produced a piece of paper from his desk, and on it was a list of words, selected as being tricky for bad spellers. He fired one word at me after the other. I spelt them all correctly. He could not catch me out on one of them. Finally the interview was over. He said he would write to me in due course. As I made my way back along the corridors the chances of a job at Maples seemed very remote.

After three weeks he received a letter saying a vacancy had occurred and that he should report in two weeks time. He would be required to live with the other trainees at 49 Grafton Street. All his meals would be provided and his wage would be 28s a month.

Norman Andrews was not the only Maples trainee of those days who found conditions in The House somewhat spartan. 'I doubt if it had altered since my father's time.' The bath-house was under the pavement, and to reach it he had to go down to the basement and cross the 'area' open to wind and rain. There was no hot water in the washroom upstairs. Over the five zinc bowls in the zinc-lined trough along one side of it were five cold water taps; on the other wall a lone rectangular mahogany-framed mirror.

The basement was the first part of the five-storey, redbrick Victorian no 49 that Patrick Rowe saw the day he reported in 1933. Patrick was taken down to it by Kendall, the fellow-trainee who had been appointed his keeper, to introduce him to the elderly female housekeeper who had her living quarters there. She took him upstairs, and after passing through the washroom she opened a door on the right.

> I found myself in a small self-contained cubicle with one sash window facing the street. The bottom of the window was obscured so that you could not see or be seen. There was an iron bedstead, and behind it a tall chest of drawers. Behind the door was a shelf at the top, with a curtain suspended from it. On the underside of the shelf were two hooks. This was to serve as a wardrobe. A cane seat chair and a very threadbare rug completed the furnishing. The ceiling was very high and the partitions of the cubicles only about seven feet high; so if you stood on your bed you could look down into the cubicle next door. I unpacked my suitcase and put my clothes away. Kendall conducted me back along the corridor past the stone staircase and into the communal lounge with its red leather, club type easy chairs and a fireplace. It all looked rather grim and Dickensian, and I suddenly felt a long way from home.

At least Patrick's cubicle faced front. Norman Andrews had one looking on to the back, and right at the top, which may have been dingier but safer. On his first night Patrick Rowe woke up to see a figure coming through his window backwards with one foot feeling for the end of his bed, stumble to his feet, lower the window and tiptoe to the door exclaiming, 'Sorry if I disturbed you, old chap.' The intruder opened the door and was gone. He had two more visitors the same night. He was dumbfounded. Seeking an explanation in the washhouse next morning he was told, on giving the number of his room, that he was in the New Boys Cubicle.

> You start in there because the window is in direct line with the railing support bar across the area. Any boys locked out after 11 at night climb the railings, creep along the support bar and enter through your window. You'll get used to it in time. The police know what goes on. They've been known to give a chap a lift over the railings before now. When the next new boy arrives you'll be transferred to another room.

Contact with directors however was seldom that close. On occasions after lunch Patrick eyed the President, Hunter Regnart, six foot tall and broad in the girth, lounging in one of the larger easy chairs in the Upholstery Department, reflecting on the excellence of the cuisine in the Directors Dining Room. 'He walked along with his jacket undone carrying all before him, his head up and looking over the head of anyone who passed him – every inch a President.'

To the young junior of the 1930s Stanley Wharton, Vice-President since 1926, was equally imposing but rather lighter in weight. He always wore an orchid in his buttonhole, one he had grown himself.

> The Board of Directors were divided into two camps. Hunter Regnart could be called the 'Government' camp; and the 'opposition' camp was led by Stanley Wharton.

From Antiques Patrick Rowe was shifted to Bedroom Furniture. The Horace Regnart tradition of accepting the work of outside manufacturers, only if it was perfect in every detail, still prevailed. When a van arrived it was Patrick's job to go out into the yard and watch it unloaded.

> I examined every piece, took out every drawer and put it back upside down to make sure it was a perfect fit. The driver had to wait until my inspection was finished. If I found any faults in it I would have it put back on the van for return to the maker. If it was a minor defect it might be something which a Maples polisher could put right, and the manufacturer would be charged with the time. I checked the invoices with the load, and initialled the invoice to show I had physically seen each item, and it would then be countersigned by Mr Cherrill the Administration Manager and again by Mr Norman Gray the Buyer.

From there to the Cabinet Department – dining-room suites, office furniture, bookcases and the rest – in charge of the Special Order Book.

> Any goods sold or required that were not standard, and were not from the showroom, had to be ordered through the Special Order book, and an estimate of their cost received. If a customer required anything made three inches longer, higher or wider, it had to be done. My job was to exert pressure on the manufacturer to supply it, or if that failed, to organise its manufacture by one of the small makers who worked exclusively for Maples – or in some cases for Maples, Warings and Harrods.

Staff were needed not only to sell the furniture and furnishing. Maples were still very much more than a retail store. Customers, not only in London but the Home Counties and beyond availed themselves of the services provided by Maples experts in restoring furniture; purifying, re-stuffing and re-covering upholstered goods; re-polishing sideboards, re-lacquering bedsteads; re-silvering, re-gilding, re-dyeing, re-making and cleaning bedding, carpets and curtains. The company still had a prominent role as auctioneers, house and estate agents, the first business they carried on outside London, at Eastbourne and Brighton, as seen, and in the 1930s continued alongside their furniture retailing. Clients had Maples' estate agency sell their properties by auction or private treaty, and find them town and country houses to occupy or for investment. Consultation, and access to their register of available properties, was given without charge. Clients came to Maples too for valuations for probate, assessments of dilapidations, fire claims. Based on Camden Depository an army of skilled workmen still gave customers a Warehousing service, including cold storage, and Removals.

The most sophisticated non-retailing activity had for long been the work undertaken by Maples Contracts Department which had grown to vast proportions through Sir Blundell Maple's relationship with Gordon Hotels and Frederick Hotels. There had been an inevitable reduction of contract work during the war but it had revived in the 1920s. The prestige to be gained from contracting Maples to furnish and decorate was as high as ever.

The British Government gave the company the contract for decorating and furnishing the British Embassy in Kabul, Afghanistan, in 1922. Everything had to be taken through the Khyber Pass on packhorse including a grand piano. The

The Imperial Hotel, Torquay.

Central Electricity Board had it take care of its new offices in Trafalgar Square, and the National Provincial Bank its city premises in Princes Street, in 1927. There were contracts for the beautiful Prince of Wales Hotel in Scarborough (1929); the Livermead Cliff Hotel in Torquay (1924). In 1926 Maples were given a contract for work on the splendid four-star Imperial Hotel at Torquay built in 1863 and still one of the most elegant on the south coast; on London's Embassy Club in Bond Street; the Café de Paris.

In 1933 Maples were contracted to supply all the china, glass, silver and cutlery for the Old Palace in Baghdad, and furniture for King Feisal's Gift House. Among the contracts awarded Maples in the 1930s were those for providing carpets and furniture for the Nuffield Wing at Guys Hospital and the private patients block at University College Hospital; furnishing the fashionable Ecu de France restaurant which had opened in Jermyn Street; supplying and fitting carpets for the largest block of flats in Europe, Dolphin Square, overlooking the Thames, and for the Royal Opera House in Covent Garden; furnishing the public rooms of the Grand Central Hotel in Belfast.

Hotel contracts were abundant, but though Maples craftsmen had applied their skills to the occasional floating hotel – in 1922 for instance they created the interior of Mr McCombe's luxury yacht *Monarch II* in 1922 – the management at Tottenham Court Road thought the time had come for greater activity in a field which, as Britain pulled out of the Economic Crisis, seemed to have so great a potential.

As a lad of 12, Herbert Henry Martyn, born in Worcester in 1842, became a student at the School of Design in South Kensington. At 14 he was apprenticed to a picture-frame maker. In 1861 an architectural carver, James Forsyth, gave Martyn, now 19, seven shillings a week to work for him as a journeyman carver. He left shortly afterwards to work – at 30s a week – for R L Boulton who was doing restoration in Worcester Cathedral. When Boulton moved his studio to Cheltenham in 1867, Martyn went with him, and seven years later set up on his own as feelance carver in wood and stone. In 1888 he

The King's Palace in Baghdad, which became the President's.

formed H H Martyn & Co as an association of art craftsmen centred on a house in High Street Cheltenham called Sunningend. Ten years later he took his son Alfred Willie Martyn into partnership. In 1900 the partnership was incorporated as a private limited company, the activities of which, conducted by some 200 skilled craftsmen and artists, embraced decorative plaster work, joinery, cabinet making, wrought iron and small castings in bronze and gun metal. In 1909 they began very large-scale casting, with 80 men taking three months to construct the massive central ceremonial gates, the so-called Cumberland Screen, at the Marble Arch entrance to Hyde Park. But more importantly, in the same year, they began what became the mainstay of the company's business, the fitting out of luxury ocean liners.

On the outbreak of the Great War in 1914 orders for artistic and decorative work almost ceased. They had already however opened an office and showroom in London at 5 Grafton Street off Bond Street, on a 54-year lease from Lord Byron. In 1915 the Aircraft Manufacturing Company of Hendon were looking for a woodworking company to which they could sub-contract the manufacture of wings and fuselages for De Havilland and Maurice Farman aircraft and, out of the three companies they examined, chose H H Martyn. One of the others was S J Waring of Liverpool. This led to A W Martyn forming The Gloucestershire Aircraft Company at Cheltenham, owned 50-50 by Martyns and the Hendon company. In 1925 the manufacture of 'Glosters' moved from Cheltenham to Hucclecote, Gloucester.

Herbert Henry Martyn, whose firm H H Martin of Cheltenham was acquired by Maples in 1937.

Large and famous as it was, the Glosters operation (taken over by Hawker Aircraft in 1937) was a diversion. By 1933, in 24 years, H H Martyn had undertaken 36 ship interior decoration contracts in their five-acre factory at Cheltenham. Their main areas of work were first class lounges and foyers, staircases, smoking rooms and swimming pools. They had built the fluted columns in the *Titanic* and worked on the refit of the *Lusitania*. In 1934 they had just started to work on their most prestigious marine contract to date – for ship no 534 which had lain rotting on the stocks at Clydebank for many months after

Metal work carried out by Martyns of Cheltenham, the architectural decorators for the ocean liner Queen Mary.

the money ran out. It was rescued by the Government's North Atlantic Shipping Act which made loans of up to £9½ million for building ships for the North Atlantic service at the time of depression and unemployment. Construction of 534 was resumed and brought Martyns a contract which included 272 light fittings in silver bronze, the first-class main staircase and the music practice room. In 1991 the *Queen Mary*, as Cunard later called the ship, is permanently moored off Long Beach, California, where tourists can still see Martyn's plasterwork, joinery and metalwork.

Following an acute difference of opinion with his fellow directors, A W Martyn had resigned from the Board both of H H Martyn and Gloster Aircraft in 1927. Like much of British industry in the Economic Crisis of the years that followed, Martyn's financial situation deteriorated and in 1934 they accepted the take-over bid offered by Maple & Co.

The new owners styled the alliance of the two famous firms 'The Maple-Martyn Organisation'. 'The change' wrote John Whitaker, Henry Martyn's grandson,[*]

> was no more popular with the staff of Martyns than when A W Martyn relinquished his control in 1927, only seven years before. The staff continued to consider themselves Martyns men, and some friction was evident between the men and the management

[*] in *The Best*, the history of H H Martyn & Co (1985). John Whitaker's mother is A W Martyn's daughter.

appointed from Maples. The men were at times assembled to be told that they should forget their past of which they were proud and become 'Maple-minded'.

Maples did the panelling in this third class lounge on B Deck of RMS Queen Mary.

Whitaker considered the takeover came about for several reasons.

> Maples were interested in acquiring ship work for their furnishings and by 1934 Martyns had built up a considerable connection and reputation in this field. The main interests of Hugh Burroughes and David Longden, principal members of the Board, now lay in the Gloster Aircraft Co rather than Martyns. There was also some commercial logic in the argument that the association of the two companies could be beneficial with the furniture and soft furnishing of Maples complementing the comprehensive architectural decoration produced by Martyns.

The range of Maples' new acquisition was certainly comprehensive. They described themselves as carvers in wood, stone and marble; modellers of decorative plaster enrichments; sculptors, architectural carvers and craftsmen; artists in wrought iron and stained glass; casters in bronze and other metals; cabinet makers and joiners; creators of memorials in stone, bronze and glass; decorations in ships, trains, palaces, cathedrals, churches, stately homes and public buildings,. From now on the work undertaken at Cheltenham was talked about vicariously as being done by Maple-Martyn, H H Martyn or just Maples. In 1936 Maples formed The Cheltenham Manufacturing Company as a subsidiary to take the place of Martyns' Furniture Department, whose speciality was wood

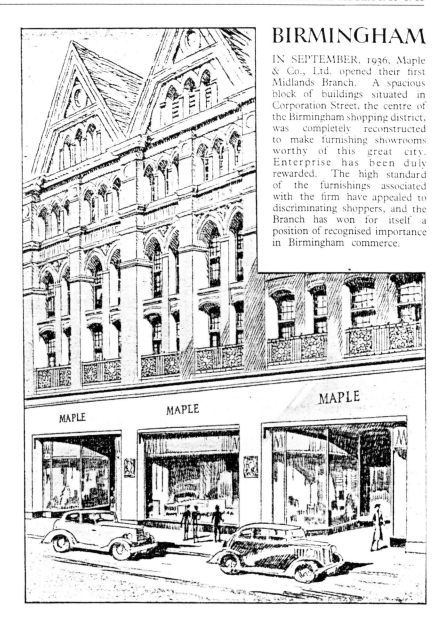

BIRMINGHAM

IN SEPTEMBER, 1936, Maple & Co., Ltd. opened their first Midlands Branch. A spacious block of buildings situated in Corporation Street, the centre of the Birmingham shopping district, was completely reconstructed to make furnishing showrooms worthy of this great city. Enterprise has been duly rewarded. The high standard of the furnishings associated with the firm have appealed to discriminating shoppers, and the Branch has won for itself a position of recognised importance in Birmingham commerce.

In 1936 Maples opened a third branch outside London in Birmingham – the store was rebuilt after being destroyed in a World War 2 air raid.

panelling. Maple-Martyn opened a modelling studio at 192 Albany Street on the north side of Euston Road.

Maples had no retail operation in the West Country, but in 1936 they leased premises for a third provincial branch in Corporation Street Birmingham, no 150. The building was gutted, passenger and goods lifts installed, staircases and windows added, and in March 1937 a fine Maples furniture store was opened with Norman Gray as Resident Director.

The stores in London, Brighton, Bournemouth and Birmingham, and indeed in Buenos Aires, Montevideo and Paris, all sold Maples furniture made in London workshops at and around Tottenham Court Road, in Highgate Road and in Drummond Street off Hampstead Road where they made chairs and upholstery; and that made by The Cheltenham Manufacturing Company. The French and South American stores were also still selling the merchandise their companies manufactured in their own nearby factories. Much of the custom came from newly weds who now more than ever started their married life not in a house but a flat.

In 1936 John Maple's great grandson Gerald Holman married Alva Burbidge, daughter of Sir Woodman Burbidge Bart, who the year before had retired as managing director of Harrods Ltd and handed over to his son Richard, the new Mrs Holman's brother, while retaining the chairmanship. Five years earlier Harrods had bought the stock and goodwill of Shoolbreds, Maples' next door neighbour in Tottenham Court Road and competitor, closed the shop and sold off the merchandise. Mr and Mrs Gerald Holman had Maples furnish the flat which they made their first home, and the bill from the Largest and most Attractive Furnishing Establishment in the World came to just over £400. The most expensive items were the weathered oak wardrobe at £6 5s and the walnut chest-of-drawers at £8 5s. But the four-piece oak bedroom suite only cost them £4 8s 6d (plus 5%) and the dark lath-back Windsor chair only 5s (25p).

As Britain – and the world – recovered from recession, and people who furnished their flats and houses at Maples felt justified in reckoning on a more settled and prosperous future, the dreams of the fanatical new German 'fuhrer' for a New Order in Europe shifted their preoccupation with home-making to one of home-protecting. After the Munich Agreement of 1938 no-one could fail to be aware of the need to take Air Raid Precautions seriously, though in true British tradition it was widely regarded as a joke – by, among others, the editor of the Clarence Athletic Sports Club programme:

A.R.P.
The Protection of Your Home Against Air Raids
Read these instructions through carefully and then destroy them

> If this country were ever at war, the target of the enemies' bombs would be Maple & Co (ask any of our Special Constables, who know many state secrets). We all hope and work to prevent this, but the enemy know the weak spots of London – the weakest of all being the beer in the dining rooms. The brains of the Clarence are listening practically all night to the wise words of our Watch Committee (W.C.) who suggest wonderful schemes to prevent surprise attack. Our call is for volunteers who can clear up the mess made by those who are subject to surprise attacks ... it's up to YOU.

In that last year of Before The War Mk 2 Maple-Martyn started work on a further contract from shipbuilder John Brown for the Cunard White Star Company's ship 552 which they decided to call *Queen Elizabeth*. The contract, worth £11,465, covered the tourist main staircase, decorative work, walls and ceilings and entrances.

The last big job for Maples' own Contracts Department was decorating and furnishing King Carol of Romania's palace in Bucharest, though the ship carrying the first consignment of furniture was sunk by the enemy in the Mediterranean where the Maples settees, carpets, and light fittings still lie.

In 1938 the Board of Maples decided that the system of remunerating directors through the dividends they received from their so-called Management Shares, which Sir Blundell Maple had instituted when he incorporated the company, was now antiquated, an anachronism out of keeping with the practice in other big companies. The shares gave their holders enormous voting powers and the ability to prevent an unwanted take-over bid. The directors of Maple & Co relinquished their rights to management shares, and from 1938 received salaries under ordinary service agreements.*

When in September 1939 Britain joined France, the USSR and the other Allies in declaring war against Hitler's Germany, Maples' workshops turned, as they had done in World War 1 25 years earlier, to making webbing and canvas equipment for the fighting services – anything from anklets to blister curtains, camouflage nets, mock guns, kapok anti-invasion booms, and some 20 million gas mask haversacks. The 124 War Office contracts were worth £17 million. Furniture stocks were high in Britain at the beginning of the war but, since timber stocks were low and Britain could not spare the ships to import any, furniture was soon in short supply. Such furniture as Maples were able to make had to conform to the single Utility range controlled by the Utility Furniture Committee chaired by Gordon Russell. 'At last,' wrote Phyllis Bennett Oates in *The Story of Western Furniture* (1981),

> the climate was favourable for good design and craftsmanship to be built into the industrial system and functional practical standards could direct the taste of the whole nation. Hitherto a return to honest craftsmanship had been equated with hand craftmanship and therefore the prerogative of the affluent; the poorer classes, thought by manufacturers to have a taste for the over-decorative, had had to put up with shoddy goods.

Overnight the great body of Maples craftsmen, salesmen, clerks, porters, drivers, warehousemen, designers and renovators shrunk. People like Stanley Darvill who had been a part-time volunteer civil defence fireman were at once called up for full-time duties. Others in the Territorial Army, in navy and airforce reserves left to join their units 'for the duration'. The scheduled compulsory mobilisation of everyone of call-up age took away the rest. Maples, like every other enterprise throughout Britain, carried on with a wartime staff of loyal men and women devoted to making the Home Front as tolerable and cheerful as circumstances permitted, and taking whatever blows the enemy delivered with resolution and infectious courage.

The jokey piece about ARP in the programme of the 1889-1939 Clarence Athletic Club 51st annual sports (which also noted incidentally the retirement of Edward Barnes, Sir Blundell Maple's faithful secretary) proved only too accurate.

The conspicuous island site at the top of Tottenham Court Road, where warlike stores were being made for the British Government, *did* become a target for German bomber pilots. The third phase of the Battle of Britain began with the

* References to 'Management Shares' continued to appear in the annual reports and accounts however. The Directors Report for the year ending January 29 1971 contained the sentence: 'On 29th January 1971 the Management Shares were converted into Ordinary Shares on the basis of one Ordinary Share of £1 for every five Management Shares of 4/-.'

Germans bombing London on September 7, 1940. At about four o'clock on Friday afternoon September 13 a single 250 lb bomb hit Block L of the Maples complex, fell through five floors and exploded in the Second-hand basement where Patrick Rowe had spent part of his training. Some 3,000 were about their work in other parts of the group of buildings, but for some reason no-one was in the Second-hand basement. The explosion destroyed expensive china and glass and French antique furniture, the Alma-Tadema 'Byzantine' grand piano and many other pianos, but did not cause the loss of even one much more expensive life. On the 16th a high explosive bomb damaged the upholstery factory at 9 Hertford Place, and the hostel in Grafton Street; and on the 19th a 500lb bomb fell on the main site but failed to explode. The site was evacuated while a Bomb Disposal Unit defused it. A time bomb which lodged at the back of Camden Depository was safely removed after ten days. On September 24 incendiaries showered down north of Euston Road, gutting the 'Stuffers Factory' in Drummond Street, half destroying the furniture warehouse in Euston Road and damaging the workshops in Stanhope Street. A 750 kilo bomb fell through what remained of the Carpet Department, travelling through six floors and burying itself in the ground without exploding.

Maples had been targeted for 14 days in September 1940, but there was worse to come in 1941. Maples premises in Birmingham were demolished by fire on April 10. The following week incendiaries began falling once more on Tottenham Court Road just after nine at night. An employee who was on duty as roof spotter described how, on hearing a colleague shout 'Incendiaries everywhere!' rushed to the delivery yard on the Gower Street side and found them burning wherever he looked. Where to start?

> We concentrated on those nearest to us, clearing them as we went, dealing with everything except the Grafton Street block which had the heaviest concentration. Within a matter of minutes however it was obvious we were going to have a major fire. The main water supplies had been hit, and we were unable to make use of the hydrants. We managed the motor pump, but it emptied 5,000 gallons emergency water tank in minutes – and to no effect. We called for assistance from the nearest Fire Service but all their vehicles were out attending to fires in other parts of London. We just had to wait for reinforcements from outside London. Our little team were utterly helpless. The fire leapt across Tottenham Place and then across Beaumont Place to all the adjoining factories.

Guided by the light of the inferno the Luftwaffe flew over and dropped high explosive bombs, making at least two direct hits. Fire engines eventually turned up from Edgware, and stayed to do what they could to prevent damage for the next 24 hours. But the fire burnt for 11 days in the centre of the island. Three quarters of the factory and showroom space of Maples were destroyed by incendiary and high explosive bombs that night. The value of the government materials and Maples furniture lost was assessed at £750,000. But during the whole of the blitzkrieg on Maples – September and October 1940 and April 1941 – not a single employee was killed. And, strangely, no part of the store's frontage was damaged. Neither did the fire have much effect on a Chinese carved jade vase which was rescued from the antiques showroom with the glass of its showcase melted round and on to it. Still embedded in molten glass it is now on exhibition in the Geological Museum, South Kensington illustrating how refractory jadeite, formerly a very pale green, had suffered little by the heat which destroyed Maples, but the glass had melted and in its cold hardened state encrusted the vase.

At five o'clock the morning after the big fire Gerald Holman walked from his flat in Notting Hill Gate on a carpet of broken glass up Charing Cross Road. With the permission of the Government he commandeered all the public telephones in Warren Street Underground Station for three days, and the place became Maples telephone exchange. Within a few days the Government gave him a provisional compensation cheque of half a million pounds to get his factories going again.

The almost total destruction of Maples Tottenham Court Road took place on the night of April 16, which happened to be the traditional day, as seen, on which John Maple opened his shop on the same site a hundred years before.

If there had ever been any thought of celebrating the centenary while Britain was engaged in a life-and-death struggle with the Nazis, Fascists and Japanese, the events of that night made it impossible. The occasion did not pass unnoticed however. *The Cabinet Maker* sent along a reporter to interview John Maple's grandson and current Vice-President, Stanley Wharton, who showed him the evidence (quoted on page 7) for believing that no 145 had been opened for business on May 13.

> Mr Wharton let me handle this old book in its faded and well-thumbed red cover. The handwriting of Mrs Maple stood out firm and clear, and one wondered how far the ambitions of Mr and Mrs Maple reached when that entry was made, and whether they were vouchsafed then a glimpse of the vast and imposing structure now covering so large a site, and famous the world over.

The edition of the magazine carrying the article headed MAPLE'S FIRST CENTURY was published on April 12, 1941. So, ended the writer,

> broad based upon the sanity and probity of John Maple, who passed all the exacting tests to which the Victorian business man was submitted in a sternly and healthy individualistic age, the noble structure of the famous 'Maples' has endured 100 years. It looks confidently forward to a brilliant future.

❧ 6 ❧

London Style Moves to County High Streets 1941-1971

WHILE the enemy were pulverising and burning Maples in London – and Patrick Rowe's family firm Mark Rowe & Sons in Exeter which they destroyed in one of their notorious 'Baedeker' raids in 1942 – they were pressurising and threatening the management of Maples in the French capital which they occupied in June 1940.

Claude Guillaume, a Frenchman who had been a resident of the hostel at 49 Grafton Street and a Maples trainee before the war, had become manager of the Paris branch at rue Boudreau and the factory at rue de la Jonquière. His English assistant G R Booth managed to escape from Occupied France and return to Britain, but Guillaume remained to do what trade he could – but under increasingly difficult circumstances. He bravely refused to fall in with any of the requirements made of him by the German Command. Outwitted and out-manoeuvered, their patience eventually gave out. 'In view of the fact that you have done nothing to satisfy my demands for a further stepping up of the work in your factory,' they wrote to Guillaume on March 4 1944,

> and that you have made no real effort to begin the mass manufacture of goods to meet the needs of Germany, I find it impossible to leave you any longer in the position of Manager of Maple & Company Limited. Further, I have twice asked you to send me a statement of the position of Maples business and especially particulars of orders received, cash receipts and payments etc. Unfortunately you have taken no notice of my demands. I have lost confidence in you because I must see at the head of your firm a person who deals immediately and energetically with the manufacture of furniture for the millions of bombed out people in Germany.

Guillaume had managed never to comply with any of the instructions he received, and by devious methods the craftsmen in the factory made certain that no piece of furniture ordered for dispatch to Germany was ever actually finished. Guillaume was removed, and two French collaborators appointed to manage Maple & Co (Paris) in his place. Hitler ordered the total destruction of Paris but its governor Von Choltitz disobeyed him, and in August 1944 surrendered the city to General de Gaulle. Claude Guillaume returned to rue Boudreau but, his health failing him, he shortly retired. C E R Ashenhurst came out from London to take over as manager after VE Day, and became largely responsible for building up the Paris business in the difficult post-war years. The Jonquière factory was sold to the French Government for £198,000, and a modern, one-storey factory build in the Paris suburb of Ivry.

In London, with strict priorities imposed on post-war reconstruction through a rigid building licensing system, it was 18 years before the whole of the Tottenham Court Road site which had been devastated in 1940 and 1941 was finally reopened for business. With the rationing of building materials, particularly steel, the time spent on Town Planning considerations and the processing of War Damage claims, and with licenses given initially only to what was considered essential building (where retail stores were low on the list), the first section of rebuilding Maples did not start until 1950, five years after the war ended, and the last section was not completed until October 1959.

Most of the cost was recovered from the Government through the War Damage Commission, but management elected to indulge in a more costly and grander style – at least £300,000 more – and looked to the proceeds of the sale of property regarded as 'surplus to requirements' fronting Euston Road and Gower Street to make up the difference. By 1959, with contracts exchanged for 70 per cent of what they were offering, they had already realised £900,000.

With reduced floor space and fewer showrooms however went reduced trade and fewer customers. Not only materials to build new houses, offices and hotels were rationed, but the furniture and furnishing fabrics to put in them. The coupon system continued for many years after 1945; return to 'normal' was gradual. It took time for the Government to recover the cost of winning a total war. Purchase Tax made so many non-essentials unaffordable. But then what was considered essential Before The War Mk 2 was now of little account. The large armies of domestic servants largely disappeared. Madam, with a part-time job and running the house on her own, wanted furniture she could clean and dust as quickly and easily as possible. Families no longer expected to live in the same house for generation after generation. People who moved house frequently had no wish to take cumbrous wardrobes and sideboards with them. 'Movement, speed and change replaced durability and permanence in the form of smaller, movable pieces, built-in furniture and stackables.' The tendency was to combine sitting room with kitchen, have a 'dining recess', have a single large living room. Elegant Simplicity with modular, demountable furniture became the fashion. The Council of Industrial Design, established by the Board of Trade in 1944, as Molly Harrison said in her book *People and Furniture* (1971), 'attuned the public to new shapes, new colours, new domestic arrangements.' The Furniture Development Council too made people in Britain more design conscious. The Festival of Britain 1951 and its South Bank Exhibition in London gave the word 'contemporary' design connotation which was particularly associated with furniture, and furniture designers like Terence Conran and Robin Day.

Those who lost out in the race to acquire what little 'contemporary' furniture came on the market, whose tastes were not yet adjusted to the New Look or were offended by the Utility ranges of the 1950s, flocked to Maples second-hand department – as Stanley Darvill found when, freed of his Fire Service duties, he returned to Tottenham Court Road.

Not everyone who had left Maples in 1939 and 1940 to help with the war effort returned. Some had died or been killed in the fighting overseas or the air raids on the home front, had retired or obtained jobs elsewhere. Those who took up where they left off found the frontage the same but much else changed. Norman Andrews, returning from Burma after VJ Day, soon discovered that many of the departments he had once known had disappeared, and those that remained greatly reduced in size. The vast pre-war stock of which Maples had boasted was now puny. The section of Soft Furnishing which he rejoined under the same two Buyers was concentrated into a small space round the well. He now had to cross over to 49 Grafton Street for lunch and tea. Only the top floor was used as a hostel for the few juniors being trained; the other floors contained the still stratified staff dining rooms. The Clarence Athletic Club had been revived, but without its Sports Ground at Mill Hill at which so many had spent their weekends Before the War. The almshouses and convalescent home at Harpenden were still functioning, however, and employees could look to an easement of their financial situation after retirement by the introduction in 1955 of a Staff Superannuation Scheme.

Prospects of the firm placing its own finances on a sounder basis came with the introduction of central bulk buying for the main five departments. The move was prompted to a large extent by the change which wartime had brought to people's shopping habits. With restricted travel by road and rail, the black-out, the air-raids, the rationing and the shortage of practically everything, people acquired the habit of relying very much more on their local shops. London's West End lost some of its mystique, and the High Streets of Britain's country

The Maples almshouses at Harpenden.

towns lost so much of what people were insinuating when they patronisingly applied to them and their merchandise the term 'provincial'.

Maples had become aware of the weakness of concentrating their retailing in London as far back as 1936 when, to add to their operations in Brighton and Bournemouth, they opened up in Birmingham. But for the threat of war which began to loom so soon afterwards, they would have gone ahead with their plan to make Maples furniture and furnishing available locally in High Streets all over Britain. With the end of hostilities in 1945 and the accumulation of the necessary funds from the sale of surplus property in London between 1946 and 1958, Maples took their pre-war plans off the shelf and established retail outlets, many with attached local factories, in eight towns north, south, east and west of London. In some they established new branches which traded under the name 'Maple'; in others they bought out old-established furniture firms which continued to trade under their own names as wholly owned subsidiaries.

The first branch store to be opened outside London after World War 2 was in Leeds where a freehold property was bought at 12 Park Row and opened under the Maples banner in April 1946. Ten years later they moved the store to the larger Headrow House, and again in 1962 to the building in Albion Street which had once traded as Denby & Spinks but in 1958 changed its name to Harrison.

The following year Maples acquired the Nottingham firms of Henry Barker and Smart & Brown which in January 1947 were amalgamated into a single company called 'Henry Barker Smart & Brown' with Donald Bett as managing-director. Their shop was in Angel Row in which the two firms had been operating separately since 1943, and had been Henry Barker's store since 1879. With the shop came a repository in Hendon Rise, and an upholstery and cabinet factory employing 30 men in St Bartholomew's Road. Henry Barker had started in a small workshop in Goose Gate, and then moved to Bridlesmith Gate, where Arthur Brown set up at about the same time as 'Smart & Brown'. The Angel Row shop was rebuilt in 1957.

In 1948 Maples gained a foothold in Bristol by buying two private houses in Whiteladies Road for makeshift showrooms, and freehold premises nearby for a factory and workshop. On the freehold site they bought in Queens Road they built a magnificent new Maples with 34,000 square feet of showroom which opened with Jack Segrave as managing director in 1954. Premises on a 21-year lease were secured in Leicester in 1950 for Maples with frontages on the Market Place and Cank Street. They installed a lift, new lighting and central heating, and the store opened for business in March 1951. A freehold factory with a floor area of more than 20,000 square feet was acquired round the corner.

Mark Rowe & Sons of Exeter had been trading as a family firm for 90 years when Patrick Rowe's father sold it in 1925. In April 1954 the company, whose store at 266 High Street was destroyed by aerial bombing in the war as seen, and been trading from a warehouse in Longbrook Street, was bought by Maples. On the original site in the High Street they built a new store which they opened that summer – 'the largest display of every style of furniture to be seen in the South West'. It continued to trade as 'Mark Rowe & Sons'. Like John Maple, Mark Rowe began as a linen draper. He set up in 1834 in the High Street premises built with bricks of East Gate over which stood a statue of Henry VII and the royal arms, which had been placed there to commemorate the king's visit to Exeter in 1497.

In 1957 Maples moved their furthest north with the acquisition of the whole of the share capital of Robson & Sons Ltd of Newcastle-upon-Tyne, founded by Robert Robson in 1835 with premises in Northumberland Street. Fifty years later they built themselves a cabinet factory on the outskirts of the town in which they did domestic and ecclesiastical woodwork. They added a removals and storage department, and from 1900 were doing panelling and furnishing in the ships being built on the Tyne by Cunard. They secured large contracts for the *Mauretania* in 1907, and the *Berengaria* in 1919. Their catalogue of household furniture – 224 pages in 1888 – was as comprehensive as Maples' own publication. In the 1920s the family opened a Robsons branch in London at 75 Knightsbridge. After the takeover by Maples the store in Northumberland Street continued to trade as 'Robson & Sons'.

Maples moved to the north-west coast in 1958 when they acquired the family furnishing and decorating firm established in Liverpool by William Ray and Jeremiah Miles in 1864 in Parker St, moving in 1901 to London Road. 'Ray & Miles Ltd' remained the name over the door after the company passed to its new owners. In the same year Maples range of furniture and furnishings became readily available to the people of East Anglia when the company took over the business established in Ipswich by brothers R D and J B Fraser in 1933. Frasers opened a branch in Felixstowe, and another in Dieppe. Like Maples they were patronised by royalty. The shop was rebuilt after a disastrous fire in 1912, and when Edwin Fraser retired in 1951 control passed to Boardmans (Stratford) Ltd. After acquisition by Maples, the store redecorated, refitted and restocked, was opened in Princes Street in October 1958 as the new 'Frasers' under the management of Jeff Hembry.

The group of 11 stores plus Tottenham Court Road had the benefit of a central bulk buying organisation based on London with a high degree of personal service – as Central Buyer Fabrics, Norman Andrews visited every Maples store at least twice a year but it took time for the idea to be accepted by provincial managers in the front line.

The cost of the 12-year push into the country was absorbed without borrowing. The financial position of Maple & Co was demonstrably strong. The balance sheet for the company's diamond jubilee year of 1950 showed fixed and current assets standing at £6,046,392. The authorised capital was £3,000,200 of which £2,800,000 was issued and fully paid. There was a reserve of £3,939,513; the profit for the year ending January 31, 1950 was a healthy £543,186; holders of Ordinary shares received a ten per cent dividend plus a five per cent bonus. Purchase tax of 66 per cent and 100 per cent was the biggest drag on profitability. The tax was payable on furniture which Maple & Co bought from outside manufacturers and might store in their warehouse for months before being sold. So they created a separate warehousing unit 'The Drummond Manufacturing Company Ltd' which could take and store goods on which PT would only become liable when they were taken over to the Tottenham Court Road showrooms and hopefully sold within days.

For a decade, complained President Charles ('Hunter') Regnart in 1950, the British furniture industry had been prevented from producing the best furniture – that requiring the skill of the best type of upholsterer and cabinetmaker. As a consequence practically no apprentices had been articled to the trade. Hard wood had at last been freed from control, but the abolition of Purchase Tax would help a crippled industry not only to survive but revive.

> In no other way can the craftsmanship be maintained and the Antiques of the future be produced. Machine made Utility furniture has and will serve a useful purpose, but it will sap the life blood of the industry if it continues to enjoy freedom from purchase tax and other controls to the exclusion of the rest and best of the products of our industry. The Government has set up a Development Council in the Furniture Trade presumably to teach us our business, yet we are restricted from teaching this body what we already know.

In spite of the penal PT, Excess Profits Tax and the controls that every chairman felt required to complain about, next year Hunter Regnart was able to announce a record increase of turnover to half a million pounds and a profit which had surged to more than £609,000.

A major contributor to that success was The Maple-Martyn Organisation, incorporating the prestigious H H Martyn of Cheltenham.

The Blitz which wrecked Maples Tottenham Court Road also laid waste the Palace of Westminster and the City of London's ancient Guildhall. When it came to reinstating the chamber of the House of Commons in 1951 the Ministry of Works found that certain woodwork could not be done by modern crafts-

H H Martyn's woodcarving studio in 1923.

The completed Speaker's Chair.

men, and sent to Cheltenham for Martyn men, the youngest of whom was over 70. They carved a new 14 ft high Speaker's Chair in six months to the design of Sir Giles Gilbert Scott similar to the one destroyed and also designed by him. Charles Gisborne who carved the canopy and the coat of arms was awarded the MBE for his work – his last job before retiring.

Martyn carvers also made the new Scott-designed dispatch boxes in purruri wood lined with the green leather used throughout the chamber called vaumol hide. They made the table too on which the boxes lie, across which front bench members of the two parties face each other in debate. From the Cheltenham foundry came 500 cast bronze grilles and gallery railings – the foundry which cast Oscar Newman's half-ton seated statue of Sir Winston Churchill for Guildhall. Of the woodwork in Guildhall Sir Giles Scott said the Martyn carvers had 'done a magnificient job, particularly with the oak panel surmounted with crown and lions'.

The four-ton £27,000 statue of Robert the Bruce cast at Cheltenham took four days to pull to Bannockburn for unveiling by the Queen to mark the 650th anniversary of the famous battle in which the Scots gave the English a trouncing in 1314. Even more massive were the two aluminium doors, 23 ft high, which Martyn cast for the new Government Office block in Whitehall Gardens now the Ministry of Defence. The Spire and Cross they made for the cathedral at Debra Libanos in Ethiopia was also of aluminium. More delicate was their trowel and mallet used by the Queen to open the National Theatre on the South Bank; and their console case for the organ in the Royal Festival Hall next door.

The Rag and Stick Men of The Maple-Martyn Organisation were much in demand for the decorative fibrous plaster work for which they had been renowned before the war – in buildings such as the City Hall, Belfast, Stormont Castle and the Royal Palace in Baghdad. After the ship *Seastan* sank with its cargo of plaster pannelling and carving, Martyns were allowed to submit a second quotation for the Baghdad contract, which never made a profit however. Half way through it the King of Iraq was assassinated, and the building became the Presidential Palace. Ted Claridge, manager of the Fibrous Plaster Department, went out to oversee the work. Fortunately

Martyns had obtained irrevocable letters of credit, so they had no fear of not being paid. They were able to save a bit of money by using the two large bronze doors still in store in London, which had been waiting since 1939 to be put into the royal palace in Bucharest, a contract aborted by the outbreak of war. What was good enough for the King of Romania was more than adequate for the President of Iraq.

Orders from another royal customer, the King of Egypt, dried up when Farouk abdicated in 1952, but Martyns had already completed the joinery and decorative work for the royal train built for him by Metropolitan-Cammell. Railway carriage work was nothing new to Martyns who in 1920 had decorated the interior of the royal train in which Edward Prince of Wales travelled on his tour of India.

The Middle East was the source of a considerable amount of work in the 1950s not only for The Maple-Martyn Organisation but Maples own Contract Department. Much of it came from the personal relationships built up by senior salesmen like Stanley Darvill who were able to assure high-ranking Arabs that by contracting with Maples they would not be dealing with Jews. That Maple & Co had no-one on its Board of the Jewish faith was easily demonstrated, but for Sharif Nasser bin Jamil, uncle of King Hussein of Jordan and Commander-in-Chief of the Jordanian Army, with whom Stanley Darvill was discussing the furnishing of his palace in Amman 'in the English style', that was not enough. Says Darvill:

> I had a letter from him saying would I please ensure that none of the furniture for which I had given him estimates and had had designed for him was made in Jewish factories. I well knew that much of the cloth with which we upholstered our chairs and

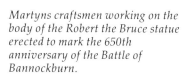

Martyns craftsmen working on the body of the Robert the Bruce statue erected to mark the 650th anniversary of the Battle of Bannockburn.

The finished statue of Robert the Bruce.

sofas had been made in factories run by Jews. So I had to have much of what had been done re-designed and re-priced. I told the affected suppliers of the position. Only after I had given Sharif Nasser a formal letter declaring that nothing Maples were sending him was made in a Jewish factory would he give the go-ahead, and agree to pay the extra sum involved.

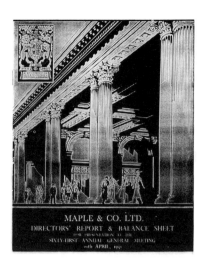

MAPLE & CO. LTD.
DIRECTORS' REPORT & BALANCE SHEET
FOR PRESENTATION AT THE
SIXTY-FIRST ANNUAL GENERAL MEETING
29th APRIL, 1952

When, some years later, Sharif Nasser bought a big estate in England at East Sheen, he sent for Stanley and asked him to have it furnished in the style he liked – in ten days. No problem.

He organised another fast furnishing operation the following year when, within the specified month, he assembled from stock, and put in place, furniture for an Australian millionaire sheepfarmer called Buckland who had bought a huge house, Windlesham Moor, where he had dreams (unfulfilled) of entertaining the Queen and Prince Philip over Ascot Week. The day before Buckland was to arrive he sent a cable asking Maples to buy him a Rolls Royce (no easy task in 1952) and engage 'a competent chauffeur' (for whom people normally had to wait six months). Gerald Holman's acquaintanceship with Jack Barclay the RR dealer of Berkeley Square did the trick. A Problem – but Maples cracked it.

It was the time when Maple-Martyn were fully stretched with the big contract for the new Southampton Passenger Terminal Ocean Dock for British Rail. This specified: 'taking over the whole of the public spaces and providing wall treatment, ceilings, decorations, partitions, lighting, heating, air conditioning, plumbing, flooring, electrical installation, sanitary fittings, kitchen equipment, loud speakers, furniture and furnishings.' The first points to attract the eye at the new terminal, ran a Press report, were the furnishings and decoration.

> Maples did a wonderful job of work in all departments, indeed to such effect that in two sets of decorated reception halls one could be excused for imagining that one had entered the latest and most up-to-date hotel on a grand scale, in which comfort was the keynote.

The terminal was opened by the Labour prime minister Clement Attlee on July 31. Since his government declined to spend taxpayers' money on a celebratory luncheon, the Cunard company, whose liners the terminal was to serve, brought the *Queen Elizabeth* alongside and invited the VIPs who had attended the ceremony to be their guests at a fitting repast in the ship's dining room.

Martyns who had done so much work on that famous vessel had an order book full of marine re-fit contracts in the immediate post-war years which they carried out on a cost-plus basis which meant none of them could lose them money. Later they worked on the new Canadian Pacific liner *Empress of Canada*, and did the first-class entrance halls and stairways, and a unique spiral staircase, in the P & O liner *Canberra*. Much later Cunard gave Martyns at £250,000 contract for panelling, ceilings and fittings in the after part of the *Queen Elizabeth II*.

Much of the success of this profitable side of the business was due to Gerald Holman as Contracts Director, who became

RMS Queen Elizabeth 2 *in 1969.*
(photo by P J Fricker)

Gerald Holman, great grandson of
John Maple.

Vice-President in 1953 when Charles ('Hunter') Regnart retired as President and was succeeded by Stanley Wharton. C C Regnart had joined Maples in 1894 and, succeeding his father as President in 1926, had held the position for 27 years.

The return of the Maple family to the two top places in the management tree came at a time of reduced turnover but no reduction in the high esteem in which after 112 years the name 'Maples' was held literally all over the world, and the confidence of its management in its ability retain it for many decades to come. 'Our reputation,' declared Charles Regnart in his last Chairman's Statement, 'and the discrimination of our buyers are well known, and the name Maples carries its own guarantee of quality and construction far above the minimum standards in question.'

The latter, voluntary and for 'constructional efficiency' not quality, had just been introduced by the British Standards Institute in place of the statutory Utility Scheme. It was the year the name Maples hit the headlines not because of a newsworthy breakthrough, but a break-in which the Lord Chief Justice described as 'one of the most serious robberies which have taken place in London for a great number of years'.

When the store had its doors closed to the public at the end of each day, a Night Superintendent remained on the premises to guard against breaking and entering, and extinguish an incipient fire for which he had the help of a couple of firemen. The routine on the evening of Thursday September 24, 1953 was the same as usual. A manager locked the door of the strong room in the basement and left the building in the trusted hands of Fred Gridley, who at eight o'clock opened the side door to admit the two duty firemen. One of them was 54-year-old George Williams who presumably had not revealed to his employers that he had seven convictions for burglary. A few hours later Gridley opened up the side door to three other men: Bill Nicholls who had had a stint as a firemen at Maples a few months back and also had seven convictions; Frank Martin, an expert safe blower with six convictions; and a fifth man who Bill said was 'a Jewish-looking man whose name he thought was Marx', Frank said was called Sid, and Gridley claimed was 36-year-old Alfred Hinds, a safe cracksman, army deserter and prison escaper of some notoriety who had been convicted eight times.

Gridley was persuaded to betray the trust which Maples put in him by promise of a £2,000 cut of the proceeds from the crime which the four men he had let into the premises he was paid to guard, were about to commit. They had rehearsed what to do on Monday, and now Gridley guided the gang down to the basement and along the maze of corridors beneath the huge building, at one point forcing a steel-lined barrier with an iron bar. When they came to the door of the strong room, the two 'geli' men, Martin and Sid/Marx/Hinds, blew it open with explosive. They did the same to the inner door behind which they found a small safe. After the cracksmen had done their work, the safe yielded £4,200 worth of cash and the unexpected bonus of duplicate keys to the main jewel safe. Gridley heard them say, 'We may as well have the lot as well as the money', and, after they had pocketed the fivers and tenners intended for Friday's wages, they ascended to the ground floor where Gridley directed them to the jewel safe. The keys opened the door and each of the drawers, from which they lifted jewellery to the value of £34,000. After letting the two safe blowers and the one-time fireman out of the back door bearing the loot, Maples Night Superintendent waited till 1 am to dial 999 and report to Tottenham Court Police Station with feigned alarm the robbery he had 'discovered'.

Detective-Superintendent Herbert Sparks was round at Maples by 8.30 the next morning. He listened to Fred Gridley's account of the evening's events. When Sparks heard that George Williams, whose criminal record he knew, had been on the premises all night as fireman and not yet gone off duty, he waited for him to leave and followed him home. At the sight of the policeman on her doorstep George's wife let cry.

'This is it! I warned you not to do it!'

'Say nothing, dear,' countered George, fearing all was lost.

'I shall tell them if you don't,' she replied.

It was a fair cop. 'All right, Mr Sparks. Let's go back to the nick. The wife knows, and I'll put my cards on the table.'

Alfred Hinds, jailed for 12 years for his part in the 1953 £38,000 robbery at Maples.

Master escaper Alfie Hinds, recaptured after weeks of freedom in 1960, is escorted to the more secure Parkhurst Prison on the Isle of Wight.

At the police station Williams made a statement in which he described all the men who had taken part. Sparks also obtained a confession from Gridley – 'I don't know why I let Williams and Nicholls influence me'. Sergeant Tiddy picked up Nicholls with a plastic bag in his hand containing £1,590 in cash and £4,000 worth of jewellery, and he too signed a full confession. When the sergeant called at Hinds house outside Staines he found him having tea with Frank Martin.

'How did you tumble us down here!' asked Frank. 'The others didn't know where we came from.'

'Would you care to say what you mean by "the others", sir!'

'Don't kid me. You know the watchmen who have been on the job with us.'

While Hinds was being searched by Tiddy he told the sergeant he would like to know who had shopped them. Having his finger prints taken at the police station, he said he supposed the missing watchman was the grass.

At Clerkwell Court on September 27 only Nicholls, Martin, Wiliams and Hinds were charged – and remanded in custody. Gridley was with them in the dock however when the case came up on remand, but then was given bail. When Hinds managed to persuade a judge in chambers to grant him bail pending his possible commital for trial, at which he intended to plead Not Guilty, Gridley asked for police protection. Gridley said Hinds had come to his house and tried to interfere with him; Mrs Gridley was in a state of nerves. After that Hinds's bail was rescinded. It was said later that Hinds had offered Gridley £500 to fail to pick him out in an identification parade. At the Old Bailey trial in December, prosecuting counsel said Gridley was genuinely frightened of reprisals if he gave evidence against Hinds, but nevertheless did so. Sparks regarded Hinds as the ringleader – 'he is a forceful personality and I am sure he has put terror into the heart of Gridley'.

Hinds insisted he was at home watching a television programme called 'The Medium' that Thursday evening, and had gone to bed at 10.30. Gridley's evidence was all lies. Both Martin and Nicholls said Hinds was not involved. In spite of his protestations of innocence, Alfie Hinds was found guilty and sentenced to 12 years preventive detention.

'This is one of the most serious robberies which have taken place in London for a great number of years', Lord Goddard, Lord Chief Justice, told Hinds. 'Whether you are the ringleader in the matter I am not going to determine, but I am quite satisfied that you are a most dangerous criminal, and that you were the person who was mainly responsible for this safe blowing.'

Gridley was sent to prison for 12 months; the others for between six and ten years. During his first two years in prison, Hinds heard the Court of Criminal Appeal had refused to allow him to appeal, and he published a pamphlet demanding a retrial which was ignored. So one night he climbed over the wall of Nottingham Gaol and escaped in a waiting car – by no means his first prison break. He was recaptured after eight months. When in 1964 Sparks wrote a newspaper article asserting that Hinds was guilty of the Maples raid, he was successfully sued by the ex-convict for libel. The man he had brought to justice was awarded £1,300 damages. There was no escaping the Reaper whose name is Death, however, though he evaded him until the year of 1991, dying in January in Jersey at the age of 73 – 'the most successful prison escaper in English history', as the *Daily Telegraph* obituarist noted, 'and one of the shrewdest legal minds never to have been called to the Bar.'

There may have been shortcomings in the way Maples picked their firemen, but selection of shopwalkers was reserved to top management. By now the company had abandoned the tradition of having all their sales staff men whom they had trained as boys straight from school whom they housed in their hostel. Frank Emes, who applied for a job as salesman in 1958, was 37 and had spent five years as a manager of competitor Perring at Richmond. He was interviewed by a director, Norman Gray; and there was no question of his joining the dozen trainees on the top floor of 49 Grafton Way.

He did start his career with Maples however on the top of Tottenham Court Road, on the third floor devoted to 'modern' G-Plan furniture under Mr Barnes who had once been on the Curtain Counter at Harrods. Like other Maples salesmen of the time he then worked his way *down* – to the coveted ground floor walked by the top Cabinet Salesmen who were appointed by the Board and had only stopped wearing morning tails in 1956. He crossed the street each day for lunch at no 49, dressed in his dark suit and stiff white collar. There was a jug of ale on the table for those who wanted it (few did) – in the Senior Buyers' dining room one floor below they could have a *bottle* of Bass. The store normally closed at 5.30, but when it stayed open to seven on Thursdays, lunch became a three-course meal with cheese and biscuits. A salesman who missed his lunch shift for any reason could go to a nearby restaurant and present the bill to Maples cashier.

Frank Emes received one per cent commission on the value of the goods he sold on top of his basic salary, plus an extra one per cent on all 'own factory' furniture and bedding. This was anything made by the company's cabinet factory in Highgate Road which had its own Exhibition Department making

stands and display material; their bedding factory in Euston Buildings; subsidiary Drummond Manufacturing Company, chairmakers and upholsterers; Cheltenham Manufacturing Company, furniture manufacturers; or H H Martyn, the architectural decorators at Cheltenham. To steer a hesitant would-be purchaser into placing a firm order, Frank could offer to give her, free of charge, a scale floor plan showing the position of and space occupied by each piece of furniture in the room she was contemplating furnishing, along with a water colour 'Perspective' of how the room would look, and a colour board with the suggested materials for curtains, upholstery, carpets, wallpaper. It was all part of their routine marketing and provided by the Studio – 'the Circus' – staffed by highly trained artists.

Frank received a third one per cent commission on anything he sold to an export customer – Maple Contracts and Export Ltd had been established as a separate subsidiary and was exporting to 80 countries round the world. With part of what he sold on a one plus one per cent basis he reckoned that in a good week in the 1960s he might sell £10,000 worth of furniture. In his last year he sold around £800,000 worth. Two-thirds of a salesman's income came from commission.

The system attracted men of the highest calibre, and gave Maples salesmen the reputation of being fully conversant with every aspect of what they were about, and becoming personally involved in each customer's requirements (none of which were ever the same), taking all the time and trouble in the world – a tradition that stemmed from the days when John Maple and Blundell Maple were there to attend to customers in person. But the Maples touch now operated well beyond the vast emporium in Tottenham Court Road to the 11 stores in the

THE HOUSE OF **MAPLE**

Tottenham Court Road, London.
An artist's impression of the new
Maples wing in Grafton Way
opened on April 25th, 1956.

Tottenham Court Road, London.
An artist's impression of the new wing in Grafton Way
opened on April 25th, 1956.

'Men of the highest calibre' – the Maples Cabinet Salesmen's Dinner.

provinces which by 1965 had been joined by shops in South-ampton (Shepherd & Hedger founded by Richard Perkins in 1819) Guildford, Woking and Richmond, Surrey. A Harrogate branch was opened in 1969.

Frank Emes's experience reflected the words of 1960s bro-chure *A Career in the House of Maple*:

> The Furniture Trade offers almost unlimited opportunity for those which enthusiasm tempered by a sense of responsibility who seek a career that is rewarding in every sense of the word. Within the trade itself, nowhere are the highest standards of quality and service more zealously maintained or greater scope afforded than in the House of Maple.

Not only the salesmen but what they had to sell, in the words of one of the 12 new-look catalogues issued in 1966, had 'the exclusive Maples style and quality: exclusive because they are made in Maples workshops for the delight of Maples cus-tomers.'

> Whatever comes out of those workshops bears the Maples stamp as ummistakably as the signed products of the old furniture masters. Indeed, Maples are themselves old masters as well as modern ones. They made furniture for the grandparents of many of today's customers. There are period pieces in the showrooms which have been inspired from the old exclusive designs treas-ured in the Maples archives. Craftsmanship does not date, and the habit of fine workmanship at Maples has come down the ages. Good taste too is traditional, and Maples have a long and distinguished record.

'Spacious, well laid out, with easy circulation from one depart-ment to another, wrote Frederick Hartley of Maples in *Investors Chronicle* at this time,

> the re-built store is admirably suited to its purpose and of course in line with the modern trend towards greater size in shops and stores generally. Cut off from the distractions of the world outside, the customer is able and encouraged to go about the serious business of choosing durable goods in the appropriate

leisurely atmosphere. In contrast to the experience in general department stores, the percentage of customers entering Maples that come to buy is extremely high – this also applies to the size of the average transaction.

For the 1960s generation too Maples, as had been said so often before, was much more than just a group of shops. Apart from buying Maples tables and chairs , beds and sofas, customers could order Maples built-in furniture; have Maples removals vans drive their possessions off to the new home or Maples mammoth depository in Camden, where the freehold site had been bought in 1956; have a Maples lighting consultant plan the way their rooms were lit; a Maples kitchen consultant advise on where best to place the cooker and the air extractor; a Maples expert clean and adapt their carpets, repair their bedding, repolish their antiques.

John and Blundell Maple's enterprise pushed into the post-Utility era of the second half of the twentieth century with renewed vigour under the leadership of Gerald Holman who in 1960 took over as President from Stanley Wharton who had been with the company for 59 years, was soon to be 80 and remained a director. Stanley Wharton joined the company in 1901 as company secretary, as seen, became a director in 1908, a governor in 1912, Vice-President in 1926 and been President since 1953. In the seven years 1955 to 1961 trading profit before tax rose from £157,200 to £379,000. It was a thriving business which he entrusted to the 53-year-old son of his sister Mildred (Mrs Frank Holman), who had already served the company 35

TOTTENHAM COURT RD.
ENTRANCE DOORS

DEPARTMENTS

BEDROOM FURNITURE
DINING ROOM FURNITURE
DRAWING ROOM FURNITURE
ANTIQUES & REPRODUCTIONS
BEDSTEADS AND BEDDING
ELECTRO PLATE & CUTLERY
IRONMONGERY & TURNERY
MUSICAL INSTRUMENTS
SECONDHAND FURNITURE
REMOVALS AND DEPOSITORY
BRITISH & ORIENTAL
CARPETS AND RUGS
CURTAINS & BLINDS
FURNISHING FABRICS
CHAIRS AND SETTEES
LINENS AND BLANKETS
ORNAMENTS AND CLOCKS
ELECTRIC FITTINGS
CHINA AND GLASS
RENOVATIONS
BUILDING DECORATION
JEWELLERY
PICTURES
NEON SIGNS

SHIP, RAILWAY CARRIAGE
AND THEATRE DECORATIONS
AND FURNISHINGS

ELECTRICAL AND SANITARY
ENGINEERING

EXHIBITION STAND
CONTRACTORS

VALUERS & ESTATE AGENCY

years. At the same time his own son, 47-year-old Philip Wharton, Gerald's cousin, became Vice-President. Philip had joined as a 19-year-old trainee in 1931, been made a director in 1941 and a governor in 1950.

The new president strengthened his Board by inviting on to it in 1961 his wife's brother, Sir Richard Burbidge Bart who had just retired as chairman of Harrods, and an insider, William Matthews who had come as a trainee in 1953 and for the previous 18 months had been superintendent of all the retail businesses outside London. Apart from these two and the two cousins and Stanley Wharton at the top, the Board consisted of eight others: Norman Gray, William Knight, Denys Oppé (of Kleinwort Benson), Donald Bett, Roy Matthews and William Foulkes.

Frederick Hartley concluded his 1962 *Investors Chronicle* review by stating that in the furnishing field, for a combination of high quality, service, range of choice and reputation, which more and more consumers were evidently seeking, Maples' position was unique.

> And no challenge to this leadership is at present in sight. In the circumstances it is reasonable to assume that any check to profitability is likely to be temporary.

An early innovation of the new president was a Group Newsletter called *The Maple Leaf*, making the enlightened choice of an experienced cabinet salesman John Pounce as editor. The first two issues of November 1964 and February 1965 were duplicated on foolscap and stapled, but from then on the quarterly illustrated issues were printed and bound. In his foreword to the first issue Gerald Holman said he trusted the Maple Spirit would continue in every increasing degree as of paramount importance in the very competitive days they were now going through.

In order more successfully to meet the competition, management changed to a five-day working week for staff. The stores were open to the public for 5½ days, but Saturday morning workers took alternative Mondays off. Sales staff had a ten-day fortnight. Management called in Harold Whitehead & Partners to report on Maples' operations and recommend ways of improving them. A commissioned public relations report hinted that a management structure that had served well in its day needed modernising; there was a need to promote and sell in the more competitive areas which now represented such a preponderance of the community's buying power, to serve those buying their first pieces of furniture as well as those buying their last. Francis H D Chowins (known universally as Fred Chowins), who headed the Whitehead examination, started with the Leicester Maples, and the measures he recommended for improvement transformed the store's performance in six months. Chowins resigned from Harold Whitehead and joined Maples as sales director. He analysed the previous six months' sales in each department at Tottenham Court Road, rationalised the stock and at once weeded out more than £300,000 worth of slow sellers. With a scientific basis for buying to public preference, turnover rose significantly. The company acquired its first managing director in the person of Donald Bett, who had been governing director in charge of dining-room furniture. Jeff Hembry was made merchandising

The MAPLE ORGANISATION Comprises—

MAIN SHOWROOMS	Tottenham Court Road, London, W.1.
WEST END ESTATE OFFICE	Grafton Street, Bond Street, London, W.1.
DEPOSITORY	Camden Street, Camden Town, London, N.W.1.

BRANCHES:

BIRMINGHAM	Corporation Street, Birmingham, 4.
BOURNEMOUTH	St. Peter's Road, Bournemouth.
BRIGHTON	King's Road, Brighton.
LEEDS	Headrow House, The Headrow, Leeds.
BRISTOL	Queens Road, Bristol.
LEICESTER	Granby Street, Leicester.

SUBSIDIARY COMPANIES:

MAPLE & CO. (SOUTH AMERICA) LTD.	Calle Suipacha, Buenos Aires, Argentina.
MAPLE & CO. (PARIS) LTD.	Rue Boudreau, Paris, France.
FRASERS (MAPLE) LTD.	Princes Street, Ipswich.
HENRY BARKER SMART & BROWN LTD.	Angel Row, Nottingham.
MARK ROWE LTD.	High Street, Exeter.
RAY & MILES LTD.	London Road, Liverpool.
ROBSON & SONS LTD.	Northumberland Street, Newcastle-upon-Tyne.

There are local factories attached to all branch businesses and Subsidiary Companies.

H. H. MARTYN & CO. LTD.	Sunningend Works, Cheltenham.
Architectural Decorators in Wood, Metal, Stone and Plaster.	
CHELTENHAM MANUFACTURING CO. LTD.	Sunningend Works, Cheltenham.
Furniture Manufacturers.	
DRUMMOND MANUFACTURING CO. LTD.	Drummond Street, London, N.W.1.
Chair Makers and Upholsterers.	
General Merchants and Exporters.	

LONDON FACTORIES:

HIGHGATE ROAD, N.W.5	Cabinet Factory and Exhibition Department.
EUSTON BUILDINGS, N.W.1	Bedding Factory.

The Maple Organisation in 1959.

director responsible for Central Buying. Under the managing director were six full-time executive directors allotted a particular function. Such wholesale re-structuring followed the death in 1966 of directors Stanley Wharton and Sir Richard Burbidge. Sir William Beale who had headed NAAFI in the war and been chairman of the food chain Key Markets joined the Board, and Chowins was made a director. Tighter financial controls and new accounting methods coincided with a physical face-lift to the whole of the Tottenham Court Road frontage.

The brief to Pollard Design Studios was to make the interior so attractive and visible that potential customers would feel impelled to come in and look around. The windows were gutted, opening up the ground floor to the street. The arcade was done away with, a canopy was thrown out over the main entrance and the window line was set back seven feet, but the fluted Corinthian columns were retained. The entrance hall was given a false ceiling and modern lighting. 'I am sure that some of the older and retired members of the staff will shudder at the changes going on,' said J M R Hastings, the general manager, 'but we must march with the times if we are to survive as a great London Store – the Largest Furnishing Store in the World.' The modernising face-lift was completed in April 1968.

'The new face of Maples,' proclaimed their PR men, 'thus peers out through the symbols of magnificent past.' It was revitalisation throughout the whole organisation. 'While doing nothing to diminish the prestige wares with which

Maples has always been identified, it wants to emphasise that side of its range which is more notable for value than being valuable. Hitherto Maples has always satisfied its customers. From now on it will aim to excite them too.'

'Many of you in London have told me of the new confidence you feel in the future of Maples,' wrote Donald Bett, managing director in *The Maple Leaf* of June 1968, 'and we must all do our best to see this enthusiasm is not allowed to fade.' The past year, he said, had been one of the most eventful in the company's long history.

John Pounce thought the modernised frontage a great success. 'The new entrance had acquired a dignity of its own,' he wrote in *The Maple Leaf*, 'and would be an undoubted attraction to draw an even wider range of the public to the ultimate benefit of us all.' They should not however forget the solid traditions of the past on which the House of Maple set its strong foundations – the unrivalled range of goods of all qualities, the service that ensures the building up of goodwill so that customers, once gained, never feel they have to look elsewhere, the expert advice and attention that customers expect and should receive. 'If the truth were known, we have no real rival today if only we all do our job as it should be done.'

'It will not be long,' said Gerald Holman, the president, 'before we shall have the whole business of the Group on an informative and modern basis.' His son Rodney Holman, who had joined the staff at Tottenham Court Road marking up goods in the office and been assistant manager of the Hove branch, instigated the opening of Maples of London in Bermuda on Front Street, Hamilton where so many British spent their holidays. Anglo-Argentinian relations had become strained once more with the re-election of Juan Peron as president in 1951 and the sacking of the Jockey Club in April 1953, which to Peronistas symbolised the 'oligarchy' whom their revolution had overthrown. Declaring a general strike a mob had attacked the headquarters of the two opposition parties and then set fire to the Jockey Club destroying all the valuable furniture and tapestries supplied by Maples. Two years later Peron had resigned and gone into exile. Maple & Co (South America)'s store in Buenos Aires thrived under resident managing director Maurice Schefer and by 1968 was trading throughout the South American continent, manufacturing its own distinctive styles of furniture. They opened a second surburban store.

In France the rebuilt and enlarged Paris factory was expanding its sales with the Common Market which the UK had yet to join. Fashions in furniture were fortunately the same on both sides of the Channel: teak was back in favour and mahogany had replaced walnut, both in London and Paris.

Although most of Maples furniture and furnishings were manufactured either in their own or other British workshops, their buyers travelled the world searching for new trends and ideas. At the big exhibitions such as those in Paris and Cologne, they either bought furniture outright or the right to make it themselves. Most of their imports came from Scandinavia, but an increasingly large amount from Spain despite a 20 per cent duty which purchases from European Free Trade

ESTATE AGENCY

MAPLES' ESTATE OFFICES are situated in Grafton Street, Old Bond Street, in the historic London home of Lord Byron. A beautiful, typical Georgian mansion, it reflects in its architecture the high standard of Maples' service. Here Maples are engaged on extensive estate management, conducting sales, preparing inventories, arranging auctions, taking over for their clients all the complicated official business associated with property. Experts on estate law are available and a staff fully acquainted with all the changing conditions of estate management as it exists to-day. This unique service is placed at the disposal of all interested in property, whether residential, industrial or official.

BUENOS AIRES

MAPLE & CO. (PARIS) LTD., Rue Boudreau, Paris, was incorporated on May 10th, 1905. For some time before Maple & Co. Ltd. had traded in Paris, establishing to the satisfaction of the Board that Maples' specialised furnishing service would command the interest of the French people.

Area (EFTA) countries did not carry. Perhaps there was scope for opening more sales outlets inside Europe? They seriously considered having a store in Brussels – they opened one later.

A general expansion of retailing in Britain was also on the agenda. 'There are a number of major cities in Britain where we still don't have branches,' Rodney Holman told the London *Evening Standard* in April 1968. 'We don't have a single shop in Scotland, for example. Of course we are in touch with estate agents, and have even looked at a place in Edinburgh. It didn't quite foot the bill so we must just go on looking.' There were 16 Maples stores outside London in 1968, and the volume of their trade was greater than that of London's.

When Gerald Holman, John Maple's great grandson who had master-minded the London rebuilding and the whole expansion programme, died unexpectedly at the age of 63 in 1969, he was succeeded as president by his cousin Philip Wharton. Sir William Beale became non-executive vice-president, and Fred Chowins assistant managing director. They needed to consolidate the progress they had made, said the new president, and maintain the momentum to achieve even better things. Richard Bett, son of the managing director, who was the director in charge of the London store, said they had every reason to look to the future with confidence now that management had the right information to enable them to take the proper decisions. And the average age of Board members was under 50.

The decisions they took in the next two years led to radical change. Confidence in the strength of the Group's financial position had always derived to a considerable extent from the value of its freehold premises of which Sir Blundell Maple had been so proud. When the new Board came to consider what their net book value might be in 1970 they concluded that the £3,980,000 given in the balance sheet was 30 per cent understated. The next year it was given as £4,292,000.

Checking the worth of their properties gave assurance at a time when the furniture trade was entering an extremely difficult period. Higher costs were eroding profit margins as never before and, with more than 2,000 employed at Maples on sales, administration and manufacture, the 50 per cent increase in Selective Employment Tax (SET) introduced in the 1969 Budget caused, in Philip Wharton's words, 'a marked lack of buoyancy in the consumer durable trades.'

To weather the storm Maples resorted to releasing capital tied up in property. Costs of their removal and storage business, started in 1895, were outstripping income, and they disposed of their Camden Street Depository which, with the sale of other smaller properties, realised £360,450. They let off part of the first floor of their Euston Road premises for a good rent. Group profits were bolstered by the earnings of Lablanc Limited, specialists in the export of antiques, which became a Maples subsidiary.* Lablanc's managing director George Whyte joined the Board of Maple & Co as managing director responsible for exports (to more than 70 countries), while Fred Chowins was appointed managing director responsible for retailing in the UK, soon to be expanded with the opening of stores in Dublin, Basingstoke, Hinckley, Kirkcaldy and Plymouth.

Donald Bett retired in September 1970 on reaching the age of 65 after 50 years' service, of which 23 had been as a director. 'In these changing times,' he said, 'I firmly believe that the future of Maples is as bright today as at any time in its long history, and I shall follow its fortunes with profound interest.' Then, to streamline the administration, the Board embarked on major reorganisation which was approved by shareholders and debenture stockholders at an Extraordinary General Meeting on January 28, 1971. At this meeting Philip Wharton said the proposal to bring the voting structure into line with modern practice had attracted much attention, but far from being an invitation to bidders it was an expression of the Board's confidence in the Group's potential. The proposed developments within the company had considerable financial ramifications, particularly with regard to its property and its value.

> The Tottenham Court Road building and site is the major property holding of Maples; it stands in our last balance sheet at £2,300,000 and was valued in 1963 at £3,230,000. It was the Board's view until recently that the chance of obtaining the requisite permission to achieve any worthwhile development on this site were remote.

They had now re-examined the whole matter. Subject to obtaining the necessary consents, the Board were advised that a new building could be erected on the site which might be completed in 1973/4. It would provide quite different accom-

---

* In fact Maples had paid £176,000 for a controlling interest in Lablanc in 1966 under an agreement by which they could acquire the balance of the share capital in 1971. George Whyte agreed to sell the balance in July 1970 for £525,000, having joined Maples Board in September 1969.

modation for the store from what it was then being used. Very careful planning would be required to achieve the best redeployment of their merchandising operation. With the necessary consents a possible figure for a valuation of the Tottenham Court Road site would be in the region of £5 million.

The reorganisation took the form of converting Maple & Company Ltd into a holding company with three operating subsidiaries, and Philip Wharton as chairman and George Whyte and Sir William Beale as Joint Deputy-Chairmen. On January 28, 1971 the Management Shares were converted into Ordinary Shares on the basis of one Ordinary Share of £1 for every five Management Shares of 4s.

The 19 retail stores in the UK, plus those in the Republic of Ireland, France and Bermuda became the responsibility of 'Maple & Company Furnishers Limited' of which Sir William Beale was chairman and Frank Chowins was managing-director, who told readers of *The Maple Leaf* he thought they now had a structure which would enable them to go forward to bigger and better things than ever before. 'Maple & Company International Limited' took over the Export Division, and the export and overseas operations of Lablanc Ltd and Maple Contracts & Export Ltd. Its chairman was George Whyte and its directors included Sir John Figgess, late of the British Embassy in Japan, and Carol Greene who had been with Lablanc ten years – the company's only female Board member. The parent company's manufacturing activities were handled by 'Maple & Company Manufacturing Limited'. Operations at Highgate Road comprised the Drummond Division, and those at Cheltenham the H H Martyn Division. Its chairman was Philip Wharton.

D J C Prout, who had been a general manager with the John Lewis Partnership, was brought in as general manager of the Tottenham Court Road store. He divided it into three sections each with an Operations Controller. This was a new departure for Maples in the day to day running of the store but, said John Pounce, was 'in accordance with modern thought'. Prout took over the chairmanship of the Retail Committee from Richard Bett which met once a month to discuss matters of sales policy.

Thus the old structure of president and governing body was replaced by the more orthodox management of a chairman and board of directors. They looked to develop not only new branches but for 'young progressive and go-ahead chaps, with their whole life in front of them' to staff them. Asked by the *Cabinet Maker* if the new look Maples, minted in 1968 and continually up-dated, was paying dividends, Frank Chowins said they were very happy with the progress made so far. 'We know where we are going, we know how we are going there, and I think we ARE going.'

The company's competitors were also going places. With the acquisition of Waring & Gillow, Harrison Gibson (Ilford) and Wolfe & Hollander, Manny Cussin's John Peters (Furnishing Stores) Ltd could claim a chain of 42 stores. Cussins had formed the John Peters Group after he had sold his own group to Great Universal Stores. Maple & Co Furnishers Ltd aimed to have 45 stores by 1975 said Rodney Holman, but it would need another 20 to cover the whole country. Plans were afoot to open in Swindon, Hull and Norwich. The latest addition was the Guernsey furniture store of Lovell & Co in St Peters Port,

Wood carver M Norman of Martyns at work on the St Paul's pulpit.

Tom Bridge and Harold Guest of Martyns assembling the St Paul's pulpit.

One of the most prestigious of the many wood carving contracts given to H H Martyn (which Maples sold in 1974) was to make, to the design of Lord Mottistone (reproduced here by kind permission of the Dean and Chapter), a pulpit in oak and limewood for St Pauls Cathedral to mark the 250th anniversary of the building's completion.

which had been renamed Maples. Provincial branches contributed 60 per cent of the Group's turnover in 1971.

Maples own-manufacture merchandise now represented only between five and ten per cent of stock. In October 1971 Philip Wharton announced that H H Martyn of Cheltenham would close at the end of January next year. 'The present difficult conditions in the shipbuilding and construction industries, on which the factory depends, have rendered it impossible for us to continue trading profitably there, and have thus made closure inevitable.' Manufacture of the Martyn range of reproduction furniture would be moved elsewhere, he said. The Sunningend premises and the company name were bought by Schindler Lifts (UK) Ltd. The workforce at Martyns was down to 300.

> Problems had faced the company as polystyrene cornices replaced plaster, and fibreglass coats of arms replaced bronze (*wrote John Whitaker in* The Best). Lower standards were accepted by architects and clients because of the high cost of 'the best'. The stone carvers were the first to go; most had finished in 1947 ... Decorative wood carving was much reduced and it was a bitter blow when the foundry had to close from lack of work.

Hardwood joinery, the traditional province of Martyns, was now being undertaken by the big builders such as McAlpine and Costain in their own departments instead of sub-contracting to Martyns.

Order books in the Furniture Industry in general however were at an extremely high level. There were £46 million worth of orders in hand for domestic furniture at the end of September 1971 compared with £36 million in 1970. The net group profit of Maple & Co for 1970/1 was £518,000 compared with £443,000 in 1969/70.

Philip Wharton still had four years of his service agreement to run, but as part of the reorganisation of senior executive responsibilities proposed in November 1971, he agreed to retire early on payment of a lump sum of £36,000. The events of the next few weeks however caused him to delay his with-

The finished pulpit in situ in St Paul's Cathedral.

drawal. On November 24 Camden Borough Council hinted that they would be willing to give planning consent for the development of the Tottenham Court Road island site. It was the signal which every property developer had been waiting for. They had showed little interest in investing in Maples the retailer, but Maples the owner of property, which they would be unlikely to have the money or the expertise to develop, was another matter. A hundred and thirty years reputation in the furniture business was an asset of little worth beside ownership of freehold premises and land in the West End of London.

∞ 7 ∞

New Pilot, Same Elegance, Different Presentation 1971–1991

ON January 5, 1972, taking their lead from the local authority, the Greater London Council gave Maple & Co outline planning permission to build on their London site a block which would include not only a (smaller) furniture store, but 171,000 square feet of offices, flats and a laboratory for University College Hospital. For their offices they could demand rent at the current rate of £7 a square foot.

Maple & Co were at once the subject of what the press called 'close City attention'. First to come up with a firm bid were Jessel Securities Limited who had quietly and quickly built up a 12.6 per cent holding in the company's shares. Jessel owned 33 per cent of the Ordinary shares of a Cardiff-based company called Macowards Limited who had ten provincial department stores and a television rental business. Their offer for control of the Maples Group was £14.4 million, or 200p a share. The offer took the wind out of the sails of Maples' own plans to finance the redevelopment of the site. Philip Wharton told shareholders on February 14 that he and his fellow directors had originally intended to announce how they were going to do it 'in the near future', but 'pending the outcome of the present offers' they had decided to postpone making any decision. Their directors, he said, had been advised by Kleinwort Benson, and they recommended them to accept the offer as fair and reasonable. 'My departure had in fact been delayed by the original announcement by Jessel Securities of its interest in Maples,' he said, 'and I shall now be resigning as chairman and a director of Maple with effect from 7 March 1972.'

It was with George Whyte, Joint Deputy Chairman, that Jessel Securities, acting on behalf of Macowards, agreed to purchase 400,000 Maples 25p shares at £2 each if the offer became unconditional by March 7. Jessel themselves by now already owned another 5,510,000 shares – 19.9 per cent. Any uncertainty as to the outcome was removed with the announcement that Macowards had had 73 per cent acceptances, and Maples shares leapt 20p to 180p.

'Maples performance has faltered amidst all the uncertainty of recent months,' commented the *Cabinet Maker*. 'Now that its future has been settled, it is hoped that its other 20 furniture shops will recover to their former standing in the market.'

There was no hesitating however by the new owners who had changed their name to Maple Macowards, and had George Cantlay of Macowards as chairman and an American, Jan van Bergen, as managing director. Fred Chowins was made a director of Maple Macowards and managing director of its subsidiary Maple & Co of which Carol Greene and Jeff Hembry (who married in 1971) were also directors. George Whyte, Sir William Beale and Denys Oppé resigned their directorships. With the retirement of Philip Wharton and the withdrawal soon afterwards of Rodney Holman, there were no longer any descendents of John Maple with Maples.

Everyone knew that 'development' of a site meant demolishing what already stood on it. But it was a shock when in mid-April came the announcement that Maples of Tottenham Court Road was to close that very summer. That major asset, said George Cantlay in his Chairman's Statement of May 30, 1972, would be developed for office, residential, laboratory and shopping use, 'and the anticipated rental income will contribute materially to Group profits'.

> Redevelopment will take approximately three years. The Tottenham Court Road store will close on 29th July 1972 and demolition will commence shortly afterwards.

Demolition? But had not the store been given an expensive modernising facelift only in 1968? Ah yes, but . . .

The 21st issue of *The Maple Leaf* dated October 1971 was the last. Editor John Pounce said he hoped to give details of the rebuilding plans, but could only quote a story in the *Evening Standard* saying showroom space in the new 'skyscraper' would be 85,000 square feet compared with 260,000. 'When the time comes you may be sure *The Maple Leaf* will carry the fullest details.'

It was not to be.

A very much smaller staff of managers, buyers and sales staff were needed for the small shop round the corner in Euston Road, which kept the name of Maples alive in London while the mammoth complex of buildings, which had risen on the site John Maple had acquired in 1841, was once more reduced to rubble and the builders moved in to construct the 'development' designed by modernist architect Richard Seifert. Norman Andrews, like most of his colleagues, was 'made redundant' with a fixed pension for the rest of his life. Frank Emes was one of the few retained to staff the Euston Road shop.

You Can't Keep A Great Store Down

proclaimed the press advertisements they ran in the summer of 1972.

It's true that you won't find Maples in Tottenham Court Road any longer. For the simple reason that our old building is coming down to make way for redevelopment.
But this doesn't mean we're getting out of town.
Maples is going as strongly as ever at 247/257 Euston Road – about 1 minute's walk from the old address.
The new Maples isn't as large as the old Maples – but in many ways it's better than ever. And on a foot to foot basis it carries more of the world's finest furniture and furnishings than anywhere else in town.
Maples of Euston Road
A living monument to that basic rule of nature.
What comes down must go up.

Advertisement 28 September 1972.

In the West End Carol Greene kept the name alive at 'Maples Antiques & Fine Art' showroom at 43-44 New Bond Street, opened in November 1972 by Bevis Hillier, editor of *The Connoisseur*.

In May the following year George Cantlay declared the market value of the Tottenham Court Road site to be £12 million, 'and on completion it will be worth well in excess of £20 million'. Demolition was completed in January 1973 and work began on the new building soon afterwards. Signs of undue strain on Maple Macowards funds 'primarily geared to expanding normal trading activities' showed in their decision to negotiate with 'major financial institutions to obtain a permanent source of finance', and get a separate Stock Exchange listing for their property interests. In July 1972 Maple Macowards had estimated the Tottenham Court Road site to be worth £17 million which compared with a book value of £2.8 million. In announcing details of a rights issue the directors said they expected to receive an annual rent of more than £1 million. The open market value of the site, said a Press report, was thought to be around £9 million. 'Maple Macowards, in which Jessel Securities has a substantial stake, will redevelop the site without outside help'. But a lot could happen in six months. Indeed between January and mid-March 1973, in the light of Phase 1 of the Freeze, the Government's anti-inflationary programme, Maple Macowards' shares fell 20 per cent to 66p, compared with a peak of 110p for 1972-3. Retail stores were relatively harder hit than many other sectors in the wake of Phase 2 and fears of a general slowdown in consumer spending.

The manufacturing activities of Maple & Co ceased with the closure by their parent company Maple Macowards of the factory in Highgate Road. The bedding factory in Drummond Street became Maple & Co's temporary administrative offices. The main activity was the furniture retailing outside London. Ten new Maples stores were opened in 1973 and another 13 in 1974. Six stores were renovated and modernised. Whereas in 1972 there were 25 provincial stores of which nine were trading under other names, at the end of 1974 there were 52 of them and all but one as 'Maples'. In London the Bond Street antiques showroom closed, but a Maples furniture store was opened in Brompton Road, Knightsbridge.

The new building in Tottenham Court Road was to have 50,000 square feet for furniture showrooms, not 85,000. Offices were to take up 100,000 sq ft, and a laboratory and flats for University College Hospital 10,000 sq ft. At the top were to be 32 private flats for outright sale. Completion was scheduled for May 1975, but in August George Cantlay had to admit that the retail area would not be ready until the end of 1975 and the residential blocks early in 1976. That represented a considerable delay over the original timetable.

> The delay in the completion and letting of the building exerted considerable pressures on the Group's cash resources, but I am pleased to be able to report that the syndicate of banks led by Morgan Grenfell has made available to us an additional facility of £1 million.

Maple Macowards' Board had reviewed valuations of their other properties and there was a deficit of £831,000. 'In view of the rise in building costs and the fall in property values generally,' he said in his Chairman's Statement of August 22, 1975, 'it is not the present policy of your Board to continue its plans for the redevelopment of a number of its properties. The year under review has been most difficult for all associated with the Group.' Fred Chowins and Jan van Bergen resigned as directors in October 1974, and Mark St Giles, the largest stockholder in Maple Macowards with 86,000 shares, resigned his directorship in July 1975, along with two other directors. After consulting their property advisers, they wrote down the February 1975 book value of the Tottenham Court Road development. In their Auditors Report on the 1975 Report and Accounts, Deloittes stated:

> The Tottenham Court Road site, which is at an advanced stage of development, is included in the balance sheet at a figure of £13,600,000, based on an assessment by the Directors of estimated realisable value, less projected completion costs. The valuation anticipates completion of the programme of letting of the major part of the finished building. In the light of the present uncertain conditions in the property market, we are unable to satisfy ourselves that this value is realisable.

Under an agreement made in October 1973 a syndicate managed by Morgan Grenfell had given Maple Macowards a facility of £15 million secured on the Tottenham Court Road site, repayable in October 1978 or earlier at the company's option, with interest at 1¼ per cent above inter-bank deposit rate.

The smaller Maples opened its new showrooms on John Maple's old site in 1975, with Chris Peddar as manager reporting to Peter Connolly who was in charge of Maples operations in Europe and Central London.

Maples retail stores made no contribution to Maple Macowards Group trading profits in 1975. They were 'badly affected by an ambitious expansion plan and the modernisation of a number of existing units. This caused undue strain on the company's finances and management. New stores are rarely profitable in the first year.' But Maple Macowards' troubles, which caused a £7 million loss in 1975, were more deep-seated than that.

They sold eight Macowards department stores to Owen Owen and closed three others. They sold their television rental business to Radio Rentals. They signed an agreement with Camden Borough Council for the sale (99 year lease) of the residential accommodation at Tottenham Court Road for £1.45 million. As soon as they had let the three floors of offices, and the retail areas, they intended to realise the freehold of the whole development. But once again Deloittes were not satisfied that its value of £14 million given in the balance sheet was realisable. They still suffered a loss in 1976 but it was down to £4 million.

Their mainstay was the chain of 40 Maples stores outside London situated in 1976 at Aberdeen, Bedford, Birmingham, Bournemouth, Bristol, Cambridge, Corby, Ealing, Eastbourne, Epsom, Esher, Exeter, Frinton, Guernsey, Guildford, Harrogate, Hove, Ipswich, Jersey, Kings Lynn, Leeds, Leicester, Liverpool, Newcastle-upon-Tyne, Norwich, Nottingham, Plymouth, Richmond, Salisbury, Slough, Southampton, Southport, Sutton Coldfield, Swansea, Torquay, Weybridge, Wimbledon, Woking, Wood Green and Worthing.

In September 1976 Maple Macowards Limited changed their name to 'Maple & Company (Holdings) Limited', and as such sold the whole of their interest in the Tottenham Court Road building, now called Maple House, for £11,250,000 – just about half the sum they reckoned in 1973. The buyer was Vipvale Properties, a company controlled by Bernard Sunley Investment Trust and London Mercantile Corporation. From this owner, Maple & Company, subsidiary of Maple & Co (Holdings), leased the 51,000 sq ft of the showroom space available out of the total floor area of 114,800 sq ft, on a 99 year lease for an initial annual rent of £125,000.

The deal resulted in a deficit for Maple (Holdings) of £2,545,000 against the book value of the property as at January 31, 1976. They estimated that the £11 million from Vipvale, the £1,450,000 from Camden Council and the money from the sale of other leases would enable them to repay the outstanding balance of the £15 million syndicated bank loan. 'The annual cost at present market rates of the borrowings to be repaid', stated George Cantlay still chairman in July 1977, 'would amount in a full year to some £1,050,000, as compared with rental income from the lettings so far achieved (other than to Maple & Company Limited) of some £528,000 in a full year.'

But then profiting from property appreciation was no longer

MAPLE MACOWARDS
140 Hampstead Road, London NW1 2PU
Tel: 387 2833 (STD Code 01)

the object of the exercise. After the sale of Maple House, said the first Director's Report of the reborn company in May 1978, 'the Group's property investment activities are no longer substantial.' It was back to what Maples knew best, to what John and Blundell Maple had developed on the site so expertly over so many years – furniture retailing. In September 1978 Peter Connolly, the director in charge of the store, said he hoped shopping there would be an adventure, with lots to look at as well as buy. And that there should be something for everyone. What he had to offer ranged from plush Italian leather and suede to reproduction period pieces and the best of contemporary British manufacturers. Wrote one reporter on the opening day:

> Certainly the juxtapositioning of styles is a stimulating experi-ence for anyone used to ranks of clean-cut sofas, pine and cane. Whatever you may think of the new branch, it certainly isn't dull. Some of the more exotic furniture and objects on display would seem to be verging on the theatrical. As you enter through the front door, there is a giant bed looking like a vast suede melon with slices cut out for access.

George Cantlay was still a director, but had handed over as chairman to David Keys of Morgan Grenfell. Alan Hogg was managing director, and Jeff Hembry, long serving Maples man, was a member of the eight-man board. The temporary Euston Road shop and the Knightsbridge shop remained open, the administrative offices were at 140 Hampstead Road. Total staff was down to 700. The re-structured, debt-free enterprise got off to a good start with a £1 million pre-tax profit in the first year. In October 1979 they acquired 92 per cent of the share capital of Armena SA who had furniture stores in Nice and Cannes for £900,000; and in November invested £146,000 in a new furniture store in Doha, Qatar in the Persian Gulf called Almana Maple. There was a retailing turnover of £28 million in 1980 (£23 million in 1979). Though the economic outlook was more uncertain than ever, the Board was confident said David Keys on April 22, 1980, 'we have both the financial and human resources to enable us to take full advantage of whatever opportunities may arise'.

But after two years their refound independence was at stake all over again. Seven weeks before David Keys signed his 1980 report he was approached by John Cussins and Manny Cuss-ins of Waring & Gillow, who held no shares in Maples, for boardroom talks about a takeover. 'The surprise bid,' said *The Cabinet Maker* before they knew the identity of the bidder, 'will certainly be viewed as an opportunist move by followers of the company.'

With the breakdown of talks with Maples board, Waring & Gillow went straight to shareholders with an offer to pay them 30p a share, which would cost them £8.4 million. David Keys and his fellow directors rejected the offer as 'completely unsatisfactory' and advised shareholders to reject it. In antici-pation of further developments the price of Maples shares rose to 31p. 'Market men,' reported *The Cabinet Maker*, 'are not ruling out the possibility of a counter offer from another retailing group – with House of Fraser a popular candidate.' Maples directors only held about one per cent of the shares, so fending off or admitting the predator in the new takeover battle lay with the small shareholders. Waring & Gillow had by now purchased a small block of some 150,000 shares at 30p. If they won their battle for Maples, Waring & Gillow said they would sell their Regent Street store to Debenhams. They pointed to the advantages of the combined purchasing power of the two groups, particularly in carpets, and the benefits of centralised warehousing and distribution. The furnishing industry in the UK, they said in their offer document, was undergoing material change likely to continue well into the 1980s.

> The growth of out-of-town discount retailers will increase the pressure on retail margins and, as we have seen, the number of high street retail furnishers is diminishing. The combined companies would operate some 126 domestic furniture and carpet retail outlets in the United Kingdom.

In their formal rejection document Maples said the bid was designed to enable Waring & Gillow to dispose of their Regent Street store with the least dislocation to themselves. Any move to another site would be costly and result in a substantial loss of business. The presence of Maples restricted Waring & Gillow's expansion within the UK, and they had little experience of overseas operation. Maples' properties had been revalued at £8.4 million which gave a paper profit of £3.2 million over book values.

Waring & Gillow bought more and more Maples shares on the stock market, which by the end of May, added to the acceptances they had received for their 35p a share bid, were just enough to enable them to declare the offer unconditional as the first closing date was reached – but only just. At the end of the day they had 50.4 per cent of the Maples ordinary shares on their side. But it was enough to give them control.

Who were Waring & Gillow? It was a company formed from the combining of two famous names in the world of British furniture. Robert Gillow set up as a master cabinetmaker in Lancaster in 1728. His son, also Robert Gillow, moved to London in 1760 and established headquarters for Gillow at 176 Oxford Street which remained the firm's home until 1906. In the 18th century they traded as Robert Gillow & Company, Gillow, Gillow & Taylor, G & R Gillow, making high quality furniture of every type at their Lancaster workshops. They became involved too in fitting out ships and yachts. In 1846 the Government had Gillow supply all the furniture to Pugin's designs for the new Houses of Parliament. In 1897 Samuel Harris, the employee who had become the sole proprietor of Gillow, sold the company to John Musker who was part of a group of London-based businessmen which included Gordon Selfridge and Samuel J Waring Junr.

The Waring family originated in Norway and emigrated to Ireland at the beginning of the 19th century where they became highly successful linen manufacturers. Samuel J Waring opened a branch in Liverpool where he not only sold his Irish linen but a range of household effects. Later they became wholesale cabinetmakers. In 1893 S J Waring's son, Samuel Waring junior, moved to London and established the Waring business in Oxford Street. Four years later Gillows merged with London cabinet makers Collinson & Lock who specialised in art furniture, and they began co-operating with War-ings, who apart from their workshops and showrooms in Lancaster, Liverpool and Manchester, had a branch in Paris. In 1903 the two firms combined with a capital of £1 million as 'Waring & Gillow', and at the same time took over Hamptons, house furnishers and estate agents. In 1906 they opened the huge Waring & Gillow emporium in Oxford Street which remained their headquarters for the next 65 years. After the collapse of the firm in 1931 and the appointment of a receiver, a new company, Waring & Gillow (1932) was formed; the Liverpool factory was closed and the Lancaster factory concentrated on its most marketable products and reproduction antique furniture. The company reached a low ebb again in 1953. It was taken over by Great Universal Stores and broken up. In 1961 the retail side passed to John Peters Furnishing Stores owned by Manny Cussins who in 1973 changed that company's name to Waring & Gillow (Holdings) Ltd. Cussins developed the carpet sales part of the business and set up the Carpet Distribution Centre in Sheffield. The famous New Oxford Street Waring & Gillow was closed in 1966, and the company re-opened in the Galeries Lafayette premises in Regent Street, which cost them £1.3 million.

Samuel J Waring junior in 1898. His Liverpool firm combined with Robert Gillow & Co in 1903 to form 'Waring & Gillow' which opened a store in London in 1906.

As soon as Waring & Gillow won control of Maples in 1980 they sold their Regent Street shop to Debenhams as they said they would – for £5.5 million. Manny Cussins said the Tottenham Court Road store would continue to trade as Maples, but with an increase of 13,000 sq ft of selling space for the kind of American furniture which Waring & Gillow had pioneered in Britain. But the Maples showroom in Brompton Road would change its name to Waring & Gillow. He looked for a 75 per cent increase in carpet turnover, and would make a major assault on quality fitted bedroom furniture. He would make better use of warehousing and establish more effective distribution; he would install computerised stock control. He told *The Cabinet Maker* in July 1980 he doubted whether there would be any High Street retailers left inside a generation other than large groups. The increase in property prices made selling off a freehold a much more profitable proposition than selling furniture. He would not be buying furniture in the future but production capacity. The large retailer would present the manufacturer with their design, specification and production requirements and take delivery. Maples had given Waring & Gillow the volume to do that on a scale not seen before. The present system of buying at exhibitions was crazy.

> Quite frankly I don't think Maples would have survived without us. They need more volume, better promotion, better merchandising and lower prices. The big change we hope the customer will notice is a sharper attitude to both merchandising and presentation – It was a considerable temptation to merge the two under our name, but it is one that must be resisted.

The euphoria evaporated in five years. Though Waring & Gillow earned peak profits of £4.82 million on turnover of £57.2 million the year before they acquired Maples, they lost £752,000 on turnover of £91 million in 1982-3. They made a profit of £314,000 on a £93 million turnover in 1983-4, but results for the first half of 1985 showed interim losses of £408,000 on sales of £47 million. Speculation in March 1985 that someone was bidding for Waring & Gillow sent the price of their shares soaring 24p to 140p. Further take-over speculation saw them rise to 158p. At the beginning of April came the announcement that an £24.9 million offer to buy Waring & Gillow/Maples had come from a new consortium called Hopecastle comprising Cyril Spencer, former Burton Group executive chairman, Ashley Meyer formerly Debenhams Furnishings' managing director, and investment bankers Albion Trust half-owned by S & W Berisford the commodity brokers. To them John and Manny Cussins handed over control.

The terms of the agreed offer were 160p nominal of Hopecastle unsecured loan stock 1990, or a 153p cash alternative. Great Universal Stores accepted the offer in respect of its 30.9 per cent holding. Cyril Spencer took over as chairman of Waring & Gillow which now had a chain of 116 stores. He told *The Cabinet Maker* he saw a great future for the high quality furniture group his consortium had acquired 'whose origins go back to the days of the great English cabinet makers Chippendale and Hepplewhite'.

> The opportunity is there to attract the upwardly mobile young professionals and executives as customers, and to increase market share, presently about seven per cent, by broadening its appeal. We shall pursue the group's policy of buying British wherever possible, and aim to make Waring & Gillow and Maples the shop windows for the British furniture industry.

Cyril Spencer had his office at 145 Tottenham Court Road, but the registered office of Waring & Gillow (Holdings) Plc was The Mount, Glossop Road, Sheffield. The chairman's letterhead read MAPLE WARING *GILLOW* – with the accent on the latter. The reign of Hopecastle was a brief one, and in October 1986 a management buy-out gave direction of the company to Cyril Spencer, Ashley Meyer, managing-director, and the rest of the board, as controlling shareholders. There had been a marked decline in turnover which, combined with integration problems and reorganisation costs, had put the company deeply in the red. The 1986/7 results of what they now called the Gillow Group showed pre-tax losses of £7.2 million on a turnover of £113 million. They made £1 million out of property disposals but had debt service charges of £3.6 million. In January 1987 they absorbed Wades Furnishers, Kingsbury Furnishers and Homestore which made Gillows the fourth largest retailer of furniture in the UK. It had 150 branches, more than 2,000 employees, one-and-a-half million square feet of selling space and a budgeted turnover of £140 million for 1987/8. Trading in the USA ceased and all management resources were concentrated in Britain.

MAPLE WARING
Gillow

It was big – perhaps over-big – and looked promising. But the prospects never fulfilled their potential. The first year's sales performance of the enlarged Gillow Group, resulting in a loss, was extremely disappointing. The stores had suffered from the disruption of a major refurbishment programme – some were renamed 'Gillow' and then back to 'Maples' – and they never recovered from lost sales. A constant round of discount sales had a depressing effect on both sales achieved and gross margins.

Cyril Spencer and Ashley Meyer resigned from the Gillow board, and the remaining controlling shareholder/directors, who had had to borrow money at interest for their management buy-out, looked outside for replacements with management expertise to generate the higher turnover needed to produce a profit and give the group much needed stability. In April 1988 they appointed as chairman Denis Cassidy, deputy chairman of Storehouse where he was chief executive of British Home Stores, and Simon Bee as group managing-director. By the end of the 1988 trading year Gillow were £2 million in the black.

But Cassidy was aware of the need for nothing less than 'a full and urgent reappraisal' of Gillow's situation. Within less than twelve months however came an approach from Allied Carpets to pay £29 million for 48 of the 87 Gillow-owned stores and nine related properties, together with the sole rights to the trading and brand names of 'Gillow', 'Maples' and 'Waring & Gillow'.

Allied Carpets had come from two carpet traders and a distributor combining to create six stores under that name in the mid-1960s. An 'Allied Carpets' company was floated in 1971. By 1978 it owned 30 stores, and in that year it was bought by Associated Dairies (ASDA), the food chain. Between 1978 and 1989 Allied Carpets diversified into upholstery, bedding and cabinet furniture and soft furnishings, sold through 86 stores.

Richard Harker, the chief executive whom Allied Carpets appointed to develop their retail strategy into the 1990s, said the acquisition would promote the company as one of the leading home furnishing retailers in the UK. 'We will harness the strong Maples and Waring & Gillow brand names in furniture and bedding to Allied's existing core.' They would be trading from 158 stores. The 48 Gillow stores had been hand-picked and were mainly in the south. Gillow retained 39 stores including the Maples of Tottenham Court Road which was renamed 'Maples International'. Their recommendation for selling to Allied was based on the need to reposition the Gillow group in the market place – a move into the middle market was being considered as a new retail philosophy.

Under the terms of the deal Gillow Plc had two years in which their 39 Maples or Waring & Gillow stores in Britain, the one in Rue Boudreau Paris and the one in Avenue Louise Brussels, could continue to trade under those names. They no longer had the store in Buenos Aires.

In the 85 years Buenos Aires had had a Maples in its midst, the name, as in France, albeit pronounced Spanish-fashion, had become a household word. The lyric of a still-popular Argentine Tango, *Y Todo a media luz* (Everything in semi-

GREAT STATESMANSHIP

GREAT CRAFTSMANSHIP

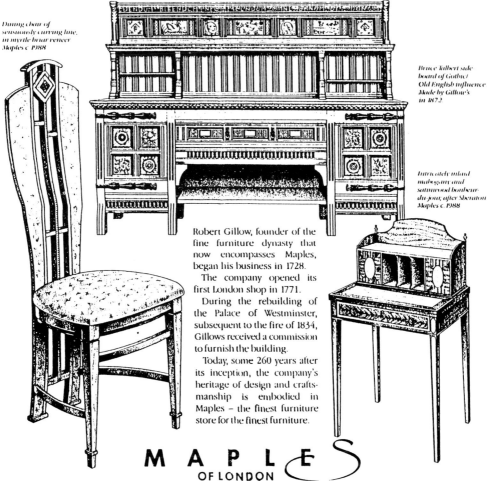

Dining chair of sensuously curving line, in myrtle briar veneer. Maples c. 1988

Bruce Talbert side board of Gothic/ Old English influence. Made by Gillow's in 1872

Intricately inlaid mahogany and satinwood bonheur-du-jour, after Sheraton. Maples c. 1988

Robert Gillow, founder of the fine furniture dynasty that now encompasses Maples, began his business in 1728.

The company opened its first London shop in 1771.

During the rebuilding of the Palace of Westminster, subsequent to the fire of 1834, Gillows received a commission to furnish the building.

Today, some 260 years after its inception, the company's heritage of design and craftsmanship is embodied in Maples – the finest furniture store for the finest furniture.

M A P L E S
OF LONDON
145 TOTTENHAM COURT ROAD, LONDON W1. Tel: 01-387 7000
A Member of the Gillow Group.

The advertising message of the now Gillow-orientated Maples of the 1980s.

darkness) tells of a boy and a girl dancing together in his poorly furnished apartment, and deploring that none of their furniture is from Maples. No matter if it was not new, so long as it was Maples. In fact the store's second-hand department in the basement was highly popular. It contained many pieces of fine old furniture rescued from British homes damaged in the Blitz of World War 2. Much of it had been brought out to Argentina in the holds of British ships sailing in ballast during the war to load Argentinian beef and grain.

The fine building in Calle Suipacha 658, with its imposing fluted columns, was still standing in 1991, but had been turned into a municipal bank. 'It is in a sad state of disrepair,' states Baron Clemens von Schey-Koromla, 'and all that the curving glass shop windows have to offer the passer-by are dingy reproductions of old Argentine film stars'.

In 1986 Maurice Schefer (who has since died) had sold the furniture operation of Maple & Co (South America) Ltd to ex-employees who formed 'New Maples SA' and opened a Buenos Aires showroom in Quintana Avenue. They failed to attract sufficient custom however and the following year New Maples was declared bankrupt. In 1991 the building in Calle Suipacha 658 still belonged to Maple & Co (South America) Ltd, in the hands of an administrator, who leased it to the Municipality of Buenos Aires.

It was upsetting for men like 80-year-old Leonard Cox who used to work there. He is now at Wrights Bazaar which sells wedding gifts, English China and silver and furniture commissioned from the same local cabinetmakers from whom Maples ordered. In his day the main business of the Buenos Aires Maples was the interior decoration of clubs, offices, hotels, private houses and yachts. In addition to the main store there was a branch in the suburb of Martinez. Originally the manager was always English like the Mr Botting whose daughter Mrs Dorothy Creiger still lived in Buenos Aires in 1991. But Raul Miserendino became General Manager after serving the firm 50 years from 1910 to 1960; then Maurice Schefer took over. When Maples first came to Argentina, reminisced Leonard Cox in 1991,

> they must have had few competitors, for they had a very extensive library of designs which no outside competitor ever had. But as time went on they had a lot of competition from a number of very able designers and well-run workshops. Swedes came from Nordiska and made very attractive furniture, but even they closed down eventually, because of lack of trade. The Locapi SA carpenters I spoke to who had worked for Maples for 20 years thought Maples had left Argentina in good time. I agree. Business had been going down here for many years, and there is a great deal more competition in the interior decorating business than there used to be.

To return to the main story, on May 15 1989, when the agreement came into force, administration of Maples, which had been done from Tottenham Court Road, split into two. Half went to the Maples building in Bournemouth – buying, merchandising, store operations – under Christopher Peddar, a long serving member of Maples management; half to the offices of 'Allied Maples Group Plc' which Allied Carpets had formed to function out of their West Bromwich office – property, warehousing, financial control.

When the new owners asked Chris Peddar what he thought Maples should now aim for, he said what it had always been famous for – selling medium to top quality furniture conscientiously, and with style.

> In recent history, in an attempt to keep up volume, we sold upholstery groups for £599. Our cheapest upholstery ought to be around £1,000. We were forced into selling merchandise at half that price. Instead of promoting furniture at the correct market profile, we adopted a cheaper marketing stance – which Maples

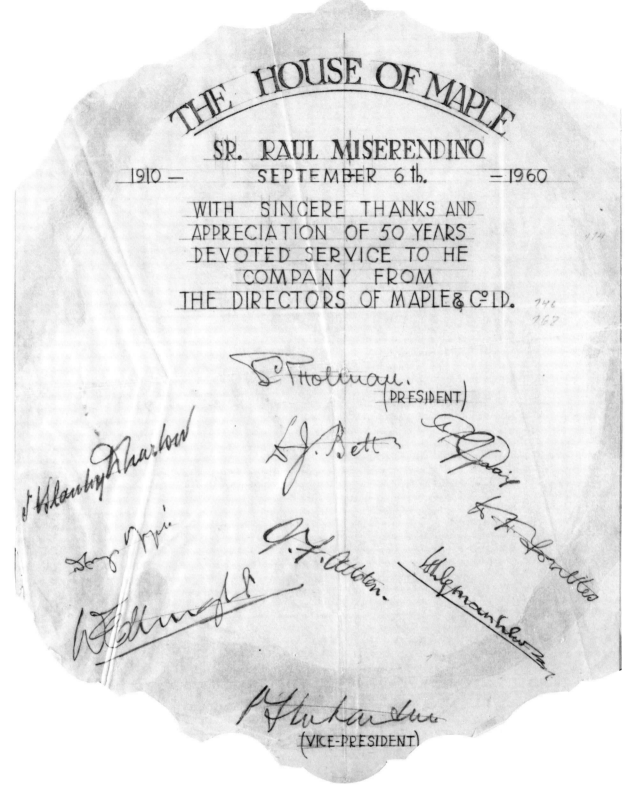

Design for the silver salver presented to Raul Miserendino on September 6 1960 after 50 years service to Maple (South America) Ltd in Argentina, signed by the London directors.

were never in. We left the volume business to others, who did it better.

Their plan was to double the number of main Maples and Waring & Gillow stores in two years. They would have furniture made to their own specification, a joint venture to be master-minded by Malcolm Walker. Half of the range would be special and 'Only From Maples' in model or cover – the design of the fabric and its colour. Within a year they hoped 90 per cent of the furniture they sold would be exclusive to Maples and unobtainable outside a Maples store. The stores themselves would be re-styled, along with the suits to be worn by sales staff. It was a scheme not imposed by outside consultants but evolved through internal discussion – and then handed to the professionals to work out. The first three pilot schemes were carried out in 1990 and 1991 at stores in Leeds, Exeter and Watford.

Seventy per cent of the competition came from the furniture departments of department stores such as Harrods and John Lewis, and from the 'quality independents' on the High Street. There was no competition in 'chain' terms, which was why Allied Maples were determined to push ahead with re-styling up-market the stores they had bought – reduced by 1991 for various reasons to 25 – and creating new ones, at least 20, making a chain of 50 by 1993.

'We have to be different,' said Chris Peddar. 'And we will be different.'

'There is simply too much sameness in retailing today,' said Grahame Winter, who took over from Richard Harker as managing-director of Allied Maples. 'Consumers can virtually go from one store to another and see a similar range of products. It is becoming more and more difficult to differentiate one retailer from another as the market currently sits.'

Everything they were doing with Maples revolved round quality, from the products to the layout of the showroom in which they were displayed. 'The concept,' Grahame Winter told *Superstore Management* in December 1990, 'is unashamedly aimed at the top end of the market place,' He was not hell bent on having 500 or 1,000 stores, but what appealed to him was a total of 250 to 275 which showed quality running right through the entire operation, perhaps in three chains and perhaps in Europe and America too.

In the meantime the £8 million investment, and the other £1 million allocated for staff training – 'investing in people' – seemed to be paying off. In the year May 1989 to April 1990 Allied Maples Group turnover rose from £169 to £248 million. Maples may have appeared to have lost its way as a furnisher after 1971, and its management, dazzled by the short term gains it could hand its shareholders through property appreciation, to have lost its furnishing nerve. But under new management it is returning to its home, to the business to which it belongs and has belonged for 150 years. And in 1992 Allied Maples made a deal with Gillow Plc, now renamed Saxon Hawk Group Plc, by which Maples returned home to the London address where this story began. That June they opened a showroom on the ground floor of 145 Tottenham Court Road which they had occupied up to 1978 but abandoned in 1989.

The new management are restoring as swiftly as they can the reputation for elegant merchandise and elegant service in elegant surroundings which gave Maples unprecedented status, of a kind that came to only a select few, as this story shows – the kind that made the name, in truth and not just a copywriter's cliché, a household word.

Chris Peddar (left) Maples Divisional Executive, John Hardman (second left) Allied Maples Chairman (1989–1991), Grahame Winter (second from right) Managing Director, Liza Goddard (right), unveiling the bust of John Maple on the launch of our first new concept store in Leeds.

Grahame Winter, Managing Director, outside Maples of Leeds on opening day.

*Traditional dining-room
furniture, still available from
Maples today, shown here in
the Bournemouth showroom.*

Maples extensive collection of upholstery shown here in their Leeds showroom.

Carpets and oriental rugs on display in the Southampton showroom.

Bedding shown here in the Cardiff showroom.

The newly introduced Lighting Department photographed here in the Watford showroom.

Maples design service available throughout new Maples stores nationwide.

*Ann Brown and Colin Elsden,
Sales Consultants, on
opening day in Leeds.*

*One of Maples newly
refurbished fleet of
delivery vehicles.*

Grahame Winter, Managing Director (left), John Keating, Watford General Manager (centre), John Hardman, Allied Maples Group Chairman 1989–91 (right) – the cutting of the Maples 150 Year Anniversary cake.

Managing Director, Grahame Winter, with Her Royal Highness Princess Michael of Kent, on Maples 150th Anniversary Exhibition at the Ideal Home Exhibition in March 1991.

150 Years of Fashion and Furniture Exhibition, fashion throughout the era.

1841

The 1900s

The 1930s

The 1960s

Limited edition bureau specially commissioned to commemorate Maples 150th Anniversary.

Specially commissioned limited edition chair to celebrate the 150th Anniversary of Maples.

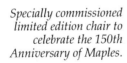

Original Gillow & Co craftsmen – photograph taken in 1887 at their Lancaster workshop (courtesy of the Lancaster Museum).

Billy Brown, at the re-launch of the Waring & Gillow Collection in Chester. Billy began his career with Waring & Gillow in 1933 at the age of 14. He was recognised as the most qualified craftsman in Great Britain for six years during his career.

Imperio sofa taken from the collection.

Limited edition pieces from the re-launched Waring & Gillow Collection. For nearly 300 years, Waring & Gillow produced some of the finest English furniture and this exquisite collection truly reflects that heritage.

Spider back chair taken from the collection.

Grosvenor Collection, a superb example of period dining furniture.

Wiltshire Collection, a classical design sofa in a modern glazed cover.

*Gillow Pembroke table based
on an original made by
Gillow of Lancaster in 1780.*

*Empire Chaise, an example
of beautiful turn-of-the-century
craftsmanship.*

Appendix 1

Sir Blundell Maple and the Creation of Frederick Hotels

In the 1880s and 90s there was intense rivalry between the major furniture/furnishing firms in London, such as Shoolbred, Maple and Gillow to win contracts to fit out the wave of new luxury hotels. Such contracts were not only extremely lucrative, the major order for the Hotel Cecil in 1895 amounted to £50,000, but provided an excellent method of displaying products to an influential section of the public and receiving widespread press coverage. During the 1880s, the firm of Maple, founded in 1841 and run by the energetic and ambitious Sir John Blundell Maple, M.P. (1845-1903), was the acknowledged leader. Maple had built up close contact with Frederick Gordon, the first great London hotel entrepreneur and won the contracts for his Grand, 1st Avenue and Metropole hotels in London and the Metropole at Brighton amongst many others.

It was, therefore, hardly surprising that Maple was extremely concerned when the highly sought after contract for the Hotel Cecil, at the time the largest hotel in Europe, was given in 1894 to the Liverpool based firm of Waring. As a result, Waring established a London showroom and began negotiations with several other firms, including Gillow, Lock and Collinson (decorative work) and Bonsor (carpeting), to form a massive combined company. The eventual result was the creation of Waring and Gillow in 1897 and the building of a huge showroom in Oxford Street in 1906.

In the close-knit world of London furniture making, Maple soon learnt of these schemes and naturally saw any new grouping as a major threat; a threat which was to be more than realised when the new firm later won the contracts for the Carlton, Ritz and Waldorf hotels, amongst others. In the booming period of hotel construction in the 1890s Maple saw a move into hotel ownership as a way of combining profitable investment with a method of keeping his company well established in the public eye. The development of Sir John's ambitions fortuitously coincided with the financial embarrassment of the Great Central Railway and the result was the creation of the Fitzroy Syndicate (Sir John major share holder) to finance and construct the Great Central Hotel. At the same time an agreement was also reached with the Bedford Estate for the Fitzroy Syndicate to run the Russell Hotel, which C. Fitzroy Doll had been planning for the east side of Russell Square.

Thus Sir John Rapidly obtained two major hotels although their location was well away from the fashionable areas of the Strand, Northumberland Avenue and Piccadilly. The new opposition was outraged and Mr S. J. Waring commented at the Waring and Gillow AGM in 1898:-

'While dealing with the subject of hotels I should like to make one point clear to the shareholders and that is that the company does not build hotels for the mere sake of furnishing them. In our view the building and owning of hotels by a furnishing company is an improprer proceeding, as, in the opinion of the directors it would be the means of inducing legitimate hotel proprietors to place their furnishing orders with firms who do not compete with them in their own business.'

Sir John was, however, busy ruffling feathers elsewhere. The close contact between Maple's and the Gordon Hotel Co. had led to Frederick Gordon becoming a member of the Maple board. Sir John was well aware of Gordon's successful record, not only in building and running hotels but also the public flotation of his firm for over £2m in 1890. In April 1897 Sir John asked if Gordon would become chairman of his new company to be called Frederick Hotels. Gordon accepted although the issue split the Gordon Hotel board and the company never quite recovered from the animosity which was generated. Sir John and Gordon eventually won the day and Frederick Hotels was officially incorporated on 1st July 1899 with a capital of £1m and to take over control of the GCH from the Fitzroy Syndicate. Apart from the Russell in London, the company built up a chain of provincial hotels and remained an important element of the British hotel scene until their integration into Trusthouse Forte in the 1960s.

When Sir John came to choose an architect for his flagship in 1896, his primary concern was to create one of London's leading hotels which would provide a suitable backdrop for the best of interior decoration that Maple's could create. In addition he wished to outdo in luxury and service, the Midland Grand at St. Pancras, which was the flagship of the London Midland Railway Co's hotel chain. The Midland Grand was generally accepted as the finest terminus hotel in London. However, Sir John was enough of a realist to see that the Great Central Hotel, located away from the centre of London, would have to rely heavily on a railway borne clientele from the Midlands and North for the backbone of its turnover. Therefore, although the hotel had to be modern and luxurious, it had to appeal primarily to the relatively traditional tastes of northern businessmen and families requiring high quality but not avant-garde, or even, in the age of the Oscar Wilde scandal at the Café Royale, risqué accommodation. He needed an architect who could produce a hotel which would rival and if possible surpass the type of atmosphere and service provided by a London club. Sir John therefore probably in close consultation with Frederick Gordon, selected R. W. Edis, who had designed a hotel at Bournemouth, but was better known for his London clubs. As architect to Sandringham and the British Pavilion at the 1893 Chicago World's Fair, Edis also had royal and nationalistic associations of particular importance in late- Victorian Britain.

Buiiding got underway in 1897 (the date cast on the drain pipe mountings) and despite the scale of the project work proceeded sufficiently speedily to allow the opening in June 1899, only a couple of months after the inauguration of the Great Central Railway's service.

(From *History of the Great Central Hotel, Marylebone*)

Geoffrey Marsh

Historical Consultant to ABE Ventures Corporation UK Limited
(reproduced by kind permission of S'International Architects)

Appendix 2

At an Extraordinary General Meeting held on November 14, 1990 it was agreed that the name of Gillow Plc should become THE SAXON HAWK GROUP PLC.

From May 15, 1991 the only Maples and Waring & Gillow stores trading in Britain were the following:

MAPLES
St Peters Road, BOURNEMOUTH
High Street, EXETER
Connaught Avenue, FRINTON ON SEA
Smith Street, St Peter Port, GUERNSEY
North Street, GUILDFORD
Western Road, HOVE
Minden Place, St Helier, JERSEY
Vicar Lane, LEEDS
Exeter Street, PLYMOUTH
Oxford Street, READING
The Strand, TORQUAY
Guildbourne Centre, WORTHING
High Street, WATFORD
Parliament Street, HARROGATE
Clarence Street, KINGSTON ON THAMES

WARING & GILLOW
North Street, BRIGHTON
Queens Road & Park Place, BRISTOL
Bouverie Place, FOLKESTONE
Paddock Row, CHESTER
North Road, LANCASTER
Belvoir Street, LEICESTER
Deansgate, MANCHESTER
Lord Street, SOUTHPORT

Appendix 3

Taste with economy

In their 1920s brochure *Modern Furniture for Modern Homes* Maples gave schedule of suggested furniture for 'a compact modern house costing from £650 to £1,000 freehold' (see page 107).

TOTTENHAM COURT ROAD
LONDON W1

MAPLE & CO

PARIS · BUENOS AIRES
MONTE VIDEO

A COMPLETELY FURNISHED HOUSE FOR £145 . 0 . 0

Suggested furniture, with prices, that can be supplied in MAPLE'S
£145 . 0 . 0 complete Furnishing Scheme.

Page	ARTICLES.	£	s.	d.
	HALL			
6	Oak Hat Rack	1	19	6
6	Umbrella Stand		9	9
8	Oak Chair, in Rexine		12	9
76	Cocoa Mat		4	0
81	Axminster Rug, 4 ft. 0 in. × 2 ft. 0 in.		10	9
81	Axminster Runner, 9 ft. 0 in. × 2 ft. 3 in.	1	5	0
		£5	**1**	**9**
	LIVING ROOM			
72	Axminster Carpet, 10 ft. 6 in. × 9 ft. 0 in.	6	0	9
—	Cedar Felt, under		8	0
92	Casement Curtains and Railway Fittings	1	4	6
8	Oak Sideboard, 4 ft. 0 in.	6	15	0
8	Oak Pull-out Table, 3 ft. 0 in. × 5 ft. 0 in.	4	9	6
8	4 Oak Chairs, Rexine seats, at 19/6	3	18	0
106	1 Mirror		12	9
8	2 Oak Armchairs at 30/-	3	0	0
106	Antique Copper Kerb Suite, complete	2	7	6
		£28	**16**	**0**
	SITTING ROOM			
72	Axminster Carpet, 9 ft. 0 in. × 7 ft. 6 in.	4	6	6
—	Cedar Felt, under		6	0
81	Hearth Rug	1	1	6
84	Art Silk and Cotton Curtains and Railways	2	10	0
37	Oak Bureau	2	9	6
24	3-piece Suite, Settee, and 2 Chairs	15	15	6
28	1 Fireside Chair	1	2	6
—	Frameless Mirror		15	0
36	Oak Book Table		14	9
107	Pewter Kerb Suite, complete	2	14	3
39	Oak Trolley Wagon		11	6
		£32	**7**	**0**
	BATHROOM			
68	White Cupboard		17	0
68	White Stool		11	0
—	Sponge Rack		2	6
—	Holder		1	6
68	Bath Seat		8	6
—	Bath Mat		7	0
83	Lino say		10	0
		£2	**17**	**6**

Page	ARTICLES.	£	s.	d.
	1st BEDROOM			
72	Axminster Carpet, 9 ft. 0 in. × 7 ft. 6 in.	3	11	6
—	Felt Paper		2	6
45	Bedroom Suite, in Weathered Oak, complete	19	15	0
45	Bed, 4 ft. 6 in., complete	13	15	0
66	Wicker Chair	1	3	6
84	Curtains and Fittings	2	15	0
106	Kerb		9	9
		£41	**12**	**3**
	2nd BEDROOM			
77	Cord Carpet, 9 ft. 0 in. × 7 ft. 6 in.	2	18	6
—	Felt Paper		2	6
42	Bedroom Suite, Oak	7	18	6
—	Oak Bed, 4 ft. 6 in., complete	5	3	9
106	Kerb		9	9
65	Cane Chair		10	6
92	Curtains and Fittings	1	7	6
		£18	**11**	**0**
	3rd BEDROOM			
83	Linoleum		10	9
81	Rug, 4 ft. 0 in. × 2 ft. 0 in.		10	9
—	Corner Wardrobe		6	6
51	Oak Dressing Chest	3	12	6
42	Cane-seat Chair		8	6
—	Oak Bed, 2 ft. 6 in., and Bedding	2	11	9
92	Curtains and Fittings		10	0
		£8	**10**	**9**
	STAIRS AND LANDING			
82	3 Slip Mats at 5/6		16	6
83	3 yards Runner Stair Linoleum		3	9
77	6½ yards Stair Carpet at 4/9	1	12	0
75	12 Oak Rods and Eyes		10	0
		£3	**2**	**3**
	KITCHEN			
70	Table, 2 ft. 6 in.	1	9	6
83	Linoleum	1	3	9
70	Chair		5	6
81	Axminster Rug, 5 ft. 3 in. × 2 ft. 8 in.		14	0
92	Curtain Material and Fittings		8	9
		£4	**1**	**6**

SUMMARY

	£ s. d.
HALL	5 1 9
LIVING ROOM	28 16 0
SITTING ROOM	32 7 0
No. 1 BEDROOM	41 12 3
No. 2 BEDROOM	18 11 0
No. 3 BEDROOM	8 10 9
STAIRS AND LANDING	3 2 3
BATHROOM	2 17 6
KITCHEN	4 1 6
	£145 0 0

COMPLETE EQUIPMENT FOR £145 . 0 . 0 HOUSE

LINENS, BLANKETS, ETC.

		£ s. d.
2 pairs Double Blankets	at 22/6	2 5 0
1 pair Under Blankets		12 9
2 Double Bedspreads	at 6/11	13 10
2 Down Quilts	at 21/6	2 3 0
4 pairs Double Sheets	at 13/9	2 15 0
4 pairs Pillow Cases	at 2/1	8 4
1 pair Single Blankets		11 9
1 Under Blanket		6 0
1 Bedspread		4 9
2 pairs Sheets	at 6/11	13 10
2 pairs Pillow Cases	at 2/1	4 2
2 Table Cloths	at 5/6	11 0
½-doz. Napkins		4 3
6 Huckaback Towels	for	6 4½
4 Turkish Towels	at 1/8	6 8
6 Tea Cloths	for	4 3
6 Glass Cloths	for	4 3
6 Dusters	for	2 1½
6 Kitchen Cloths	for	4 3
2 Kitchen Table Cloths	at 4/9	9 6
3 Roller Towels	at 2/3	6 9
		£14 7 10

IRONMONGERY AND TURNERY

		£ s. d.
1 Baking Tin		2 0
1 Hand Bowl		9
1 Enamel Bowl		1 6
1 Grater		5
1 Bread Bin (2 loaf)		2 0
1 Bread Knife		2 3
1 Bread Platter		2 3
3 Canisters	for	5 6
1 Chopping Board		2 0
1 Clothes Basket		3 3
1 Clothes Horse		5 9
1 Coal Scuttle		5 3
1 Cork Screw		8
1 Colander		1 4
1 Dust Bin		7 6
1 Dust Pan		2 0
1 Egg Slice		9
1 Whisk		9
1 Toasting Fork		8
1 Gravy Strainer		1 8
1 Kettle		2 0
1 Knife Board		1 6
1 Mincing Machine		5 6
1 Pail		1 6
1 Fry Pan		1 6
1 Paste Board		4 3
12 Patty Tins	for	6
1 Salt Cellar and Pepper Pot		10
1 Kitchen Poker		1 0
1 Rolling Pin		6
4 Aluminium Saucepans (2, 3, 4 and 6 pints)		11 0
1 Enamel Soap Dish		1 0
1 Dredger		9
1 Tray		3 6
1 Tin Opener		6
1 Towel Roller and Brackets		1 9
1 Vegetable Press		9
1 Wire Sieve		1 0
3 Wooden Spoons	for	6
1 Hair Banister Brush		3 6
1 Whisk		3 6
1 Long Hair Broom		5 6
1 Bass Broom		3 6
1 Carpet Broom (Whisk)		5 6
1 Dusting Brush		2 6
1 Hearth Brush		2 0

IRONMONGERY AND TURNERY—contd.

	£ s. d.
1 Nail Brush	6
1 Scrubbing Brush	1 2
1 Bass Brush	1 6
2 Plate Brushes	3 6
1 set Shoe Brushes	3 6
1 Lavatory Brush	1 6
1 Carpet Sweeper	12 9
1 Wringer, 14 in. rollers	16 3
1 Wood Folding Stand for Wringer	5 9
	£8 1 6

CHINA AND GLASS

	£ s. d.
Dinner, Tea and Breakfast Services for six persons	3 11 0
Glass Services for six persons	
6 Port Glasses	
6 Sherry Glasses	
6 Claret Glasses	1 8 6
6 Champagne Glasses	
6 Tumblers	
1 Decanter	
Kitchen China and Glass	1 10 6
	£6 10 0

CUTLERY AND PLATE

		£ s. d.
6 Table Knives	for	9 0
6 Small Knives	for	8 0
1 pair Carvers		12 6
6 Table Forks	for	15 0
6 Dessert Forks	for	11 3
4 Table Spoons	for	10 0
6 Dessert Spoons	for	11 3
6 Tea Spoons	for	6 3
		£4 3 3

ELECTRIC FITTINGS

	£ s. d.
Hall Lantern	13 6
Living Room Pendant and Shade	1 2 6
Sitting Room Pendant and Shade	1 2 6
Sitting Room Standard Lamp and Shade	1 17 6
1st Bedroom	13 6
2nd Bedroom	8 6
3rd Bedroom	7 0
Bathroom. 1 Glass Shade	2 3
Kitchen. 1 Glass Shade	2 2
	£6 9 5

EXTRAS
CLOCKS AND ORNAMENTS

		£ s. d.
Living Room.	Clock	1 10 0
	Ornaments	1 0 0
Sitting Room.	Clock	1 13 6
	Ornaments	1 5 0
2-Valve Wireless Set with Loud Speaker		4 19 6
		£10 8 0

SUMMARY

	£ s. d.
Linens, Blankets, etc.	14 7 10
China and Glass	6 10 0
Cutlery and Plate	4 3 3
Electric Fittings	6 9 5
Ironmongery and Turnery	8 1 6
Extras	10 8 0
	£50 0 0

TOTTENHAM COURT ROAD
LONDON W 1

MAPLE & CO

PARIS · BUENOS AIRES
MONTE VIDEO

PLAN

showing average size rooms in a small modern house

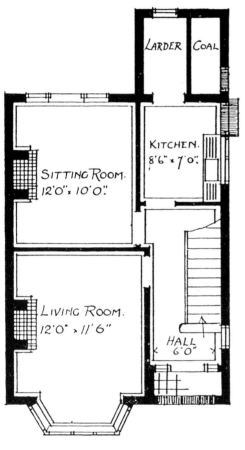

GROUND FLOOR PLAN.

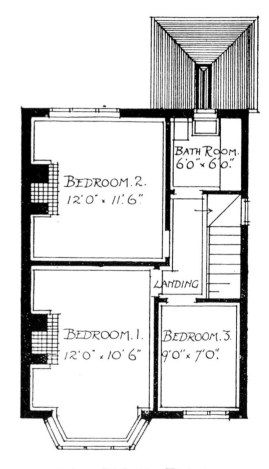

FIRST FLOOR PLAN

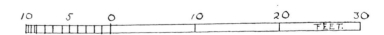

Bibliography

The First 75 Years

Pigot's *Directory of Sussex*, 1839

Post Office London Directories 1841–1864

Annual Register 1841

Hone's Year Book, 1838

Bryant Lillywhite, London Coffee Houses, Allen & Unwin 1963

P G Hall, *The Industries of London since 1861*, Hutchinson 1962

Elizabeth Burton, *The Early Victorians At Home*, Longmans 1972

J Gloag, *The English Tradition in Design*

Sir Ambrose Heal, *The London Furniture Makers from the Restoration to the Victorian Era*, Batsford 1953

The Heal Collection (ref BX 107–162 re Maples), Local Studies Library, Swiss Cottage Library, London Borough of Camden

J L Oliver, *The Development and Structure of the Furniture Industry*, Pergamon Press 1966

Irene Clephane, *Our Mothers*, Gollancz 1932

E Beresford Chancellor, *London's Old Latin Quarter*, Cape 1930

Pat Kirkham, Rodney Mace and Julia Porter, *Furnishing the World*, The East London Furniture Trade 1830–1980, Journeyman 1987 for The Geffrye Museum

Pauline Agius, *British Furniture 1880–1915*, Antique Collectors Club 1978

The House Furnisher & Decorator, no 1, vol 11, January 1, 1872

Charles Eastlake, *Hints on Household Taste in Furniture, Upholstery and Other Details*, 1878

The Cabinet & Upholstery Advertiser, vol 1, no 1, June 23 1877; October 13 1877; April 27 1878; June 8 1878

Joan Evans, *The Victorians*, Cambridge University Press 1966

Philip G Cambray, *Club Days and Ways*, The Story of the Constitutional Club 1883–1962, The Constitutional Club

Illustrated London News 1886; June 17 1893 ('The Influence of Commerce')

The Maple Leaf 1964–1971

Herts Advertiser, May 24, 1885; November 1900

Evening Standard November 24, 1887

The Times

Daily Telegraph

The Sessional Papers of the House of Lords 1888 (51 & 52 Victoria), vol xii. Reports from Select Committees of the House of Lords & Evidence. 'Sweating System – First Report'. Sir Blundell Maple's evidence June 22, 26, 29; July 3.

Memorandum of Association, Maple & Co, April 8 1891

Vanity Fair, June 6 1891

James Pope-Hennessy, *Queen Mary 1867–1953*, Allen & Unwin 1959

Kenneth Rose, *King George V*, Weidenfeld & Nicolson 1983

J. Williams Benn (ed), *The Cabinet Maker and Art Furnisher*, The Trade Journal of all who beautify the home, 1891, 1892, 1902, 1903, 1904, 1989, 1990, 1991

Audrey Kennet & Victor Kennett, *The Palaces of Leningrad*, Thames & Hudson 1973

Miriam Kochan,*The Last Days of Imperial Russia*, Weidenfeld & Nicolson 1976

Andrey Biely, *Petersburg*, 1953

Laura Cerwiṇske, *Russian Imperial Style*, Barrie & Jenkins 1990

W R Merrington. *University College Hospital and its Medical School, A History*, Heinemann 1970

Colin Ford & Brian Harrison, *A Hundred Years Ago*, Allen Lane 1983

Punch, March 29 1899

Maple & Co, *Illustrations of Furniture*, 1898, 1912, 1930

A Foreign Resident (T H S Escott), *Society in the New Reign*, Fisher Unwin 1904

Frederick Litchfield, *Illustrated History of Furniture*, Truslove & Hanson 1907

Alison Turton & Michael Moss, *The House of Fraser*, Weidenfeld & Nicolson 1989

The Second 75 Years

Maple & Co. *Inexpensive Furniture for Modern Homes, A Few Examples of Chairs & Settees A Few Examples of Wood & Metal Bedsteads –* 1930s

John Whitaker, *The Best*, H H Martyn & Co, Specialists in Architectural Decoration, 1985

Gabor Denes, *The Imperial*, The Life & Times of Torquay's Great Hotel, David & Charles 1982

James R Scobie, *Buenos Aires, Plaza to Suburbs 1870–1910*, Oxford University Press 1974

Sir Gordon Russell, *Looking at Furniture*, Lund Humphries 1964

Molly Harrison, *People and Furniture*, A Social Background to the English Home, Ernest Benn 1971

Mary Jane Pool (ed) *20th Century Decorating, Architecture & Gardens*, Weidenfeld & Nicolson 1980

The House of Maple, brochure intended to mark the centenary of 1941, but owing to the war published in 1948; with an up-dating supplement in 1959 offered as 'a souvenir of the opening of the "New Maples"'.

David Joel, *The Adventure of British Furniture*, Ernest Benn 1953

Daily Telegraph, and *The Times*, January 7 1991 – obituary of Alfred Hinds

Patrick J M Rowe, *Recollections or the Ashes of Time* (ms), 1990

Frederick Hartley, 'Maple – store with a difference', *Investors Chronicle*, May 25 1962

ᘓᗢ   ᘓᗢ

Index

Note: figures in italics denote illustrations

OTHER BOOKS BY Hugh Barty-King

A Country Builder Richard Durtnell & Sons 15 1–1991
The Worst Poverty, A History of Debt and Debtors
Quilt Winders and Pod Shavers, the story of the English cricket ball and cricket bat makers
New Flame, a social history of Town Gas
Round Table, the search for fellowship 1927–1977
G S M D, a hundred years of the Guildhall School of Music and Drama 1880–1980
The Drum (for the Royal Tournament 1988)
Making Provision (for the UK Provision Trade Federation)
Expanding Northampton (for the Northampton Development Corporation)
The Baltic Exchange, the history of a unique market
The AA, the story of the Autombile Association 1905–1980
Girdle Round The Earth, Cable and Wireless and predecessors 1851–1979
H M S O, the first 200 years of Her Majesty's Stationery Office 1786–1986
Scratch A Surveyor . . . Drivers Jonas 1725–1975
Eyes Right, the story of Dollond and Aitchison, opticians, 1750–1985
Light Up the World, the story of Dale Electric 1935–1985
Sussex in 1839
Sussex Maps and History (with Valerie Scott)
Harold Evans's Front Page History 1900–1984 (text)
Rum Yesterday and Today (with Anton Massel)
A Tradition of English Wine
A Taste of English Wine
Cork on Cork, by Sir Kenneth Cork with Hugh Barty-King